Broadcast Newswriting:

THE RTNDA REFERENCE GUIDE

Mervin Block

Radio-Television News Directors Association
and
Bonus Books, Inc., Chicago

Library of Congress Cataloging-in-Publication Data

Block, Mervin.
    Broadcast newswriting : the RTNDA reference guide/Mervin Block.
        p.   cm.
    Includes index.
    ISBN 1-56625-017-X : $29.95
    1. Broadcast journalism—Authorship. I. Radio-Television News Directors Association. II. Title.
PN4784.B75B557   1994
808'.06607—dc20   94-29925

Bonus Books, Inc.
160 East Illinois Street
Chicago, Illinois 60611

02 01 00 99 98   5 4 3 2

Printed in the United States of America

To Julia B. Hall.

*She edited this book to a fare-thee-well—and wondrously
well. She helped shape it, reshape it and shipshape it.*

Man is a tool-using animal. . . . Without tools he is nothing, with tools he is all.

Thomas Carlyle

Contents

Chapter		Page
1	Write to the Point!	1
2	Loopy Lapses and Sappy Synapses	12
3	Why?	17
4	The Writer's Struggle	24
5	Rewriting Wire Copy	28
6	Righting Wrongs	32
7	Newspapers: Handle with Extreme Caution	43
8	Rereading, Rethinking, Rewriting	55
9	Thou Shalt Not Bury a Verb in a Noun	59
10	*Ing*lish	63
11	Missing Links	70
12	Be Your Own Editor	81
13	Verbless Sentences	99
14	"Tennis-Ball Writing"	103
15	Writing Tune-Ups	107
16	A Second Look	123
17	Thou Shalt Not Scare Listeners	130
18	Don't Make a Long Story Too Short	137
19	Dial 911 for Help	144
20	No Headlinese, Please	150
21	One-Word Openers	154
22	Looking for Trouble	158
23	*As* You *Like* It?	162

Chapter		Page
24	Empty Vessels	166
25	Thou Shalt Not Give Orders	170
26	Hedge-Hopping	174
27	Accentuate the Positive	178
28	Can You Spot the Mistakes?	182
29	Perils of Polls, Pollsters and Polling	189
30	*You* and *I*	194
31	Transitions	201
32	"Remember, They're Only *Half*-Listening"	206
33	News Is Not Us	210
34	Windy Scripts	214
35	Do Drop the Ball	218
36	A New Look at "New Look"	222
37	The Power of Short Words	228
38	Words to Watch: The Worst 40	232
39	News Retardants	237
40	*Sources? What Sources?*	241
41	*Exclusive!*	248
42	What's Next?	252
	About the Author	257
	Index	259

1

Write to the Point!

Words are a writer's tools, so this book is a tool chest for professionals. It's full of tips. Tips about words—about writing, about language, about journalism. These tips are illustrated by examples from broadcast scripts: radio and television, local and network.

All these scripts, excerpted or printed whole, *were* broadcast, and they are presented in this book word for word. Many need help. Many are beyond help. But these scripts can help *us*—when we look at the corrections and rewrites.

Just as physicians learn from post-mortems, so writers learn from dissecting scripts. By finding mistakes in the scripts of others, writers see how to avoid making mistakes themselves. The poet Nikki Giovanni says, "Mistakes are a fact of life," but what counts is our response. The way we respond to these scripts can lead to gain without pain, because all the mistakes were made by *other* writers.

This *Guide* is based on "WordWatching," my column about broadcast newswriting published by the Radio-Television News Directors Association. Pre-1987 columns from RTNDA's monthly magazine, *Communicator,* have been reprinted in *Writing Broadcast News—Shorter, Sharper, Stronger.* Same author, same theme: Write right.

But this book is more than a collection of columns. I've rearranged, reedited and revised the originals, and in many cases expanded them. I've also written a fresh

1

chapter (this one) featuring top tips of the trade. As a result, the manuscript has developed into a manual of tips and guidelines to better writing.

Whether you consider your writing beyond reproach or beyond repair, feel free to roam through these pages. And for a refresher, you can read the rest of this chapter. (If you think you're a finished product already, you're already finished.)

Yes, you *will* be tested—when you write your next script. And your next. And your next. So watch your words.

They say writing news for broadcast has only two rules:

Rule 1: Write the way you talk—or should talk.

Rule 2: Never forget Rule 1.

Those basic rules can help, but they are distilled from many specific working rules that writers must absorb—and apply. And writers need to make these rules part of their *modus operandi* (and *modem operandi*). The result: scripts that are clear, concise and conversational.

Writers are quirky, and many scoff at rules—writing by them or living by them. So let's call these rules *tips*. If you don't accept tips, call them *steps*—**The 39 Steps:**

1. Think *listener*, not *reader*. Your listeners get only one crack at what you write. They can't read your script, or replay it, or reflect on it. So make sure each word can be understood, no word misunderstood. According to the English critic Cyril Connolly, "Literature is the art of writing something that will be read twice; journalism what will be grasped at once." Broadcast journalism must be grasped even faster—in the twinkling of an ear.

2. Read—and *understand*—your source copy. Read it from start to finish. Occasionally, source copy buries the lead or puts material relevant to you at the end. Also, don't write what you don't understand. If you can't get a clear explanation, write around the murky point. And when in doubt, leave it out.

3. Underline, highlight or circle key facts. If you mark your source copy vividly (with a red or orange pen), key facts will jump off the page. After you've read your source copy or notes, you can go back and easily spot those key facts for your script. And when you've finished writing, you can go back and check—and double-check—those facts easily, quickly, accurately.

4. Don't write yet. Think! What's this story all about? And what's the best way to tell it so listeners don't have to sort out what you're saying or what you mean? So they can latch on to it the first time around—the first and *only* time. In a field where verbosity is verboten, what's the best way to say what you have to say—effectively *and* economically? The writing coach Don Fry sees it like this: listeners don't need a perfect lead, or even a great lead. Just a good lead.

5. Don't start with *There is* or *It is*. They're dead phrases. But there are exceptions ("It's raining"). Find an action verb that will make your sentence move. Watch out for—and avoid when possible—stretchers, words that lengthen sentences: *that, which, there, of, the* (before plural nouns) and *to be*. For example: "He seems to be angry." (*To be* need not be.)

6. Don't write a first sentence with the main verb in any form of *to be*. *Is, are, was, were, will be* are linking verbs and don't express any action. Exception: "The big bad wolf is dead." *Is* is O.K. when the sentence is short and dramatic. And it works even better when you end the sentence with a strong one-syllable word. In *is complaining, is* is an auxiliary (or helping) verb, not the main verb. Other linking verbs also go nowhere, do nothing: *may, might, could, should, seems, becomes, has, looks.*

Also lackluster in a lead: a verb buried in a noun. For example, the noun *collision* lacks the impact of the verb *collided.*

7. Don't back into a story by starting with a participial phrase. It delays introduction of the subject and leaves listeners waiting. And wondering. By the time the sentence unspools and reaches the subject, listeners must rewind mentally to reassemble the parts. That's why, without even thinking, you don't open conversations with participial phrases: "Feeling hungry, I'm going out to eat."

8. Don't start with a question. Why not? Opening questions tend to sound like quiz shows or commercials. They can be hard to read, bring an answer you don't want, and trivialize the news. Questions delay delivery of the news. Besides, listeners are looking for answers, not questions.

9. Don't start with a quotation. Listeners can't see quotation marks. Unless a newscaster introduces a quotation by first telling *who* said it, listeners have every right to assume the words are the newscaster's own. **Put attribution before assertion.** That's more than a mere tip. It's a law. On the books (and in the books) since the earliest days of broadcast news. And for good reason: That's the way we talk. You wouldn't tell a friend: "'The sky is falling.' That's what Henny-Penny says." You'd probably say, "Henny-Penny says the sky is falling."

When does a story need attribution? Typically, when an event is not seen or covered by your reporter or by a wire service that you treat as staff, or when information seems doutbtful, or when you think listeners might wonder about it.

Even in a story that needs attribution, not every sentence may need it. In a sentence where attribution *is* needed, it sometimes can be tucked into the middle: "'The sky,' Henny-Penny says, 'is falling.'" That isn't a Grade A sentence, but it *is* legitimate because the attribution (*Henny-Penny*) precedes the predicate (*is falling*). Hanging an attribution onto the end of a sentence—"according to Henny-Penny" or "Henny-Penny said"—is print style. Broadcasters should *never* do it. The law's the law. (Although this book is generally conversational, some attributions in the text are set down, naturally, in print style.)

10. Don't start with a personal pronoun. When you're off-duty, you don't start conversations that way. You wouldn't walk up to a friend and say, out of the blue, "She told me Jim invited her to lunch." Who's *she?*

11. Don't start with an unknown or unfamiliar name. Before using a name, if a name is needed at all, use a title: *State Treasurer Kay Cash.* Or a label/description: *the first winner of the state lottery; a woman in a flak-jacket, a bank clerk out for a stroll.*

12. Don't start by saying someone is *making news, making headlines* or *making history*. Everyone mentioned in a news story is making news. Leave headlines to newspapers and history to historians.

13. Don't start with *as expected*. News is the *un*expected. Otherwise, it's usually not news; *as expected* or *as predicted* detracts from whatever follows. And don't say, "We begin with. . . ." Listeners know when you've begun. Another non-starter, "Topping our news tonight," sounds like Reddi-Wip.

14. Don't use *yesterday* or *continues* in your first sentence. In today's world, yesterday seems long ago. And don't use yesterday's news today. If something happened yesterday but has not been reported, use the present perfect tense: "A Rubetown mechanic *has been convicted* of flying a kite in a basement." If *yesterday* is absolutely needed, you can use it in your second sentence. Or later in the script. *Continues* tells a listener only that whatever has been going on is still going on. Find another angle and another verb, a muscular verb.

15. Don't characterize news. Don't call it *good, bad, dramatic, exciting, funny, frightening, amazing, alarming, shocking, disturbing, troubling* or *interesting*. Just <u>tell</u> the news. And make it interesting. What's good for some listeners is bad for others. You're safe, though, when you're specific: "Mayor Marshall got good news from his doctor. . . ." Don't call a story *unusual*. News *is* the unusual. When a Boy Scout helps an old woman cross the street, that's not news. If he trips her, *that's* news. If she trips him, you could earn a merit badge.

16. Don't raise questions you don't answer.

17. Don't be intimidated by rules for writing. Newswriting isn't an exact science. Go ahead: bend a rule—or break one. But *only* when you can improve a script. As the poet T.S. Eliot said, "It's not wise to violate the rules until you know how to observe them."

18. Don't parrot source copy. If you borrow a clever phrase from wire copy, writers at other stations may be doing the same. An alert listener hearing your script may remember the phrase from another station and figure that you've swiped it. So say it in your own words: plain, precise words. Beware of clichés, jargon, journalese ("strife-torn Bosnia," "cyclone-ravaged Bangladesh," "his newspaper-heiress wife"), legalese, euphemisms, sibilants and superlatives. Don't use a hypewriter.

19. Refrain from wordy warm-ups. Get to the point. If you don't see the point in the source copy, here's one way to find it: Think HEADLINE. Imagine that your local newspaper is going to banner the story across page 1. How would the banner condense it? Take those words and add only as many words as needed to flesh out those bare bones to make a sentence. Even if that approach doesn't work completely, it can nudge you in the right direction.

But don't use headline words: *hike* (headline word for "increase"), *pact* (contract), *probe* (investigate), *vie* (compete), *laud* (praise), *blast* (denounce), *slay* and a slew of others. We don't use those headline words when we talk. Not even in newsrooms. So please don't tell your news director you want a *hike* in your next *pact;* he might tell you to take a hike. Also, don't take your cue from headlines and write about an accident or disaster by starting with a boxscore: dead, injured, missing. First, set the scene. Then, report the casualties: "An explosion in a chemical plant near Muleville has killed ten people. . . ."

Another way to see the point (from another writing coach): Pretend you're phoning in a story to 911: "A man has been shot at Oak and Polk. Looks dead. The shooter is a woman. Tried to rob him. She got away in a car. An Olds. A new Olds. Green. Here's the license. . . ." In summarizing a story for the 911 operator, you'll probably wind up with a mental road map—and a good route. As Yogi Berra might have put it, "If you don't know where you're going, you'll wind up somewhere else."

20. Start strong. Your first sentence is crucial. Ordinarily, your second sentence should answer any question(s) raised by your first sentence. And your third sentence should answer any question(s) raised by your second sentence. Well begun is half done.

21. Write simply. Don't try to impress anyone with big words, fancy words, foreign words. Use short words and short sentences. That's how people talk. Edward R. Murrow once said: "You are supposed to describe things in terms that make sense to the truck driver without insulting the intelligence of the professor." Save the big words for Scrabble.

22. Write the way you talk. Yes, I've said that before, and I reserve the right to say it again—and again. Write the way you talk, unless you're from the Bronx.

23. Go with S-V-O: subject, verb, object. That's the best sequence for a sentence. It's the way we speak: "Jane [subject] told [verb] me [object] she wants out." You wouldn't say: "'Out.' That's what Jane told me she wants." Nor would you say, "'Out' is what Jane wants, she told me." Nor would you say, "'Out,' Jane told me, is what she wants." Avoid those missteps by sticking with the standard pattern of English speech and starting with the subject, *Jane*. If a subordinate clause intervenes with a fact that's essential, give it a sentence of its own. The more closely the verb follows the subject, the easier it is for the listener to follow.

The S-V-O pattern is especially important in writing news for broadcast. Most source copy comes from news agencies, and most of it is written for the eye, not the ear. Because that copy is intended for readers (newspaper, newsletter, magazine), it must be translated into language that listeners can grasp. Instantly. Only when you write in broadcast style can listeners process your words at the speed of sound. That style, the same for radio and television, has evolved to meet the particular needs of *listeners*. Think of *listeners*. Always. All ways.

24. Write news, not olds. News is what's new. Focus on action, not reaction (unless you are writing a follow-up).

25. Use familiar words in familiar combinations. Use common words that are easily understood. Never use a word you don't fully understand. But using familiar words in a script isn't enough. Familiar words must be combined in a familiar way. The words tumble from our keyboards and stream into listeners' ears so swiftly our listeners don't have time to decipher unfamiliar combinations. To mix metaphors (and semaphores), their train of thought goes off the track. Or out the window.

26. Activate your copy. Use action verbs, and write in the active voice: "The bus hit a tree." Packs a punch. The passive can be awkward: "The tree was hit by a bus." But when the action itself or the receiver of the action is more important than the doer, the passive may be preferable: "Mayor Marshall was indicted today. He's accused of bribery and conspiracy. . . ." In this case, the doer is whoever indicted the mayor. And only a grand jury indicts people. So mention of the grand jury can be deferred or omitted. The focus of the story is the mayor, not the grand jury. (Also, don't compound a crime by writing that indictments were handed *down*; they're handed *up*.)

27. Watch out for *we, our, here*. Those words are blurry. When a newscaster says *we*, is she referring to herself, her newsroom, her station, her nation? When she says *here*, where is that? Her town? Her studio? Her desk? When she says *our troops,* does she mean that her station maintains a militia?

28. Humanize and localize your scripts. Write about *people,* not *personnel.* Look for a local peg. And in writing about accidents and disasters, put people before property.

29. Limit a sentence to one thought. Listeners can't read your scripts, let alone re-read them or re-think them. Make it easy for your listeners, half of whom are probably only half-listening.

30. Put your sentences in a positive form. Try to avoid *not* and *no.* The old song says it best: "Accentuate the positive, eliminate the negative, don't mess with Mister-In-Between."

31. Try to put the word or words you want to emphasize at the end of a sentence. Build up to your key words, the words you want to stress. Prepare your listeners for what they *don't* know by starting a sentence with what they *may* already know, "Mayor Marshall." Then work your way toward what's most significant: "Mayor Marshall said his proposal to rebuild City Hall is dead." That construction creates suspense as the lead climbs to the peak. Then, after the sentence reaches the key word, *dead,* it should stop. "No steel" said the Russian writer Isaac Babel, "can pierce the human heart so chillingly as a period at the right moment."

Yet, some newswriters would invert that sentence: "Dead. That's what Mayor Marshall says his proposal to rebuild City Hall is." Scripts backing into a story that way—with shock leads or with the bottom line at the top—violate the rules of good writing, good storytelling and good sense.

32. Use connectives—*and, also, but, so, because*—to link sentences. No matter what a well-intentioned schoolmarm might have told you, it *is* permissible to start a sentence with any of those words. When you tie sentences together, the listener has an easier time following the thread. Also helpful in tying sentences together are possessives: *his, hers, its, their.* Let's say you write: "Police searched the suspect's car for clues. The car was. . . ." You can tie that second sentence in with the first more smoothly by writing, "*His* car was. . . ."

You can also improve your copy with words like *new, now* and *but.* Would you ever turn away from a newscast when the first words you hear are: "A new study says. . . ."? *Now* can serve as a quick transition. And *but* can alert the listener to a catch. Or a contrast. Or a conflict.

33. Use contractions—with caution. Contractions are conversational and save time. But we need to be careful with a few. For example: *can't.* A listener can miss hearing the *t.* Without it, the sentence means the opposite. So it's often better to write the word in full, *cannot.* That way, your listeners cannot get it wrong.

34. Use present tense verbs where appropriate. When your mayor says he's going to do something, you can go on the air one hour later or twelve hours later and still use *says.* And you can use *says* in several successive sentences. *Says* has several advantages: it's neutral and, like a good stagehand, it does the job, it's unseen and it moves the show right along. But you can cause a real problem when you use a synonym for *says* that doesn't fit (*vows, states, declares*) or one that colors the story (*claims, admits, insists*). So avoid heedless (and needless) variants.

35. Place the time element, if needed, *after* the verb. Listeners expect the news to be today's. They take *today* for granted. More inviting or arresting than *today* is a verb reporting action. Also, *today* before the verb sounds odd. No one talks that way. Ever. Never. You wouldn't tell someone, "I today ate too much for lunch."

36. Omit needless words. Use few names, few numbers, few facts, few words. Ask yourself: is each word indispensable? If it's not necessary to leave it in, it *is* necessary to leave it out.

"Vigorous writing is concise," Strunk and White say in *The Elements of Style:* "A sentence should contain no unnecessary words, a paragraph no unnecessary sentences, for the same reason that a drawing should contain no unnecessary lines and a machine no unnecessary parts. This requires not that a writer make all his sentences short, or that he avoid all detail and treat his subject only in outline, but that every word tell."

Likewise—and like the wise—David Lambuth says in *The Golden Book on Writing,* "The fewer the words that can be made to convey an idea, the clearer and more forceful the idea." Go, and do thou likewise.

37. Read your copy to yourself, aloud. What counts in broadcast news is not how it looks but how it sounds. If it sounds like writing, rewrite it. As we know all too well, in newsrooms we often don't have time to rewrite—or even to write. But when we do have time, remember: the art of writing *well* lies in rewriting what you've already rewritten.

38. Scrutinize your script one last time: Is it accurate? Is it fair? Does it flow? Then let it go: turn it in.

39. Pray. (And polish your résumé.)

2

Loopy Lapses and Sappy Synapses

Little lessons from our loopy lapses:

"She was the first woman to win a Grammy for best female country vocalist." Sounds as though previous winners were androids, androgynes or animales. The redundancy in the script should be have been caught by someone on staff—or distaff.

"Our __ ___ is standing by live in Durham with new information tonight." Always good to hear that reporters standing by are still alive. And good to hear that they have *new* information. And good to be reminded that tonight is still tonight. Some newsroom advisers dote on *tonight* and *live*, but far more important—all the time, today and tonight—is lively writing.

Like all scripts reprinted in this book, these are run word for word:

"Two Green Bay police officers are nursing minor injuries tonight following a fight today. Police say it happened this afternoon at a. . . ." It takes a contortionist, or distortionist, to inject *tonight* high in most *today* stories. How can an average listener adjust to three time shifts—*tonight, today, this afternoon*—in six seconds? Those fast shifts can leave a listener woozy. And isn't a police *officer* a captain or lieutenant?

A man with a fervent following among verbivores, Robert Burchfield, the former chief editor of the Oxford English Dictionaries, has written, in a guide for the BBC, "Do not use [*following*] instead of *after* or *as a result of;* it is poor syntax and obscures the sense, as in *Police have arrested a man following extensive inquiries.*" So follow his advice: when you mean *after,* use *after.*

"A dangerous trend among some children is worrying some doctors in our area." *Some* sentence! Two *somes* in a row turn a script into a wastebasket case. Advice for writers: Next to his dog, a man's best friend is his wastebasket.

"The mother accused of trying to use murder to help her daughter become a cheerleader again said she's innocent." *Use murder?* No. And *again* is a swiveling modifier; it looks backward and forward, leading to ambiguity. Does *again* mean the daughter wanted to become a cheerleader again or does it mean the woman pleaded not guilty again? If she had pleaded (not *pled*) not guilty previously, is the second pleading still news in a distant city? The first time, it *is* news. The second time, it's a twice-told tale.

"A faulty hydraulic line is at fault for yesterday's fire at the Imperial Food chicken processing plant which killed 25 employees. Oil spilled from the line and vaporized. The vapors came in contact with. . . ." Too bad the script didn't come in contact with an editor. A *faulty* line at *fault?* Come on! Even more serious: when someone affixes blame, attribution is a must.

"People who live near the intersection of Route F and Highway 65 want the state to build an overpass there. They say the intersection, located about a mile south of Ozark, is dangerous and needs to be redesigned. A spokesperson says a large number of accidents in recent months prompted a citizens group to form. . . . [Better: "prompted formation of a citizens' group."] **Too many accidents there has convinced a lot of people something needs to be done."** *Has* they? Accidents *have.* Also: Delete *located;* the meaning remains the same. That *spokesperson* is a spokesman or spokeswoman. *Spokesperson* is a synthetic word (*man-made?*) that has the stuffy stigma of bureaucratese.

Spokesperson is best left unspoken—unless you're in *Middlesex* County.

"Two men robbed and assaulted a Wake Forest University student yesterday in his dorm room. Officials say the incident was the third recent assault on the campus. A news release from the university says 20-year-old Van Vahle heard a knock on his door about 1 A-M. Vahle opened the door to find two armed men, who got away with seven dollars, a portable stereo and other property." In the first sentence, *yesterday* should be expelled. In a story about a robbery, a writer should not be quoting a press release. The writer of the press release doesn't work for you; he's writing it for his boss. The writer of that script should have talked with city police, campus police or the victim. Or touched *all* bases. If the writer confirmed the information, he needn't mention the release. If all else failed, he should have found a university official—not a *spokesperson*—and attributed the information to him. (Is an official source who doesn't want to be identified a *spooksperson?*)

My most memorable lesson about handouts came from my night city editor on a Chicago newspaper. His nightly battle cry was "Don't be a handout reporter," but he handed me a fistful of press releases trumpeting the impending arrival of the movie monarch Louis B. Mayer. An hour later, the editor asked me what time Mayer's train would be pulling into the Dearborn Street Station. I told him, and when he challenged my answer, I cited the handouts: one from the Santa Fe Railway, one from Mayer's studio (Metro-Goldwyn-Mayer), and one from his destination, the Ambassador East Hotel. All agreed on the time. But that wasn't good enough for my boss: "Call the stationmaster and *find out.*"

"There have been two traffic fatalities reported so far this Labor Day weekend. Two men died this morning in a bizarre double-motorcycle accident." That's the whole script! Bi-*zarre*! Tantalizing us by saying an accident is bizarre and then not telling us anything about it is, well, bizarre. *Die* is dull. People die in bed, quietly. Those men were *killed,* violently. In the next script, we'll see how another newscast handled the same story:

"The first two traffic fatalities this holiday week-end came in a bizarre accident in Caswell County. The state highway patrol says one motorcyclist died early this morning [use *today*] **when he swerved to miss a man lying in the road. But the man was killed seconds later when a second motorcyclist hit him. Authorities identified those killed as 42-year-old Harry Leon Elliott and Kerry Leroy Turner."** Delete *bizarre.* Save it for something really bizarre, such as the Addams family. The accident *was* unusual, but most news is. Were the two cyclists traveling together? Who were they? From where? Why use the age of one man and not of the other? If we have confidence in the authorities, and if they are authoritative, let's skip the attribution at the end and say simply that the victims *were* Elliott and Turner. And skip the middle names. But which man was the biker? And which man had been lying in the road? And why?

"The country is heading for an all-time record-breaking [*record* suffices] **federal deficit. Based on a ballooning deficit for August, economists say the fiscal-year deficit by the end of September will be at least 280-billion dollars. . . ."** Some economists may have their heads in the clouds, but have you ever known any economist based on a ballooning deficit? Here's what *was* based on the ballooning deficit: an estimate or a conclusion. Make sure *your* modifiers don't dangle.

"It's got all the elements of a great spy novel, only this story is true . . . and it's sending shock waves from Washington, D-C, to Moscow. A former C-I-A agent and his wife were charged today on suspicion of acting as double agents for the Kremlin . . ." Don't waste time comparing a story to a novel. Or a movie. Or any other story. Go ahead and tell your own story. *Charged today on suspicion?* No need for *suspicion.* They were charged with spying—as double agents—for Moscow. As for *shock waves,* don't let them be sent anywhere, except the journalese junkyard.

"There's a war going on along the coast tonight . . . a war between neighbors. The battleground: Laguna Beach. The reason for the battle: a 15-hundred dollar tree-house . . . that's blocking one neighbor's view. . . ." *War?* If you call that squabble a *war,* what do you call the "brain-spattering, windpipe-slitting" battles elsewhere? No wonder George Bernard Shaw said the press seems unable to discriminate between "a bicycle accident and the collapse of civilization." Perhaps we can curb any temptation to magnify minor events, and also put them in perspective, by heeding Quentin Crisp's quip: "You should treat all disasters as if they were trivialities, but never treat a triviality as if it were a disaster."

"The Durham city council declared war on crime. . . ." Time for all of us to declare war on clichés like that. And war on weary words like *bizarre.* And war on our loopy lapses and sappy synapses.

3

Why?

What's the most important question in the universe? One savant has answered, *"Why?"*

"Why?" indeed. In writing news for broadcast, we seldom have time for the traditional five W's—*who, what, when, where, why* and an occasional *how*—that offer a framework for a newspaper story. Even when we have enough time, we seldom need them all. Some stories cry out for a *why,* and newswriters often fail to hear that cry. Let's look at several examples.

"A 19-year-old Bois D'arc man is charged with shooting one man and beating another. Police say Zachary Hays shot one victim with a shotgun and beat the other with a wooden club. The incident happened at Hays' home early this morning. He has been charged with first- and second-degree assault and armed criminal action. Prosecutors have recommended bond be set at 25-thousand dollars. Hays will go before a judge tomorrow."

Why did Hays do what he allegedly did? Who are the "victims"? Burglars? Friends? Why were they in Hays's home? How did the trouble start? Had they all been drinking? What condition are the "victims" in? Who *is* Hays? Is the gun his? The club? *Why* is he going to court? Arraignment? Bond hearing? Why does the writer say Hays *will* go? No one knows what someone else will do. Maybe Hays will refuse to go. It *is* safe to say Hays is *scheduled* to go. But he could go on the lam. One more

17

question: why did the producer let that script go on the air? Why, oh, why?

"A suburban Kansas City teenager will spend the next 10 days at home, suspended for setting off a tear-gas canister in school. The youth told police he didn't know what was in the canister before he pull [that's how the script spelled it] **the pin near a lunch line Friday. The school was evacuated twice and eventually closed two hours early. A girl with asthma is in the hospital in fair condition."** Alas, the script is not in fair condition. How does the writer know exactly where the boy is going to spend the next 10 days? There's no basis for saying the boy will be at home all that time. Chances are, he'll stay home only when there's no place else to do nothin'. All the writer knows for sure is that the boy was suspended from school for 10 days. Is it a *high* school? (Some teens are in grade school.) Is the boy 13? Or 19? As for *youth,* it's not a conversational word. Do reporters who use *youth* on air also use it off-air? Where did the boy find the canister? In the school? How many students were affected by the early closing? The last sentence of the script, about a girl with asthma, seems unrelated to the story. Had the girl been standing in the lunch line? Near the lunch line? Too bad the newscaster, ultimately responsible for every word in the newscast, was out to lunch.

"A Suamico couple and their son, accused of selling beer to minors, are expected to go on trial to-day. 51-year-old Norbert Szprejda, his 47-year-old wife, Jean, and 21-year-old son, Joseph, are all charged in connection with a beer party in late April. Three Green Bay men died in a traffic accident shortly after they fled the party. The Szprejdas are charged with illegally selling beer to minors. Their trial will be held in Brown County Circuit Court." That's the whole script. After hearing about three men who *fled* a party, thoughtful listeners—yes, many listeners are thoughtful—who don't remember the six-month-old case will wonder *why?* Did the three men really *flee,* or was the writer careless in choosing a verb? If they did flee, why? (Were they men or teenagers?) And was their fatal traffic accident related to the party? If so, how? Had they been drunk? What kind of a party would cause anyone to flee? (If they had run out of beer, maybe they ran out for more.) Another script, from elsewhere (where *else?*), tells of two young men charged with murdering the father of one of them. After 60 seconds of details but no hint of the reason for the homicide, the script closes:

"Authorities speculate that the motive behind the murder was revenge. They say Anthony Rindahl [the son] **blamed the death of his mother on his father. 44-year-old Gail Rindhal** [the mother] **was killed in late July when the semi-truck she was driving was struck by a car near Wisconsin Rapids."** That's all, folks. Why did the son blame his father? Was the father driving the car that struck the semi? Why was the mother driving a semi? Was she upset after a violent argument with her husband? Did he send her out into a storm? Why didn't the producer toss the story back to the writer? Why? (Warning: Never call a father's murder of his son "sonnycide.")

"A Joplin manufacturing plant [better: *A Joplin factory*] **is on fire this morning. The Joplin fire department says the fire at Eagle-Picher Industries, Incorporated, was reported shortly after midnight this morning. A fire official tells ___ News there is much concern about lithium being stored at the plant because the chemical is water-reactive. The lithium is used in the manufacture of batteries at the plant. Firemen continue to battle the fire this morning** [we're not deaf; we heard the first two *this mornings*]. **There is no official word yet on the amount of damage, and there are no confirmed injuries."** Why suggest there may be *un*confirmed injuries? Why doesn't the writer tell us what *water-reactive* means? Why is the writer so wordy? Is it the thought of batteries that energizes him to keep on going, and going, and going? Why didn't the writer ask himself, "Why? Why? Why?"

Some wisenheimers may dismiss *why* as just a crooked letter. But even though a word to the wise (and otherwise) is seldom sufficient, a casual look at broadcast scripts makes it clear that newsrooms need more *whys-guys*. Many more.

Too many news scripts are like chop suey: they consist of odds and ends, they lack substance, and they're hard to untangle. But one hour later, I don't crave more.

Let's look at a few of those broadcast scripts, reprinted here in their entirety:

"Police in western Virginia have a 23-year-old man in custody following a high-speed chase where [*where?*] **three police cruisers were damaged.**

"The chase began in Montgomery County and ended in Carroll County. The man had 15 police cars involved in the pursuit at one point, and was finally stopped at a roadblock on Route 77."

When it comes to a verb with verve, *have* is a have-not. It's a linking verb and expresses no action. Better: "Police in western Virginia chased a motorist for X miles and caught him near. . . ." If we had answers to our questions, we could write a far better lead.

Why did police chase the man? How fast did they go? How far did they go? How long did the chase last? We don't need to know the speed and the distance *and* the duration, but we do need to ditch *high-speed* chase. Did you ever hear of a *low-speed* chase, except for O.J. Simpson's (if you call trailing someone 50 miles to his home—discreetly—a chase)? As for *following,* make it *after.*

How were the cruisers damaged? Anyone hurt? (If a policeman is put out of action, don't call that a cop-out.)

Where along Route 77 was the roadblock? You need at least two coordinates to find the position of a point on the map.

The suspect didn't arrange the chase, so he didn't *have* the police cars *involved;* who'd want so many chasers, or any at all?

Who *is* the suspect? Does he have a name? An occupation? Is he from our town? Was he armed? Any shooting? Did he surrender tamely? In custody *where?* What has he been charged with? So many questions unanswered, the whole story becomes questionable. Next case:

"An unusually high bond was set yesterday for a 16-year-old boy who allegedly pulled the trigger of the gun that killed his 15-year-old classmate. Judge Michael Buckley set bond for Larry Sims at three-million dollars. Sims will be tried as an adult for the shooting death of Datagnan [D'Artagnan?] **Young in the halls of DuSable High School."**

Why is the writer so wordy?

What is Sims charged with? And why should we have to guess?

Did Sims have only one classmate? If not, I'd say "*a* classmate." Rather than classmates, they might have been only schoolmates. What class were they in—sophomore, junior? Their ages differed, perhaps by almost two years. In any case, the shooting took place in only *one* hall of the school. Also, Sims will be tried *in* the shooting death; *for* implies guilt. As a criminal lawyer I know says, "All my clients are presumed innocent—until proved broke."

Why call a 16-year-old, especially one being tried as an adult, a boy?

Why did he (allegedly) pull the trigger? *Pulled the trigger of the gun that killed = shot and killed.* Or shorter still: *shot dead.*

Where? The script was broadcast by a big station, reaching into several states, so the writer should identify the city where the action occurred.

Why was the bond so high?

Why did the writer use *yesterday* in the first sentence? When we listen to news, we want to find out about *today. Yesterday* seems long ago. As a listener, my reaction is: if it occurred yesterday, why are you telling me today? If you did tell me yesterday, why are you telling me again today?

"A city panel is recommending changes in the building code—to relax some fire prevention requirements. Under the proposal, shelters for the homeless would no longer be classified as places of public assembly and would no longer be required to have fire alarm and sprinkler systems. But several aldermen warn that measure could pave the way for fire hazards at shelters."

Why does the *city panel* want to end the requirement that shelters have fire alarms and sprinklers?

What *is* the *city panel?* Does the writer mean a committee of aldermen in the city council? Or a committee in the Department of Housing? Or a committee of building owners?

When the writer says *is recommending,* does he mean *is going to* (if so, when?), or does he mean the committee *has* recommended? What is the status of the recommendations? Have they already been presented to someone? Who?

What does the fire commissioner have to say about the recommendations? What does an advocate for the homeless have to say?

Speaking of panels (to reach for a transition), let's look at some hardwoods:

"McNeese State's basketball program has been placed on two years' probation by the Southland Conference. The announcement follows three months of investigation." That's all there is, folks, the whole script. Why was the program put on probation? (And why not the editor?) Next:

"A Forest City company is helping to launch what may be a bid for the Presidency by a seventh Democratic candidate. The Cycle Satellite Company will be broadcasting an announcement out of [should be *from*] Des Moines tonight by Chicago industrialist Bill Farley. The announcement will be made available to T-V stations across the country." At first, it seems the company may be helping finance the candidate. But we don't know that he is a candidate, only that he may be-come one. Would he be buying satellite time to tell the country he is not a candidate? Either the writer didn't have enough information, or he didn't set it down clearly. Sounds like his editor was asleep at the switcher.

Next:

"A man on Richmond's ten-most-wanted list is in custody in the Washington, D-C, jail, where it turns out he's been for several months. Richmond officials say they had suspected David Phillips was in the D-C jail, but had to wait on [should be *for*] **fingerprint identification because he has used** [should be *had used*] **an alias. Phillips has been replaced on the ten-most-wanted list by Donald Lucas, who's wanted for the murder of his wife."**

Why does Richmond want Phillips? *Why* did Richmond officials *suspect* he's in a D. C. jail? And *why* had he been arrested in D.C.?

Why? may be the most important question in the universe, but we often don't know—or can't learn—the *why?*s of a story. Even when we do, we often don't have room—or reason—to include the *why?*s in our copy. But in some stories, *why?*s are crucial, even imperative. What we need are editors who scrutinize scripts and know when to ask *why*. That's what we need: more *why?*s guys.

4

The Writer's Struggle

Simple stories are often hard to write. But newswriters must get a good grip on them so they can also handle not-so-simple stories. "Only those who have the patience to do simple things perfectly well," Schiller said, "acquire the skills to do difficult things easily."

Newsroom oldtimers tell newcomers: Just write the way you talk. Good advice. But a writer has to do far more than that. Besides, how many of us talk well? So let's hopscotch the dial and sample some scripts gone wrong—and see how to right them:

"The St. Paul Civic Center is launching a bid for the Minnesota North Stars to play at the center. Currently, the professional hockey team plays at Met Center in Bloomington. Civic Center Executive Director David Rosenwasser says. . . ." *Launching a bid* is newscasterese. It doesn't sound like anything you'd say in real life. It's about as unreal as another phrase some newscasters use: *unveiling a budget.*

If you were talking with a friend after work and describing what you had covered at City Hall that day, would you say, "The mayor *unveiled* his new plan (or new budget)"? Or *launched* something? Ships are launched, products are launched, careers are launched, and space cadets go out to launch. But bids aren't launched. More to the point: "The St. Paul Civic Center is going to try to get the Minnesota North Stars to play at the center." (Maybe the director of the rink, Rosenwasser, should call himself Frozenwasser.)

"Also tonight in Metarie, news of the death of a man who was reputed to be the godfather of the oldest Mafia family in the nation.

"Carlos Marcello died today at the age of 83.

"The Jefferson Parish Coroner's office confirms Marcello died at his home in the New Orleans suburb . . . but did not have a cause of death. He had been in failing health for years." Starting with *also* makes the item sound like an also-ran. The use of *tonight* in that story seems like an effort to make the story newish—as though *today* is long gone. Listeners know that it's night outside (and inside, too), so it's distracting to hear *tonight* and then hear in an instant he died *today*.

A reminder: after you report a fact, you don't need to say it has been confirmed. If a tip or a hunch or a rumor or a story has not been confirmed, you don't know whether it is a fact and have no business telling it as a fact. But once you have presented it as fact, don't follow up by saying someone has confirmed it. The writer could have said in the third sentence, "But the Jefferson Parish coroner says he doesn't know the cause of death."

Let's rewrite the script: "The mobster Carlos Marcello is dead. He died at home today in a New Orleans suburb, Metairie. He was 83 years old. Marcello's health had been failing for years, but the cause of death has not yet been disclosed. He is said to have been the godfather of the oldest Mafia family in the country."

Next: **"Leading our offbeat news at this hour, this has been International Women's Day, in case you didn't know, reason enough for some Russian women to march in the streets.** [Voice-over] **Their pot-and-pan-beating, however** [better: *though*], **took a nasty turn. No more working women and mom's apple pie.** [What does that mean?] **This crowd was yelling for Boris Yeltsin's hide. . . ."** If the phrase *in case you didn't know* helped a story, you could use it in almost every script. Some writers think it's cute. It's not. It adds nothing. Nor does *offbeat*. Nor *at this hour.* If a word or phrase doesn't add, it detracts. *Mom's apple pie?* In Moscow? Perhaps Moscow, Idaho. Or Odessa, Texas. Or St. Petersburg, Florida. The leading item doesn't need to be heralded as the leading item. And calling that news violates Truth-in-Advertising laws.

"Outback's appeal to the City Council put Councilman Milton Williams between a rock and hard place, forcing him to balance the wishes of his constituents against the economic needs of the community." Please don't ever put anyone between a rock and a hard place. It's in the heart of Clichéville, and no one should go there, let alone get stuck there.

"And in sports, we'll go with ___ ___ and golfer Perry Moss to the Big Water, plus we'll tell you about tonight's L-S-U match-up with California . . . So stay with us." In that tease, *plus* is a minus. *Plus* is a preposition meaning *with the addition of:* "Two plus two is four." Some experts accept *plus* as a noun ("It's a definite plus"), an adjective ("Her writing is a plus quality") and a conjunction ("The rain plus [meaning *and*] the wind make for hard driving"). But experts agree *plus* can't be used as a conjunction introducing an independent clause (a group of words with a subject and a verb). *Plus* would have been proper in that script if the writer had not used a verb (*tell*) after *plus*: "*Plus* a report on tonight's L-S-U game with California."

As for *Stay with us,* it's unbecoming for a newscaster to plead with listeners to stay tuned. Wouldn't you frown if, part-way down this page, I urged readers, "Stay with me." Wouldn't you say to yourself, "This guy has no class. If he were saying something worthwhile, I'd stay with him to the end. Gladly."

"Florida law states that—quote—'Any person who willfully, maliciously and repeatedly follows or harasses another person commits the act of stalking'—unquote." That sentence means the same without *quote* and *unquote*. Almost never does a writer need *quote,* an intrusive, hackneyed word. And how can you *unquote* something? An even more annoying term used by some newscasters: *close quote.* But most irritating of all is the public speaker who says, "quote, unquote" and waggles two fingers of both hands to carve quotation marks in the air. Ugh. And you can quote me.

When a quotation is worth quoting, it's best, in almost all cases, to paraphrase. But if you *must* quote someone word for word, you can set off the quotation through skillful delivery or by prefacing it with a device like "In her words." Or "As she put it."

A rewrite of the script: "Florida law says anyone who willfully, maliciously and repeatedly follows or harasses someone is stalking." More natural, isn't it?

The best broadcast newswriting doesn't sound like writing at all. The journalist Lincoln Steffens is credited with saying, "The great struggle of a writer is to learn to write as he would talk."

And you can add, "—and to talk as he *should* talk."

5

Rewriting Wire Copy

Newsrooms often treat wire service copy as though it were a sacred text, not open to challenge, criticism or correction.

Wire copy does look impressive—printed so uniformly, marching along, line after line: no smudges, erasures, X-outs or strike-overs. But the people who write for the wires are as fallible as the rest of us. And judging by some recent news stories, even more fallible. Here's a recent example, probably delivered as is by many newscasters:

"Rudolf Hess, one-time deputy to Adolf Hitler, is said to be hospitalized in West Berlin with pneumonia. The 92-year-old Hess was taken from Spandau prison, where he's serving a life sentence, to a British military hospital. There's no word on the type of pneumonia Hess is suffering from, or his condition."

Hess's name isn't universally recognized, not even in newsrooms. In writing for broadcast, we don't start cold with names of people who are unknown or unfamiliar.

One-time means only once, but Hess served Hitler for many years. I certainly wouldn't call John Adams a one-time President. (Hess's flight to Scotland in 1941 raised the question of whether he was a two-timer.)

Said to be = reportedly. We use *said to be* when we can't confirm a fact. We aren't in the business of circulating rumors, so we should save it for a story that we can't nail down. The wire copy, from a broadcast wire, presumbly was based on a longer "A"-wire story. If the

28

wire copy said *reportedly,* then *said to be* is proper. But the next sentence of the script says, without qualification, that Hess was moved from the prison to a hospital. And the last sentence of the script adds, again without qualification, that Hess *is* sick. (What needs qualification is the *editor.*) And why does the writer take time to tell us he doesn't know the type of pneumonia Hess has? If the writer hadn't mentioned it, I can't imagine that any listener would phone a station and ask, "Say, what type of pneumonia does Hess have?"

Better: "A deputy to Adolf Hitler—Rudolf Hess—has been moved from prison to a hospital. He was taken from Spandau in West Berlin with pneumonia. He's 92 years old, and he's serving a life sentence [for war crimes]. No word on his condition." [Broadcast scripts use brackets—like those enclosing *for war crimes* and enclosing this sentence—to present optional material that can be used on air if time allows or can be easily bypassed.]

Another snippet of wire copy, datelined Beirut, was sent to me by an astute wordwatcher, Bill Kitchin, news director of WLKC-FM, St. Marys, Georgia:

"One of the hostages held hostage in Lebanon says another American captive is dying." A hostage is someone held hostage. So what kind of writing did that writer write?

Another broadcast-wire story—two paragraphs joining two unrelated occurrences:

"Twenty-six people are dead in a ferryboat accident at the entrance of a Belgian harbor. The British vessel overturned today with more than 500 people on board. Hundreds have been rescued, but 240 people are still missing.

"The U-S Coast Guard says some crew members might have to abandon ship in the Gulf of Mexico. A grain-carrying freighter is flooding uncontrollably in gale-force winds."

The first graf would be far stronger if it led with action. Instead, it starts with a number and an inert verb, *are.* The item also uses an adjective (*Belgian*) when the noun form (*Belgium*) would be more readily understood.

Why did the ferry overturn? Collision? Flooding belowdecks? Too many people on the port side? Too many on the portly side?

Better: "A ferry overturned in the English Channel today, and 26 people drowned. Hundreds of people have been rescued, but more than 200 people are missing. The accident occurred off Belgium at the entrance to a harbor."

My version is based on two assumptions: that the scene was *in* the Channel (otherwise, I'd say *near*) and that the victims drowned. *Ferryboat* is a long word for *ferry.* Yes, *ferry* is a homophone, but I doubt that any listener would think the story is about a topsy-turvy fairy. Later, a newscaster said the ferry had been *uprighted*—an ugly non-word that should have been uprooted.

As for the second paragraph of the wire service item, a listener would probably assume from the first line, quoting the Coast Guard about "some crew members," that it's related to the first graf. Or that the crew is aboard a Coast Guard ship. Halfway through the second item, the listener would realize it had nothing to do with the ferry.

A grain-carrying freighter doesn't hold water with me; it's not conversational. Sounds like wire-service language, known as *wirese* or *journalese.*

A gale is a storm with steady winds from 39 to 54 miles an hour. Are *gale-force winds* in that range but not steady? That's more than most people know or care to know. I'd call it a storm. Or I'd call it a storm with winds exceeding 30 miles an hour. Or, if facts warrant, a storm with winds up to 55 miles an hour. Or just a plain old gale. Here's an improved version, written to follow the ferry story, with a transition to shift the scene:

"In the Gulf of Mexico, a storm has caused a freighter to flood uncontrollably. And the Coast Guard says some crew members might have to abandon ship. The ship is carrying grain."

I'd like to know how many are in the crew, how close they are to rescue, their nationality, the name of the ship, its position, size, registry and where it's bound. But they haven't abandoned ship yet, so I wouldn't go overboard.

While we're afloat, I want to hoist a salute to the writer who first referred to the garbage scow roaming the seas looking for a dumping ground as the *garbarge*. I heard it on WCBS-AM, New York City, and maybe someone there deserves the credit. I say *maybe* because I can't ignore an observation by William R. Inge, Dean of St. Paul's Cathedral: originality is undetected plagiarism.

I also want to salute a world-class wordwatcher, David C. Frailey of Dallas, who informed me of the republication of Ambrose Bierce's *Write It Right*. (But I'm ignoring Dave's description of the book as ambrosial.)

6

Righting Wrongs

Good writers must never stop learning the write stuff but also never stop *un*learning the wrong stuff: we need to rid ourselves of all we know that just ain't so.

Writing well isn't enough. We also must make sure that what we've long taken for granted is still true. Otherwise, we'll write scripts spoiled by the wrong stuff—wrong words, wrong information, wrong implication.

To get it right, we must feed our curiosity, read hungrily and store trillions of bits of data in our mental computers. For those who don't have that much storage capacity, the best alternative is knowing where to turn: the right expert, a savvy shopmate, a solid reference shelf.

You can test *your* data bank by trying to spot what's wrong with these network scripts, starting with a commentary on a current visit to this country by British royalty:

"When King George the Sixth of England decided to grace Chicago with his presence in 1939, some reporter asked the Republican mayor of Chicago, William Hale 'Big Bill' Thompson, what form his reception of the king might take. Mister Thompson replied that he would punch the king of England in the snoot—a sort of indigenous folk greeting in Chicago that is still widely practiced to this day."

As Mayor Richard J. Daley of Chicago once replied to a reporter's question on another subject, "That's not even true enough to comment on." But let's examine that script anyway—and every which way. The author Herman Kogan says he was never able to authenticate any threat by Thompson to punch the king and dismisses it as myth. Kogan's (and Lloyd Wendt's) book, *Big Bill of Chicago,* quotes Thompson as saying only, "I wanta make the King of England keep his snoot out of America." And he didn't say it in response to a reporter. Another kink: in 1939, Thompson was a *former* mayor. He allegedly threatened to punch the King in 1927, when Thompson was campaigning for reelection. He won, but he left City Hall in 1931. The king at that time was George the Fifth, not the Sixth. And *neither* king ever visited Chicago.

After I spotted one error—Chicago's mayor in 1939 was Edward J. Kelly—I tracked down the rest of that trivia.

Too bad the commentator, a media critic, went ahead and wrote what had apparently been long buried in his mind—and lost in the myths of iniquity—without checking to see whether it was correct. As for that *indigenous folk greeting in Chicago that is still widely practiced,* that's not even true enough—or comprehensible enough—to comment on. More than 450 years ago, Erasmus wrote, "Be careful that you write accurately rather than much."

"Thirteen of the 14 cars of the express derailed before the mail train struck, slicing through the last two cars of the passenger train, where most of the dead and most seriously wounded were found." People hurt in accidents are *injured.* People are *wounded* when they're shot, stabbed, hit by shrapnel, or stung by a critic.

"Overnight temperatures in the upper 20s caused minimal damage to Florida orange crops, but that was chilly enough to ice some vegetables before their time, with considerable damage reported to lettuce, squash and cucumber crops in Florida." *Minimal* means "the smallest in amount or degree"; it's often confused with *nominal,* which means "in name only." A better word to describe the damage is minor or slight. Damage would have been minimal if one section of one orange had gone bad.

"Now, an early read of this would be that Secretary of State Shultz did not get his optimum out of the summit and that Defense Secretary Caspar Weinberger . . . may have gotten at or near his optimum." Since when is *read* a noun? (*Reading* is acceptable.) Another word that sticks out is *optimum.* It means "the best or most favorable condition, degree or amount." So why use a three-syllable word of Latin origin? And why not say it simply, in plain English?

"The Soviet Union has about 700 daily newspapers, with a total circulation of 83-million readers. The United States has almost 17-thousand daily newspapers, with a circulation of about 63-million readers." Circulation is measured in copies sold, not readers. Total circulation of U.S. dailies approximates 63 million, but the number of readers is estimated at more than twice that total. Further, the eagle-eyed, owl-eared Lynn Slovonsky has caught an even bigger boo-boo: The number of U.S. dailies is not 17,000, but 1,700.

"A high-level meeting between U-S and Vietnamese officials to discuss the M-I-A issue may not happen as soon as the Vietnam government has been saying." High-level meetings don't *happen;* they *occur.* Or *take place.*

"The churches were full on Sunday, even in those places where damages made indoor services impossible." *Damages* is money ordered to be paid as compensation for injury or loss. The church incurred *damage.*

"His forum was a speech to French lawmakers. . . ." A speech is not a forum. A forum is a place or even a radio or TV program.

"U-S warships launched a new convoy in the Persian Gulf today, escorting two U-S-flagged Kuwaiti tankers." Ships are launched, and carriers launch aircraft. Convoys are *formed.* And an anchor who doesn't know the difference should be keelhauled. Or the newsroom should drop anchor.

"... **ambulances waited at dockside. Shortly after the Preserver anchored, the ambulances sped off into the night.**" When a ship goes alongside a pier, it doesn't anchor; it ties up.

Now, for two local examples, unequal time:

"**The trial of a convicted mass murderer has been postponed.... Daniel Remetta is accused in the shooting death of a ... clerk two years ago.... Remetta has already been found guilty of three counts of first degree murder in Kansas, one murder in Florida, and is a suspect in a Colorado murder....**" Remetta was convicted of several murders, but he did not murder a large number of people at one time, so he's not a mass murderer. People who commit a string of murders as he did are called *serial* killers. Instead of writing that he *has already been been found guilty of three counts of first-degree murder,* it's better to say he has been *convicted of three murders.*

"**Police launched a manhunt throughout the West Wednesday for two suspects in the slaughter of five people in an auto garage, a crime similar to the 1929 Saint Valentine's Day Massacre.**" What the two crimes have in common is that they took place in garages. But in the St. Valentine's Day Massacre, seven men were killed, six of them gangsters, shot by four gangsters posing as policemen, hardly similar to what little we knew about the shootings in Pasco, Washington. (Animals are *slaughtered;* humans are *massacred.*) Just tell us what happened today. Don't reach for a comparison that is distant—and distracting. That's one way to keep from going wrong. Right?

A grab bag of glitches, gaffes and goofs:

"**Her and her parents retained an attorney and agreed to pay him one-third of any damages that they might recover in a civil lawsuit.**" Her is a bad girl, that network reporter. When a pronoun is the subject of a sentence, it should be in the nominative case. So in that excerpt, *her* should be *she*. By the time a reporter reaches network, she should know instinctively and without a moment's thought that you can't take a noun in the objective case (*her*, the object of a verb or preposition) and turn it into a subject in the nominative case (*she*). A writer should already know that, well *before* reaching network. Perhaps by fourth grade.

More network problems:

"Despite what happened at Tiananmen Square, or perhaps because of it, the Chinese don't want to think about politics much these days. What they are thinking about is how to cash in on the world's fastest-growing economy." We can't know what someone else thinks, let alone what someone else doesn't want to think about. We can only know what someone says, what someone does, and what someone *says* he thinks. How can anyone know what one billion people are thinking? Or one million, especially when it's known that that correspondent does not speak Chinese and is only visiting China? How many people told him, "I don't want to think about politics"? One? Two? Ten? Did he extrapolate the answers of a few persons to the whole populace?

"And right now, Lani Guinier, the nominee, is in meeting with President Clinton, and his staff is telling us that he feels very badly about the way she's been treated." We should all feel bad about the way *English* is being treated. People feel good or bad or somewhere in between, but people don't feel *badly*, except, perhaps, a ham-handed safecracker. *Badly* is an adverb. Adverbs, as you know, modify verbs. *Feel* is a verb, but it's a linking verb. Linking verbs—*is, was* (and other forms of *to be*), *seem, feel, taste, look, sound* and several others—do not express action. Linking verbs link the subject to a noun or an adjective and merely describe or explain the subject.

"I'm going to be honest with you. You look to me like someone who was in a car accident." Whenever someone says he's going to be honest with you, hang onto your purse or wallet. *Going* to be honest with you? When someone tells you that, you wonder whether that means that up until now he hasn't been honest with you.

"Some good news about the economy today, but even the good news isn't all that good." *Some* is flabby. So is that lead. Why take time to call the news good and then take more time to backtrack and say it's not good? What's a listener to make of all that backing and filling? The net result is zero—plus irritation. Besides, why call news good *or* bad? Our job is not to characterize the news but to tell it. Listeners will decide for themselves, if they wish, whether it's good or bad.

"In Washington tonight, a major development on the consumer health front. Federal officials say they have decided to ban those so-called anti-smoking products which are sold over the counter. Starting December first, the ban will affect dozens of non-prescription pills, tablets, lozenges and chewing gum, all supposedly made to help you quit smoking. The government says they just don't work. The ban will not affect nicotine patches and other products which are [*that are* is preferable, but neither is needed] **prescribed by doctors."** *In Washington* is not intrinsically interesting. A listener who hears a story start that way isn't going to quickly turn up the volume. It's the kind of opening that news pros call a yawner. Does *tonight* mean the *development* was announced after 6 p.m.? Or did the *development* occur sometime during the day and the writer think that *tonight* could pep it up?

"In *Anyplace*" is a weak way to start—unless. Unless it serves as a transition to a story closely related to the previous story. Or unless it's one of several items under an umbrella lead that can be delivered bing, bing, bing. For example:

"The United Nations called on its members today to send emergency food supplies to Starvenia.

"In Washington, President Thresher said she'll send wheat and meat.

"In London, Prime Minister Piccadilly said Britain will send fish and chips.

"And in Paris, President du Jour said France is sending bread and cheese."

The rest of that network script also needs rethinking—and rewriting. "A *major* development"? What other kind would an evening newscast bother to report? Yes, we might report something minor, but would we call it *minor?* As for *the consumer health front,* avoid *front*s unless you're writing about war, weather, or people who put up brave fronts. Let's rewrite the script:

"All those anti-smoking products sold over the counter have been ordered <u>off</u> the market. The government said today it's banning them as of December first: non-prescription pills, lozenges and chewing gum. The ads claim they help smokers stop, but the government says those products don't work. The ban won't affect nicotine patches and other remedies doctors prescribe." Original script: 78 words. The rewrite: 59 words. Q: Which is shorter, sharper, stronger? A: The script doctor's prescription.

"Chicago White Sox catcher Carlton Fisk established a new record for games caught last night." How many games could anyone have caught last night? An editor should have caught that—and put *last night* after *record.* Also, *new record* is an old redundancy. The editor should have deleted *new.* If someone sets a record today, it must be new or it wouldn't be a record. *Established* should be *set.* And the editor should be benched—or traded.

"The flood waters are rising; there's no denying it. More than 20 businesses are already closed, and as the muddy Mississippi grabs up more land, even. . . ." Who's *denying it?* Why inject a negative element? Put statements in a positive form; Strunk and White stress that point. After all, who'd ever say, "Don't forget the Alamo"? Or "Don't forget Pearl Harbor"? Remember! Not for nothing do Strunk and White stress the positive.

Would the National Bureau of Standards rate these network scripts (a) standout, (b) standard, or (c) ____?

"Efforts by Congress to save American jobs by putting restrictions on cheap clothing, textiles and shoes now flooding the U-S marketplace from abroad today failed." The more closely the verb follows the subject, the easier it is for the listener to follow. The verb, *failed,* is the last word, too far from the subject, *efforts.* Also, *today* is confusing because in that position it's a squinting (or swiveling) modifier: it might modify either the element before it or after it.

"Stunned by the loss of space shuttle Challenger and crew and then a string of other rocket failures that left the U-S without a way to put big payloads into space. . . ." Any idea what the subject of that dependent clause is eventually going to be? Do you ever hear anyone (besides anchors) talk that way? Well, here's the main clause: **"NASA today tried on several fronts to put failure behind and get back into the space business."** Why put *today* before the main verb? And when did NASA *leave* the "space business"? In the '60s, Ed Bliss, the editor of the "CBS Evening News," taught me to use "U-S" mostly as an adjective (*U-S State Department*), not a noun (*the U-S*). Doesn't "the President of the United States" sound more robust, he asks, than "the President of the U-S"?

Editors are paid to say no, and Ed knew how to say no, nicely. As the educator Vernon Stone says, "One Ed Bliss is worth a thousand Max Headrooms."

"Seven years ago today, Iranian students seized the U-S embassy in Teheran, taking hostages they held for 444 days. Today, seven years later, the story. . . ." With multiple *todays* and *sevens,* that writer must have been in seventh heaven.

"As autumn rushes remorselessly now toward winter, many in the northern latitudes think with longing about spring and summer. . . ." The writer should be remorseful for using *remorselessly* instead of *relentlessly,* for using *now,* and for writing *think with longing about* instead of the simple *long for.*

"The quest for the perfect tan could become increasingly dangerous, even deadly, according to a preliminary E-P-A report." *E-P-A* should be spelled out in the first mention. In writing for the ear, attribution should not be tacked on at the end of a sentence. Putting *according to* or *he said* at the end of a sentence is print style. The writer could have said: "The quest for the perfect tan could become increasingly dangerous, even deadly. According to a preliminary report from the Environmental Protection Agency, acquiring a tan is. . . ." Or skip that *according to:* "A preliminary report by the Environmental Protection Agency says. . . ." Where attribution is needed, attribution precedes assertion.

"Failure of that structure, the F-A-A says, and I quote, 'could lead to sudden decompression.'" Almost never is there a need to say *quote.* Certainly not in that case. The words inside the quotation marks are not distinctive and mean the same without the marks.

"The President called for a, quote, 'long-term solution, not a Band-aid approach to the farm economy.' Unquote." Better: "The President called for a long-term solution for farm problems, not what he called a 'Band-aid approach.'" As the author Jacques Barzun writes: "How can anything be unquoted? Very likely, the original term heard over the air was *end quote.* Whatever it was, the unnecessary phrase shows how a foolish usage winds up in nonsense."

Much sense has been written about staying away from *quote* and *unquote.* For almost 50 years, experts have been telling broadcast newswriters to avoid them. In almost every case, remarks worth quoting can be boiled down, and reporters can usually do a better job than the original speaker by paraphrasing them. If the speaker's very words need to to be preserved—because of their uniqueness, or flavor, or impact—a writer can use an attribution that is conversational: "She put it this way," or "In his words." Another approach: make it clear that someone is being quoted word for word—if the quotation is short and noteworthy—through skillful delivery.

"The Pepsi Company, which brought carbonated cola to the Russian people ten years ago, confirmed today it plans to open—get this—a chain of pizza parlors in the Soviet Union." Get this, Mr., Miss, Mrs. or Ms. Writer: You don't have poke me in an eye—or ear—to get to me.

"It's no secret that interest rates are way down, and now with a surplus of new cars waiting to be bought, the automakers are slashing. . . ." If it's not secret, why proclaim it? Avoid starting a story with a negative assertion. Also, cars don't wait to be bought; dealers try to sell 'em. And when the writer says *"the* automakers," he is referring to *all* automakers. Another script: **"But so far, the problems have been few."** No need for *the.* In most cases, there's no need for the definite article, *the,* before a plural noun.

"__ ___ has been investigating the health risk at the food table." I've heard of a kitchen table, a water table and the periodic table, but until now, I've never heard of a *food* table. Have you?

"Security forces in Chile have shot and killed three people and used water cannon and tear gas to turn back thousands of demonstrators today. It was a protest strike against. . . ." Why not use *shot* alone instead of *have shot?* We usually use the present perfect tense—*have shot*—to avoid *yesterday* in a first sentence or when *today* would be awkward. But we don't combine the present perfect and *today.* As for the first word in the script's second sentence, what's the antecedent of *it?* A strike *is* a form of protest, so why a *protest strike?* Better: "Security forces in Chile shot and killed three demonstrators today. And they fired tear gas and water cannon to turn back thousands of other people. The crowds had been protesting against the. . . ."

"Good evening. It has been a sight which the public rarely sees. [Why not just go ahead and tell us the news? If the sight weren't rare or unusual, it wouldn't be leading the newscast.] **In Washington today** [borrring], **the man who will likely be the new director of the C-I-A has been giving public testimony on how he thinks the agency should be run and how he thinks it has behaved during the Iran affair. Robert Gates is the professional intelligence officer nominated by the President. . . ."** "Give testimony"="testify." As an adverb, *likely* is commonly preceded by a qualifier, such as *most, quite* or *very.* The phrase about how the C-I-A *has behaved* should precede the one on how Gates thinks it should "behave." And a better verb than *behave* is *perform.* Further, *the man who will likely be the new director,* as the anchor put it, did not become the director. Predicting is perilous, another reason a newswriter has no business being a Newstradamus.

The Bureau of Standards' rating of those scripts? Substandard.

7

Newspapers: Handle with Extreme Caution

Newspapers can easily become noosepapers—with broadcast newswriters left out on a limb, hanging, or hanged.

Yes, papers *can* mess us up, unless we use them properly. And cautiously. This network TV script shows how not to:

"The Philippine military planned the murder of opposition leader Benigno Aquino last year. Carried it out. There was a cover-up. [The anchor sounds sure as shootin'. Based on his certitude, I assume the script is based on irrefutable fact.] **Those are the findings of the official commission of inquiry, according to today's Washington Post.** [Oh, so those judgments at the outset are not absolute. They're the findings of a commission. At least, the Post *says* those are the findings. In other words, *findings* that are thrice-removed. Had the findings already been made public? Did the Post have a pipeline? A pipe dream? The attribution at the end of the sentence is print style, not broadcast style. If you need to use a newspaper story, identify the paper in *our* style: Attribution *before* assertion.] **The paper quotes a senior official on the panel as saying that ranking officers were involved in the plot, and that President and Mrs. Marcos were not."**

Better: "The Washington Post says an official Philippine commission has found that the opposition leader Benigno Aquino was assassinated by the military. The Post quotes a senior member of the commission as saying. . . ."

43

Why did my first sentence use the passive, *was assassinated,* instead of the active voice? If I had used the active, "The Washington Post said today an official Philippine commission has found that the military assassinated the opposition leader Benigno Aquino," the key idea and key words—that the military did it—would be submerged in the middle of the sentence. Instead, I built up to the key words and put them at the end, where they receive the greatest emphasis. Also acceptable: "A Philippine commission reportedly has found that the assassination of the opposition leader Benigno Aquino was carried out by the military. The Washington Post also reports that. . . ."

A local radio script:

"Philadelphia's police department needs a lot of work [So does this script. The first sentence sounds like an editorial.] **. . . So says a report due out today. In a published preview this morning . . . the study blames poor promotion policies . . . low education requirements . . . and the failure to give the commissioner needed authority to hire key people."** Writers who pepper their copy with periods (". . ." and ". . . ." or even longer strips of dots) usually don't know how to punctuate. And writers who start with a bold statement and append "So says" or "That's what so-and-so says" probably don't know an airdate from an Airedale. Where was the preview printed? (The Philadelphia *Inquirer.*) Who conducted the study? And what does the commissioner say about all this?

Another radio script:

"Controversy continues to simmer over First Deputy John Jemilo's rejection as a finalist for the job of Chicago's next police chief . . . but Police Board President Wilbur Daniel tells the Sun-Times the resignations of two board members aren't part of it. . . ." Another wrong way to use a newspaper. We don't know for sure *what* Daniel told the paper; all we know is what the paper says Daniel said. The reporter might have misunderstood what Daniel told him, assuming Daniel did talk with him. Or a copy editor might have inadvertently changed the meaning of what Daniel said. So it would be better for a broadcast newswriter who's rewriting the newspaper article to say only that the *Sun-Times* quoted Daniel as saying something or other. That way, the broadcast writer would not be blindly accepting the paper's assertion. Still better: phone Daniel and find out for yourself what he has to say. As for the opening words of the script, *Controversy continues: controversy* is exhausted from overuse; and *continues* is a weak verb for a lead. Maybe we should be grateful, though, that the writer didn't say, "Controversy erupted. . . ." Also: was First Deputy Jemilo *rejected* or was he not selected? And what does *aren't part of it* refer to? A plot? A purge? A putsch?

How would you have handled this big newspaper story if you worked in Chicago? Would you have grabbed the story and gone right on air with it? The *Tribune* reported the death of one of the city's leading politicians, Vito Marzullo, at age 91. And it quoted James Daley, identified as a brother of then Mayor-Elect Richard M. Daley, as saying the deceased "was a great fellow and a great friend of my dad's." The story ran a full column—with a four-column head—in its late Sunday edition, April 23, 1989.

The next day, the Trib ran an even bigger (five-column head) and better story: how the deceased was *not* dead, and how the mixup happened. A man *had* died that Saturday night in Marzullo's apartment building—Marzullo's brother-in-law. A tipster mistakenly told the Trib the dead man was Marzullo. In its explanation, the Trib said it had phoned a fire department dispatcher and that he confirmed the tip. The Trib said it had not phoned Marzullo's home. The Trib's explanation didn't say Richard M. Daley has no brother James. (*Time* magazine of May 8, 1989, described the Trib's obit as front-page. It wasn't; it was page 1 of section 2.)

Almost a year later, March 3, 1990, Marzullo did die. So any Chicago stations that had rushed on air with the premature story of his death could now report that he *had* died—"as we first reported."

The *Tribune*'s most widely publicized blunder was the banner headline of Nov. 3, 1948: "DEWEY DEFEATS TRUMAN."

Truman wasn't the only man the Trib dispatched prematurely. On July 22, 1992, it acknowledged describing Murray Kempton as "the late New York Post columnist." The Trib's correction said he is "alive and now writing for New York Newsday."

And the *New York Times,* the premier U.S. daily newspaper, has sent more than one man to an early grave. On April 17, 1994, the *Times* admitted: "Because of an editing error, an article yesterday about the victims in the downing of two American helicopters over northern Iraq included one officer among the dead incorrectly. Brig. Gen. Scott Pilkington, the overall comander of the military field operation, was not killed in the incident."

Newspapers can also bring the dead back to life. The International Edition of *USA Today,* Oct. 14, 1992, acknowledged listing the late actor Yves Montand as celebrating a birthday.

And in some cases, death is not the end. The *New York Times* ran this long correction Jan. 22, 1994: "An obituary of the Rev. Norman Vincent Peale on Dec. 26 misidentified his last published book. It was 'Bible Power for Successful Living,' edited by Donald T. Kauffman, who assisted in the writing; it was not 'This Incredible Century.' The obituary also misstated the total sales of 'This Incredible Century.' The number was 74,373 through December—not nearly 20 million, which is the figure for 'The Power of Positive Thinking.' And the obituary misstated the number of languages in which 'This Incredible Century' has been published. It has come out only in English, not in 41 languages."

The *Times* reported a family reunion (June 10, 1989) and listed as a guest the chief judge of New York state's highest court—but he died in 1945. And in 1991, the *Times* conceded (Sept. 26) that it had misstated, two weeks earlier, the cause of death of one of the defendants in the Salem, Massachusetts, witchcraft trials in 1692.

The newspaper makes mistakes even when writing about itself. In reporting about first-quarter earnings, the *Times* said (April 21, 1994), it had "referred incorrectly to a projected figure of $160 million. It is the expected depreciation and amortization expense for the year, up from $129 million in 1993. The company says it does not issue projections for operating profit." The correction continued: "The article also referred incorrectly to the major source of a 62 percent improvement in the company's first-quarter earnings. The company said the gain resulted largely from rising revenues for The Times and the regional newspaper group, not just for The Times."

When it comes to big numbers, mistakes also tend to be big. Even huge. The *Times* said (April 4, 1991): "The Economic Scene column in Business Day yesterday misstated a projection by two economists at the Federal Reserve Bank of New York for the annual loss in national output if the low savings rate of the 1980's persists through the 1990's. It is $750 billion, not $750 million." The gap (or chasm): $749,250,000,000.

Even on long-established phenomena, papers err. The *Times* admitted (Sept. 23, 1993): "An article yesterday about a New Jersey celebration of the autumnal equinox misstated the time of the vernal equinox. It is in March, not June. A picture caption with the article misstated the date of the celebration. It was on Sunday, not Tuesday." And *Chicago* magazine reported (September 1991): "The *Tribune* apologized for incorrectly reporting the times for sunrise and sunset, and then for reporting a total eclipse of the sun four days before it occurred. The *Sun-Times* said in a correction that it got the eclipse wrong, too, but by only one day."

The *Wall Street Journal* acknowledged (March 21, 1994): "Armand D'Amato, brother of Sen. Alfonse D'Amato is not in a federal penitentiary. This fact was misstated in Thursday's Politics & People column. . . . He is free on bond. . . ."

A similar error incriminated the governor of Arkansas. The *New York Times* had summarized an article incorrectly, the paper said (June 3, 1994): "The Governor, Jim Guy Tucker, has not admitted loan fraud, has not entered into a plea agreement and has not been charged with wrongdoing."

Another multi-part correction ran in the *Times* two days later: "A chart last Sunday showing the corporate holdings of Rupert Murdoch's company, News Corporation Ltd., referred incorrectly to five units. Barnes & Noble Inc. was never owned by Mr. Murdoch or any of his companies. The San Antonio Express-News was sold by News Corporation in 1992. Fox Television Stations has 184 affiliates, not 140. The Herald & Weekly Times Ltd. is an airline, not an air cargo carrier."

Even brief cutlines under photographs can carry wrong information. "A picture caption yesterday about the civil war in Angola," the *Times* said (May 10, 1994), "referred incorrectly to an examination being performed on a crying child. He was being weighed and measured as part of a nutritional analysis, not measured for a coffin. . . ."

Under the head "GREAT MOMENTS IN FACT-CHECKING," the *Washington Journalism Review* reported (June 1994) the *Los Angeles Times* had run this retraction: "JoAnn Strougher has never run a crack ring as stated in a picture caption. . . ."

The *American Journalism Review* reported (February 1994) that the *Tallahassee Democrat* had said it "incorrectly stated that [one] child's father was a veterinarian; he was a Vietnam veteran." Well, at least they didn't call him a bottle-scarred veteran. Or a battle-scared veteran.

The *New York Times* said (July 12, 1992) the architect Frank Lloyd Wright started out in Oak Park, "nine miles east of the Loop." Just east of the Loop, though, is Lake Michigan. But *Barron's* (March 30, 1992) placed Chicago on the shores of Lake Erie. An even more disorienting upheaval occurred at the *Norfolk Virginian-Pilot*. *The New Yorker* reprinted (Feb. 22, 1993) a recent correction from the Virginia paper: "The map . . . published in Monday's editions contained the following errors: Libya was labeled as the Ukraine; Bulgaria and Romania were transposed; Bosnia-Herzegovina was identified as Bosnia . . . the Crimean Peninsula appeared twice on the Black Sea. . . ."

In an elaborate correction, the *Times* said (Jan. 31, 1993):

"The New York Times made a long, valiant effort to report Chemical Banking's earnings the week before last, but for every step forward toward precision, it seemed to slip two steps back. First came an error in a brief earnings report, followed the next day by a correction. But that correction somehow managed to address only part of the error, and the proper correction appeared the following day, surely ending the matter. But it was not to be. Last Sunday the Business Diary reached through this thicket of confusion, plucked out the wrong figure yet again and used it in a chart. So, in what The Times sincerely hopes is the last word on the subject, here is what Chemical earned in 1992: $1.09 billion. To repeat: $1.09 billion. . . ."

Even owning up to mistakes can lead to mistakes. The *Fort Worth Star-Telegram* printed 601 corrections or clarifications in 1993, according to a column by the paper's ombudsman. A regional editor estimated in the column (May 1, 1994) that the paper had printed 200,000 articles in 1993. That total, he said, helps put the number of corrections in perspective. Another regional editor also was quoted in the column: "Everything we do as journalists has the underlying principal: Be fair and be accurate. Making an error undermines that, not [sic] matter how 'small'—from spelling and grammar to the bare facts. Every error costs us credibility." Yet a proofreader didn't catch the *not* that should have been *no*. And failed to catch the misspelling of *principle*. Still another reminder that we must be alert, be careful, be skeptical. And beware.

Errors sneak into newspapers every day, but we usually don't know where, unless someone complains and the paper prints a correction. Or unless the story is one we happen to be tracking down. Or unless it's about us. You can get some idea of the prevalence of mistakes in even the country's best newspapers by reading the boxes set aside for corrections and editors' notes. "We run corrections, " Jay Mathews of *Newsweek* wrote (in *The New Republic* of May 18, 1992), "but anyone who has worked as a reporter or editor knows how narrowly the correctable mistake is defined and how many errors never get corrected. The real problem is not so much mega-booboos . . . , which tend to get noticed and fixed, but the innumerable little errors. Spreading from newspaper to television to magazine and back again, they are magnified by repetition into bigger ones, and nibble away at press credibility."

Another source of erroneous or false stories is hoaxes. Most people who hatch hoaxes phone newsrooms and depend upon gullible newsmen to breathe life into their humbug and give it wings. "Be constantly on guard against hoax attempts," warns the *Reuters Handbook for Journalists:* "Be suspicious and check sources. Do not use news until its authenticity has been proved. . . . Regard all information you receive by telephone as suspect unless you know the caller. If you do not [know the caller], ask for full name, title and telephone number. Also ask for the switchboard number to call back on to ensure that the call is coming from the company identified by the caller.

"Make an independent check of the name and number, then telephone back. Get confirmation that it was indeed this person who telephoned you. Use the same precautions with unsolicited material received by fax or telex.

"Be on guard against April Fool hoaxes and all fantasies such as the birth of five-legged sheep, human pregnancies lasting 18 months, the marriage of 100-year-old sweethearts, perfect bridge hands and miracles."

When we consider those erroneous stories, we see that broadcasters need firm guidelines in using newspapers:

1. Proceed with extreme caution. A sage once said, "How many pens were broken, how many ink bottles were consumed, to write about things that never happened!"

2. Don't accept whatever you read as fact. No matter how respected the paper, how prominent the byline, how well written the story, newspapers are bedeviled by mistakes. The best papers carry hundreds of thousands of facts every day, and though they strive for accuracy, they generally slip up in a few places. Reporters make mistakes, editors make mistakes, typesetters make mistakes, proofreaders make mistakes. We all make mistakes. (I hope you don't find any of mine—or too many of mine.)

3. If a newspaper has an important exclusive or another worthwhile story you want to broadcast, how do you know what to believe? Even if 99 percent of what you read in the best newspapers is right, how can you tell which one percent is wrong? If you don't have the time or resources to confirm a story or dig it out on your own, go ahead and rewrite it. But make sure you credit the newspaper (in broadcast style). One selfish reason: You won't be sticking your neck out; you'll be sharing—or shifting—responsibility.

4. Don't steal stories from newspapers, even if it's only petty larceny.

To sum up: Keep your nose in the news but your neck out of the noose. Newspapers do serve a purpose—as tip sheets. But, as the English writer Samuel Butler said, "The most important service rendered by the press is that of educating people to approach printed matter with distrust."

Do you ever hear stories that have as many holes as fishnets? Well, how many holes can you find in these broadcast scripts?

"A great white shark was spotted some 300 yards off Santa Cruz. Tim Morley of the Santa Cruz harbormaster's office spotted it off Lighthouse Point. He said he went out in a 15-foot boat and the shark was longer than the boat."

Spotted twice in a row? A spotted shark? *Then* what happened? Why did Morley go out? Did he row, sail, or motor? (In a Santa Cruzer?) How far did he go? What did he do when he got there? Did he try to catch the shark, club it, shoot it, shoo it, muzzle it, nuzzle it, feed it, film it—or just measure it? When he approached the shark, what did it do? How close did Morley get? Did the shark endanger any swimmers, surfers or sailors? Anything unusual about the shark's visit? The script says Tim is *of* the harbormaster's office? What does *that* mean? Is he the harbormaster? A deputy? A gofer?

No script—and that one is reprinted in full—could or should answer *all* those questions. But the writer should have the answers so he can make an intelligent assessment. Does he have a story?

The first sentence of the script is good. As soon as I hear *great white shark,* I'm hooked. But where do we go from there? What's the point of the story? Why should we care? Is there any conflict, struggle, suspense? Is it a story of man against nature, man against the supernatural, writer against the clock—or producer against the insatiable maw of all-news?

With so many questions unanswered, the best thing the producer or editor could have done with that shark story is to toss it back.

Now what about this script—also reprinted in its entirety:

"And a birthday today. Author Joseph Wambaugh is 52." So what? How many listeners recognize his name? Two percent? And how many who know Wambaugh's name care about the anniversary? Even if a listener is inspired to send Wambaugh a card or a wombat, where would the listener send it? The script should include the title(s) of his most widely known book(s). But why bother at all with that non-news item? Use your time, energy and resources for news, not for trifles lighter than air.

Although the next story is heavier than air, the script itself needs more heft:

"The former executive director of Goodwill was sentenced to five years in prison yesterday for his ill will. [The *Goodwill—ill will* combo may sound pleasing to the ear, but the name of the organization is not Goodwill; it's Goodwill *Industries*. Because *yesterday* in a first sentence is usually a dirty word, it's advisable to use the present perfect tense and say he *has been sentenced*—omitting *yesterday*. The grammarian John B. Opdycke writes, in *Get It Right!*, "The present perfect tense (sometimes called simply the perfect tense) should be used to indicate something that has recently happened or that frequently or continuously happens, without fixing the time definitely."] **"54-year-old Harry Woodward Junior of Winnetka pleaded guilty to charges that he diverted charitable funds for personal use.** [Better: ". . . pleaded guilty to diverting charitable gifts to his own use."] **It was the second sentence handed down against Woodward.** [That sentence is unnecessary, as the next one shows.] **Last month, Woodward was sentenced to eight years on similar charges in federal court**. [Better: "Last month, a federal judge sentenced him—on similar charges—to eight years." But the writer neglected to tell us that the latest sentencing took place in a state court.]

"Both sentences will be served concurrently." Again, the writer shortchanged us. How much money did the defendant steal? Answer: $220,000. And how much money was he convicted of taking in the federal case? $480,000. Almost certainly, the writer was informed of those amounts. If he wasn't, he should have found out.

Are you satisfied with the next script, also from Chicago?

"Charges have been dropped against two men who sat in jail for more than a year awaiting their trial for murder and armed robbery, and a man already in

prison for robbery has been indicted in the crimes. Derrick Hamilton and Eugene Williams repeatedly denied shooting and robbing a man last year at the Granville El[evated] platform. Today, charges against them were dismissed, and Calvin Binion has been accused of the crimes." That's the script in full. Well, I'd rather hear the story's details than the two suspects' denials. They didn't do it? (That's what they all say.) Why were they charged in the first place? *Why* were the charges dropped? *Why* did the grand jury indict the man in prison? And listeners outside Chicago might wonder, in what city did the story occur?

I've taken the liberty of rewriting the script (who's to stop me?), using only the few facts in the script: "Two men jailed in Chicago on a murder charge for more than a year have been freed, and a man already in prison has been indicted for murder. The victim was robbed and shot last year on the Granville El platform. Today, charges against Derrick Hamilton and Eugene Williams were dropped." My version also is inadequate because it lacks important information, but at least it's more airworthy, and just one phone call to the police or prosecutor would probably fill in the blanks.

This TV script starts with voice-over:

"A confrontation at this house has some police officers in San Gabriel worried about AIDS. The officers were trying to subdue a man when he came at them with a four-foot pole. They shot him with an electronic tazer gun like this one, opening a wound that spattered blood on several officers. It was then that the man informed them he has AIDS. Several officers are reportedly having an AIDS antibody test. The suspect is being held under observation."

That script has so many holes, I'm afraid the only treatment that could help would be insertion in a shredder. So I'll limit myself to just one question: *Why* were police trying to subdue the man? *Why? Why* don't writers answer more questions than they raise? *Why,* oh, *why?* That's why every newshound should be a *Why*maraner.

8

Rereading, Rethinking, Rewriting

"There is no such thing as good writing," Mark Twain said, "only good rewriting."

And editors might add, "There's no such thing as good reading, only good *re*reading." Rereading of source copy and rereading of what you have just written. Then, a good rewriting.

A good rereading—aloud, to ourselves—can catch all sorts of slips before our words go on air. Do you see where these broadcast scripts slipped?

"In Lake County tonight, there is a new development to report about a head-on car crash . . . that killed six people in Antioch. [The lead presents no real news. Obviously, the story is new and a development or else it wouldn't be on a major-market newscast. Many stories, if not most, consist of new developments. It's best to go ahead and report the news. Yes, rather than take time to trumpet what you're going to tell us, just tell us. You don't walk up to a friend and announce, "I'm going to say hello. Hello."] **"The county coroner's office is saying that the drivers of both cars were legally drunk at the time of the accident.** [Unless you're writing about a different jurisdiction, *county* is superfluous. The coroner is commonly a county officer. *Is saying that* can be reduced to—and improved by—*says*. The writer is already focusing on the accident, so *at the time of the accident* is unnecessary. *Legally drunk* means the alcohol content of the drivers' blood exceeds the legal limit. But in a script

55

about *illegal* conduct, the term *legally drunk* sounds contradictory. The drivers were *illegally* drunk.] **"The crash occurred last Sunday on State Highway 59. . . ."**

The news in the script is that both drivers were drunk. So the key word is *drunk*. But it's lost in the word-hash. Let's try to fix it: "The Lake County coroner says that in the car crash that killed six people, including the drivers, both drivers were drunk. The head-on crash occurred Sunday on State Highway 59 in Antioch. . . ."

Another candidate for rereading—and rewriting:

"13 fraternity brothers at the University of Southern Maine are looking for a place to stay tonight. The Sigma Nu house on School street in Gorham was heavily damaged by fire this afternoon. A carpenter working on a remodelling project discovered the fire in the attic.

"Firefighters from Westbrook and Scarborough helped out this afternoon. The fire was tough to contain because it was inside the walls and ceilings. Fire damage appears to have been confined to the third floor and attic, but there is smoke and water damage elsewhere. The university is making arrangements for the students who lived in the fraternity house."

If the writer had reread his script carefully, he would have caught an apparent inconsistency: in the first sentence, he says the frat members are looking for a place to stay. In his last sentence, he says the school is making arrangements to house them. If the last sentence means the school has found lodgings for them, would the frat members still be looking? This next script also needs a good rereading—and rewriting:

"They've finally figured out why all those electric garage-door openers were acting up in the San Francisco Bay area, opening the doors at random. [A definite article, *the,* is unneeded before *doors;* it seldom is with a plural noun. Better: "opening garage doors."] **"The Navy has finally** [two *finally*s in two sentences?] **come clean in the door-jam[b] case, admitting it was using a transmitter on Mount Diablo to relay satellite messages**

to a ship after the vessel's other system broke down. [*Admitting* suggests wrongdoing. Better: *acknowledging.* Why shift from *ship* to *vessel?* Don't strain for synonyms. Preferable to *vessel's:* a simple *its. Other system? What other system?*] **"Residents welcomed the Navy's new open-door policy."** [*Home owners* is better than residents; it's specific. The Navy's transmissions were causing those private doors to open, so how can residents welcome the *open-door policy?*]

A script from Canada:

"This time yesterday we were telling you about a howling blizzard blowing across Atlantic Canada. The storm is offshore now, over the Atlantic this morning, after leaving a few centimetres of snow in Halifax, but up to 30 centimetres in. . . ."

Why start by telling us what you told us 24 hours ago? People tune in to get the latest news, not a recap. Better: "The blizzard that was blowing across Canada has now blown out to sea."

"An eleven-year-old firesetter from Biddeford will be tried for murder as a juvenile—not as an adult." By calling the kid a firesetter, you've convicted him before the trial. We're familiar with *trendsetter* and *pinsetter,* but *firesetter* is not ready for air—or the *typesetter.* It's too hot off the keyboard.

"Given the weekend activities at the White House, it's clear that there has been a change of style as well as occupant. ___'s ___ _____ is watching the early days of the Bush Presidency:" The opening word, *Given,* is a poor word to start a script. Better: "The weekend activities at the White House make it clear that not only is there a new occupant, there's a new style." *Given*s should be restricted to stories about formal debates and Mike Tyson's first wife.

"The workshop—in conjunction with the American Association of School Administrators——is the first of 50 to be held in every state." Let's see: $50 \times 50 = 2,500$. Or did the writer mean "the first of 50, one in each state"?

"Prime Minister Mulroney has appointed two new people to the bench. . . ." New *people?* What *had* they been, scarecrows?

"Tomorrow, Maine's Bishop Edward O'Leary will be passing the reins of the Catholic church to a new man. Bishop O'Leary is retiring after 14 years at the head of. . . ." Does a religious institution have reins? A new *man?* What was he previously, a nun?

A recent study has found that news directors and educators say writing is the most important criterion of quality in a TV newscast. Six years ago, a similar study was conducted with similar findings. But this time news directors mentioned writing far more frequently.

Yes, writing *is* important, but here's a plug for both *re*reading and *re*writing.

9

Thou Shalt Not
Bury a Verb in a Noun

A new commandment: Thou shalt not bury a verb in a noun. Nouns are the bones that give a sentence body. And verbs are the muscles that make it go. If your first sentence lacks a strong verb, your script will lack go-power. Let's examine a broadcast script—sentence-by-sentence—and see how it goes, or stalls:

"An Amtrak train derailment in northern Colorado . . [the script uses two dots] **and passengers called it a nightmare of flying bodies . . . screaming and fear."** [The noun *derailment* conceals a much-needed verb, *derailed*. As a result, the first verb in the script is *called,* which goes nowhere. If you visualize the train's jouncing off the tracks, you'll realize *called* is uncalled for.]

"Two engines and five cars jumped the tracks . . . with four of them sliding into the Fraser river." [Does *them* refer to the cars or a combination of cars and engines? But before the writer starts to inventory the rolling stock, I wish he'd tell me about the people. After I hear of an accident, my first question is: anyone hurt?

[How deep was the water? How far into the river did the train go? Is the site in the wilderness? What's the nearest town? Was it dark? Where was the train going? Where was it coming from? Name of the train?]

"Officials say the roadbed was weakened by melting snow . . . and slid out from under the rails last night." [*Last night?* Was that also when the train derailed? Were the officials from Amtrak or the county?

59

Wouldn't Amtrak officials prefer that the accident be regarded as an act of God rather than the result of Amtrak negligence? Or do they blame that French painter, Toulouse-Lautrec (too-loose la track)?]

"31 passengers and 18 crewmen were taken to local hospitals . . . either for treatment or observation." [At long last, we hear about the injured. Put *49 people* near the top and provide the breakdown of the two groups later. No need for *local*. And no need for *either,* either. We assume that people are taken to the nearest hospitals. If they're flown to Anchorage, say so. Were the injured taken from the scene by raft? By mule? By chopper? How many people were on board the train? Or is 49 the total on board? Better: "All [?] 49 passengers and crewmen were taken to hospitals. Some of them were treated for shock and minor injuries [if the facts warrant], and some were admitted for observation."]

"Fortunately . . . there was only one serious injury." [Strike *fortunately.* For the person injured, it wasn't so fortunate.] **Obviously . . . it could have been a great deal worse."** Strike *obviously.* If anything is obvious, there's no need to say *obviously.* And if something is not obvious, a writer would be foolish to add *obviously.* So it's best not to use the word at all. Besides, any accident or natural disaster—especially an earthquake that kills tens of thousands of people—*could have been a great deal worse.*

Fortunately (and unfortunately), that script could *not* have been a great deal worse.

This next script also buries a verb in a noun:

"A law that was passed as a way to stop prostitution may be changed soon . . . because of a complaint by a member of a film crew. [Better: "because a film crewman *complained.*"] **The man wanted a masseuse to give him a massage but found out that it is illegal in Tacoma for a woman to give a massage to a man.** [This implies that it's illegal for a woman to massage her husband.] **The Tacoma city attorney found**

out about it [What does *it* refer to? And *found out* so soon again?] **and decided it was time to do something about changing the law . . . which women's groups and the city's own Women's Rights Division have advocated for some time."** That's the script in its entirety. What's the news in that story? Ay, there's the rubdown! The script says the city attorney "decided it was time to do something about changing the law," but *what?* And is he doing it? Is he drafting a bill for introduction in the city council or the state legislature? Or what? So why does the lead say the law may be changed—and soon?

Why the ellipses? Could it be that writers who use those dots don't know how to punctuate properly? Three or four dots may be useful to indicate the anchor's voice is to trail off. But, otherwise, standard punctuation marks can do the job.

A network burial of a verb: **"The Supreme Court, by a five-to-four ruling, said today that discount houses can continue to sell some quality goods even though the product manufacturers don't want them to. . . ."** The specifics of the court's vote should be deferred. Whether the vote was unanimous or a five-to-four squeaker, the ruling carries the same force. Better: "The Supreme Court *ruled* that discount houses may still sell certain goods even though the makers of the goods want the discounters to stop. The vote was five to four." Not every story needs a *today,* so I left it out. Newscasters often refer to the Supreme Court as "the high court," but isn't it "the *highest* court"?

Another network burial: **"The Dow-Jones is at 22-19, a gain of 13 points."** Better: The Dow-Jones has *gained* 13 points. It *stands* at 22-19." Burying a verb in a noun usually leaves a sentence weak. Better: "A writer who *buries* a verb in a noun usually weakens a sentence."

Can you see where the next writer went wrong?

"Fawn Hall is coming out with a book, but don't expect any 'kiss-and-tell' secrets from her days working for Oliver North. Hall, the former secretary, says her

story is about her childhood, growing up in a family of civil servants, working for the government. Well, she's hoping you'll read it, anyway. And she's undoubtedly having more fun writing it, since she's working on the book on the shores of Malibu." Eight *ings*: *coming, working, growing, working, hoping, having, writing, working*. The pinging of the *ing-ing* is vexing. So is the naive tone. Unless Miss Hall says she's going to tell us what went on in Colonel North's office, day *and* night—the shredding, altering, destroying, falsifying, removing, concealing, obstructing and lawbreaking—who cares that she's writing a book? In any case (even a *book* case), how can anyone say at this point that she's *coming out with a book?* Even if she has a contract and submits a completed manuscript, her publisher might not accept it. Further, both Fawn Hall and Oliver North need to be identified.

This sentence in the script throws me: **"And she's undoubtedly having more fun writing it."** More fun than doing what? And since when is writing fun? Anyone who thinks writing is fun hasn't done it—or hasn't done it well.

Oceans have coasts, lakes have shores, rivers have banks. Malibu does have a shoreline, and boats head for its shore, but have you ever heard anyone talk about "the *shores* of Malibu?"

Undoubtedly makes me doubt. It's a word I avoid using. But if I were told I must put it in a sentence, I'd try this:

"Undoubtedly, Miss Hall is not going to make any great books or any great bucks." I refuse to fawn.

10

*Ing*lish

If it's true that we learn more from our failures than our successes, these flops have a lot to teach us. A lesson from network television:

"The latest news on inflation is less optimistic." They say an optimist is a person who hasn't yet heard the day's news. But whatever they say, only a *person*—not news—can be optimistic.

The last sentence of that script also needs help: **"The Dow was down more than 62 points."** The verb *was* is a linking verb and doesn't convey action. The writer needs an action verb like *fell*. Or *sank*. Or *slid*. Or *slipped*. Or *skidded*. Or *dropped*. Or *tumbled*. But *was* doesn't move. Join the action faction.

Another script that doesn't move, or makes the wrong moves:

"Well, investors pumping dollars into stocks today. [That doesn't sound like anything a grown-up would say. Certainly not to another grown-up. If the writer were reporting at midday, he'd be justified in saying investors *"are* pumping" dollars into stocks today. But *pumping* by itself is not a verb; it's a participle. A participle has no tense; it functions as an adjective, never as a verb. To pump iron into his sentence, the writer of this night-time script on national television should have used a finite verb, one that has a tense. Or he could have used an auxiliary verb (a form of *be, do, have* and others) with *pumping* and produced *were pumping*. Why did the writer avoid the past tense *pumped?* Is a puzzlement. A strong verb is what makes a sentence move. Not a pulpy participle.]

The script continues:

"The Dow Jones Industrials at a record high tonight. [Another sentence without a verb. In fact, a stream of sentences without verbs.] **The rally supported by a rebound in the high technology sector.** [Without the auxiliary *was, supported* is a past participle—and acts as an adjective.] **It was only Friday that we were having problems in the technology sector.** [*We?* He? Not me.] **For the day, the blue chip index up 49.57.** [Again, no verb.] **The Dow tonight at 2870.49.** [There he goes again.] **A day of light trading, however.** [He weakens his sentence fragment by tacking on *however.* Let's shift the emphasis to the key word: "But trading was *light.*"]

"Almost 137½ million shares changing hands. [Still no verb. Maybe it's a stunt: he wants to see how far he can float through the air without touching solid ground. Better than *changing hands: were traded.*] **Advancing issues beating out decliners by a margin of 11 to 4.** [Still no verb. The *ing-ing* of participles carries no zing. And *11 to 4* is not a margin; it's a ratio.] **The New York Stock Exchange Composite Index up strongly; up 2.86.** [The lack of a verb makes this incomplete sentence weak *and* wordy. Better: "The New York Stock Exchange Composite Index *rose* two-point-86."] **The S&P 500 moving to that new record high, gaining 6.07 on the day.** [*That* refers to an item near the top of the program. *On the day* is superfluous. **"And a new record high** [*new record* is an old redundancy] **for the Standard & Poor's 500 index as well. The S&P closing above 360 for the first time ever** [another redundancy]." Newcomers to this country whose English is wobbly lean heavily on participles instead of verbs with tenses. You might call that language *Ing*lish. The writer of the script, by relying on verbless sentences, winds up with sludge.

A local TV script: Near the end of a piece about a baby shaken violently by a guardian and gravely hurt, a reporter wrote:

"Dakota County Attorney Jim Backstrom is asking the Minnesota legislature to amend the malicious punishment statute by creating stiffer penalties for shaken babies that suffer great bodily harm. . . ." Penalize shaken babies? Why not penalize writers who cause great mental harm?

Another excerpt from TV: **"Researchers say if you want the oatmeal or oat bran to work, you've got to keep eating it."** Only ruminants (cattle, sheep, goats, deer, camels, giraffes), which chew their cud, could keep eating it. Better: ". . . you must eat it regularly."

A Midwestern TV script: **"Residents of London are in shock tonight** [highly unlikely during an evening newscast in the Midwest because at midnight in London, most people are asleep or trying to sleep]. **Terrorists today** [*before* the verb? no] **attacked the very heart of their** [the terrorists'?] **government.** [*Very* adds nothing to *heart.* Next, voice-over.] **The Irish Republican Army is claiming responsibility for launching three mortars** [the IRA fired mortar *shells;* no one can "launch" mortars] **from this van, at the home of the British prime minister. The terrorists then set the van on fire and fled.** [You'd think they'd at least have the decency to wait for police.] **Four people suffered minor injuries** [weapons *wound.* Better: "Four people were wounded slightly"], **but no government officials were hurt. . . ."**

Other local scripts:

"An underground leftist group apparently allied with Iraq is claiming credit for the murder of a U-S civilian in Turkey." The group may *claim*—and they say they deserve—*credit.* But we say "claim *responsibility.*"

"The less invasive procedure centers around a laparascope, a long metal instrument. . . ." Impossible: a center can't fit *around* anything. It "centers *on.*"

"President Bush's proposed national energy policy is under close scrutiny by several key senators. [Scrutiny is close examination, so *close scrutiny* is redundant.] **The President's plan went before the Senate Energy Committee today and received a less-than-warm welcome. . . .**" Strong newswriting is positive, not coy or negative. *Less than warm* = lukewarm.

Last (and perhaps least), another local TV script: **"In world news, the saying a woman will change her mind is sometimes true even if she's the leader of a country. . . ."** That's *world news?* (The transition—*In world news*—is not needed. It's never needed.) It *is* true that women change their minds. But so do men. So what? What does that have to do with the story?

If anyone should have changed his mind, it was the writer. Also, the editors who approved that script—and all those other scripts—should have changed their minds and their scripts.

As soon as writers see how *not* to do it, they're halfway home. These network scripts can help light the way: **"Still on the same subject, along with the winter weather has come the winter flu. The Centers for Disease Control in Atlanta now says a severe flu epidemic has swept across the entire country, with all but three states reporting cases of the type-A flu. And, sadly, the C-D-C expects it will get worse."**

Let's look at the transition: *Still on the same subject* deserves a prize for banality—and nonsensicality. The script, reprinted in its entirety, follows a package about the harsh winter, so the anchor could simply start: "Now comes the flu." If he's feeling extravagant, he can use five words instead of four: "Along with winter, the flu."

Sadly? If we're going to sprinkle subjective adverbs in scripts, we can apply *sadly* to almost every story from Belfast to Belgrade to Bujumbura—and from burgs 'n' 'burbs between.

A C.D.C. spokesman told me the correct usage is "The Centers for Disease Control *say*"—not *says*. He also said flu is not seasonal and that there's no such thing as *winter* flu. Our scrutiny of that script brings to mind Mark Twain's criticism of asserted defects in less than one page of *The Deerslayer:* "[James Fenimore] Cooper has scored 114 offenses against literary art out of a possible 115. It breaks the record."

Twain went on to urge that a writer "say what he is proposing to say, not merely come near it; use the right word, not its second cousin; eschew surplusage . . . ; avoid slovenliness of form; use good grammar; employ a simple and straightforward style." *Still on the same subject,* Twain also said, "The difference between the almost right word and the right word is really a large matter—'tis the difference between the lightning bug and the lightning."

So let's rewrite that sick script: "The government says a severe flu epidemic is sweeping the country. All but three states have reported cases of type-A flu. And the government expects the epidemic to get worse."

On second thought, the revision can be revised. That revision reduced *Centers for Disease Control in Atlanta* to *government,* but we can dispense with the first attribution. We can safely assume the C.D.C. wouldn't falsely announce an epidemic. So let's present it as what an old city editor of mine called "a true known fact": "A severe flu epidemic is sweeping the country. All states but three report cases of type-A flu. And the Centers for Disease Control in Atlanta say it'll get worse." (I include *Atlanta* because it'll cue some listeners to recall in a nanosecond, "Oh, yeah, that's that federal outfit.")

Another network script, after a story about the so-called suicide doctor: **"More medical news now.** [Each of those words can be jettisoned. *Should be* jettisoned.] **There's a new study out tonight that says that prostate cancer is diagnosed at a later stage in black men in this country than in whites. The disease is the leading cancer killer in all men, but blacks are 80 percent more**

likely than whites to get prostate cancer and twice as likely to die from it." There's that *there is,* a dead phrase. And the sentence is further sapped by two *that*s. It's also weakened by *out tonight.* Those two words were probably intended to make the news seem newsier. (*Diagnosed* was used correctly; a condition is diagnosed, not a patient.)

Cancer killer? Cancer does kill, but *cancer killer* should be excised. Cancer doesn't kill intentionally, so the disease can't be called a *killer.* Also: a *cancer killer* sounds like a substance that kills cancers. For example: *weed killer, pain killer, time killer.*

Better: "A new U-S study says prostate cancer is diagnosed in black men later than in white men. The disease kills more men than any other cancer. Blacks are 80 percent more likely than whites to get prostate cancer and twice as likely to die of (not *from*) it."

The anchor began his next lead-in, **"Turning overseas now, Bosnia's warring factions. . . ."** *Turning overseas?* If a story comes from Alaska, would you preface it with "Turning northwest?"

Another script from the same 'cast: **"An American diplomat kidnapped in Yemen five days ago is free tonight. Haynes Maloney, head of the. . . ."** *Tonight* again. If Maloney was freed that day, *is free tonight* is correct, but weak. And possibly deceptive. To say he *is* free doesn't tell us whether he has been free for an hour, a day, or a week. Better: "A U-S diplomat kidnapped in Yemen five days ago has been freed." The rewrite gets rid of the wishy-washy *is* and transforms the adjective *free* into a verb. The use of the perfect tense—*has been freed*—gives the story a sense of recency, if not immediacy. *Is,* a linking verb, expresses no action. Verbs can make sentences go. Or, in the case of *is,* go limp. That doesn't apply when *is* serves as an auxiliary (or helping) verb, as in *is running.* The advice to avoid *is* and other forms of *to be* in a first sentence applies only when *is*—or *was* or *are* or *were*— stands alone, without a participle (*running*).

The artificiality of inserting *tonight* in a story that broke during the day can be seen in another piece on the same newscast. The anchor said in his lead-in, "**In Chicago tonight, there's a spirited, even confrontational debate under way, and three dolphins are caught in the middle, literally** [a word that adds nothing, *really*]. [The network]**'s ___ ___ on what's wild, what's not and what's the difference.**" But the reporter began, "**In Chicago today.**" And nowhere in his script does the reporter use *tonight*. I, the jury, find: the anchor shaved the truth—and nicked its jugular.

Another network newscast also infected by *tonight* fever: "**More weather trouble to report tonight. Hurricane Calvin is threatening the southwest coast of Mexico tonight with top winds of. . . .**" The script came after a flood story. So let's try this: "More weather trouble. Hurricane Calvin is threatening the southwest coast of Mexico with top winds of. . . ." That ditches *tonight* and *tonight*. ("*Tonight,* and *tonight,* and *tonight,*/ Creeps in this petty ratings pace from script to script,/ To the last syllable of reordered time. . . .")

Those duds may cause critics to say many a script should be scrapped and many an editor sacked. But I say: we need more editors, and more editors must edit. And we need more writers who realize that good writing is the sum of many small things done right.

11

Missing Links

Too bad that milk cartons don't carry appeals for the folks missing from so many newsrooms: editors. Their absence causes many newscasts to leave listeners with a sour taste—or a blank look.

"The Civil Air Patrol, in addition to helping find missing aircraft, also teaches aerospace education to young people." *Teaches . . . education?* Forget about *missing aircraft.* Find those missing editors.

"Health officials are keeping their eyes out for red measles. . . ." Bulging eyes? Sounds like Graves' disease. The idiom is "keep an eye out for." Even if you are using a plural subject (*health officials*), it sounds better to keep *an* eye out. Rely on your ear.

"Hitting the big 'four-oh' is something most of us would rather not face." [Rather not live to 40? Speak for yourself, Jack. Or Jill. The script goes on to tell of a governor who hit 40.] **"And if growing older lacks dignity, the governor is making up for it with dignitaries."** The writer's implication that growing older lacks dignity might leave some listeners indignant. And the implication that you can acquire dignity by hobnobbing with dignitaries is something most listeners won't dig.

"Highway patrol officials say a Jefferson City man is dead this morning after the car he was driving ran off Highway 134 and overturned several times just south of Osage Beach in Miller County. Troopers say 29-year-old Elmer Stockman was thrown from the

wreckage of his car and died later at a Columbus hospital." Thrown from the wreckage? That's one for Ripley. Once the moving car overturns and shudders to a stop, the inert wreck can't fling the driver out. A story about a one-car accident needn't start with the source. If you have confidence in the troopers, go ahead and say—without attribution—that a motorist was killed. I wouldn't write that he *is* dead because *is*—or any form of *to be*—is deadly. It doesn't express action. Often, when you find *after* in your first sentence, you're telling the story in the wrong sequence. So you should switch what you have *after* to *before.*

When a prominent person dies, it is acceptable to write: "Churchill is dead. He died today at. . . ." That works because the story is big and the sentence is short. And it's driven home by *dead,* a one-syllable word that starts and ends with a *d,* giving it a firm thud. At the end of that broadcast script, we don't need *later.* The driver couldn't have gone to the hospital and died there earlier.

Better: "A Jefferson City motorist, Elmer Stockman, went off the road [today?], his car overturned, and he was killed. The accident occurred on Highway 134 near Osage Beach in Miller County. Stockman was 29 years old." What about Stockman? His occupation? His family? What caused the accident? Mechanical failure? Below the original script, the writer supplied another version of the story (for another newscast) that said the driver lost control of his car. That information should have been used in the first version—with attribution. Any evidence of speeding or drinking? Was he wearing a seatbelt? What time was the accident? On his way home from work? Church? A party?

"Where is the hurricane presently, and where is it headed towards?" That network anchor's question to a meteorologist is windy. *Presently* means "soon," not "now" or "at present." When you ask where the hurricane is, the *is* says it's blowing at this very moment, so you don't need *now.* And in this country, the word generally used is *toward,* without the *s.* But in *where is it headed towards,* the preposition *towards* is unneeded—and untoward.

"Good evening. Here's what's happening. . . ." Newscasters needn't announce they're going to give us news. Newscasts present what *has* happened, usually not what *is* happening.

"A deadly explosion at a Texas chemical plant tops other news of the world this morning. [Newscasts are expected to lead with the top story, so there's no need to call the top story the top story. Or to say, "We begin with . . ." When an anchor begins talking, we can tell he has begun.] **Fourteen employees of an Atlantic Richfield plant in Channelview, Texas, are** [a form of *to be*] **dead this morning. The explosion happened late last night at the plant** [where else?] **in a suburb of Houston. Witnesses described a flash and a ball of fire that looked like a rocket. No word yet on what caused the blast."**

Better: "An explosion in a Texas chemical plant has killed 14 workers. (By using the present perfect tense *has killed,* we avoid the static *is.* And we don't want to use *last night* in the first sentence.) The explosion occurred last night at an Atlantic Richfield plant in Channelview, near Houston. (What those witnesses say is not unusual, except for the *ball of fire* described as looking *like a rocket.* How can a sphere look like a cylinder? Let's skip it.) No word on the cause."

Another script: "[Voice-over] **The charge: flying under the influence of alcohol, on a flight between Fargo, North Dakota, and Minneapolis last March. . . ."** What did the network anchor mean—in July, 1990— when she said "last March"? She would have removed doubt by saying "in March" or "this March." Or "four months ago." No time element is advisable at the *end* of that sentence: you don't want to end with weak, incidental or irrelevant words.

Another network anchor: **"Although the Persian Gulf crisis broke into the headlines just four weeks ago,**

it's already become a factor in political races around this country." Why mention newspaper headlines and publicize the competition? Better: "Though the Persian Gulf blew up a month ago, it has become an issue in U-S political races."

Where, oh, where have our editors gone? Without them, *we*'re lost.

The search for missing editors has turned up more batches of scripts lacking their fingerprints. So searchers must move firmly. Let's set up a hotline to help find the missing editors and offer rewards for information on their whereabouts. No questions asked. No questions, that is, except those raised by recent broadcast scripts:

"All across the Midwest today, small towns and big cities prepared for an earthquake that has been forecast for Monday. [Voice-over] People from Indiana to Arkansas are all talking about the shaky forecast which comes from New Mexico climatologist Iben Browning. He says the New Madrid fault will produce a major quake in the next few days. The U-S Geological Survey says there's no scientific merit to Browning's prediction. But thousands of people are gearing up anyway. Communities are holding emergency disaster drills, residents are stockpiling food and water, and some schools have even. . . ."

The trouble starts with the first word: *all* is a risky word because it's all-encompassing. It creates the impression of millions of people preparing for the quake. But soon we tumble into an abyss caused by an internal inconsistency: The fifth sentence says *thousands* of people are preparing.

In the second sentence, the writer again uses *all* and implies that the forecast is the hottest topic around. Even though we don't know what was being said anywhere in the Midwest, let alone everywhere, we surmise that most people in most places were not spending much time, if any, talking about the forecast.

If the writer had tried to calibrate the reaction in the Midwest instead of exaggerating with *all*, he might have been on safe ground. Even *almost all* and *most* (more than 51 percent) would have been tall talk. *Many* seems like too many, *some* sounds soggy, and *quite a few* is untrue. And with tens of millions of people in the Midwest, *thousands* are barely a trace. Why not stick with what's probably the news agency's safe estimate—*thousands?* That way, you have no need to characterize that as *not many, barely any, almost none,* or *a drop in the bucket.* The number speaks for itself.

Another fault: the writer doesn't identify the state where the town of New Madrid, the expected epicenter, stands (or trembles), or where the fault line runs. (The script was not written in Missouri or the Midwest.)

Let's rewrite it: "The government says the forecast of an earthquake in New Madrid, Missouri, is groundless. [Voice-over] Though the U-S Geological Survey dismisses the forecast, thousands of people in the Midwest are preparing for a quake. . . ."

"In news from Washington . . . Last night we told you that outgoing Florida Governor Bob Martinez was in line to become the nation's next drug czar. Today, President Bush made it official. The President's choice ran into immediate opposition. . . ." As long as newscasts present only news, there's no need to label an item as news. In fact, what comes next is not news. And it's not from Washington. Rather, it's *olds.* And it comes from the newsroom. Someone there wants to take credit for what was a widely circulated story the station almost certainly was not the first to break. Listeners tune in to get the latest news, not the latest recaps of yesterday's news. Nor the latest boasts. And what did the President make official? Putting Martinez in line?

"Rumors have run rampant in the Army since the first soldiers left for Saudi Arabia. First, the rumor that. . . ."

We're not in the business of publicizing or circulating rumors. We check rumors, and if they're true—and newsworthy—we report them. As fact. Not rumor. We're not rumormongers. Rumors have run rampant in armies since the Battle of Jericho. Even before ancient armies fought, soldiers helped sustain themselves with their sense of rumor.

"Flooding in Washington State is finally on the wane." Does the writer mean the floodwaters are rising more slowly, or are they receding? The lead sentence has two problems: the only verb is *is,* which expresses no action. And *on the wane* is not conversational. Only Elmer Fudd would say, "It's waning."

"And better late than never. Rolling Stones lead singer Mick Jagger and model Jerry Hall have finally tied the knot. Their publicists announced today that. . . ." For that introductory cliché, better never. *Tied the knot* is also a cliché. How about just saying they *married?* Or perhaps *were married?* (Don't say that a couple *got* married or *got* divorced. Or that anyone *got* dead. Got it?)

The writer and editor Wolcott Gibbs told copy editors at *The New Yorker:* "Our writers are full of clichés, just as old barns are full of bats. There is obviously no rule about this except that anything you suspect of being a cliché undoubtedly is one and had better be avoided."

"A milestone will be reached between the British and the French tomorrow. The famed channel tunnel linking Britain and France will connect. It's taken 12-thousand workers three years to join Cheriton, England, with Sangatte, France. There's still more work to be done before automobiles [why not *cars?*] **can drive on to high-speed** [why not *fast?*] **trains and go from shore to shore in 30 minutes. The trip currently** [why not *now?*] **takes an hour on the water.** *Famed* is not a spoken word; *famous* is. Neither word helps a listener who has never heard of that tunnel. Nor does it help someone who *has* heard of it. The tunnel hasn't yet connected the two countries, so is it famed *or* a tunnel? At the end of the second sentence, *connect* is a transitive verb and requires an object. The last sentence of the script also is hazy. Better: "By ferry, the trip now takes an hour."

"You've heard the story before: a lady goes into a store . . . buys a hundred dollar's worth of groceries and only pays 85 dollars. How does she do it? With coupons. _____ _____ has another story of how coupons can get you. . . ." Yes, we have heard the story before, and we don't care to hear it again. Newswriting requires the skill to introduce—and tell—an old, or much-used, story in a new way, without proclaiming that it's a thrice-told tale.

"A slight winner on Wall Street today. The Dow Jones Industrials gained nearly six points to close at. . . ." Who's the winner? Even when the Dow goes way up, some people lose. For example, traders who short a stock in hopes that it will go down, can lose. And investors don't win or lose until they sell. But listeners who must grapple with poorly written scripts *do* lose.

Editors, wherever you are, please phone in. We miss you. And every script needs you.

Wouldn't it be dandy if the search for missing editors were joined by Interpol. Many of the editors may be overseas, so perhaps the international police network could track them down. Some may be lolling at a luau in Luanda, lying low in Liechtenstein, or praying at Lourdes for deliverance from an affliction of scruffy scripts. Lord, who can blame them? Consider these recent broadcast stories:

"What possessed 25-year-old Roy Koutsky to wreck his own house in Hollywood with a shotgun? Koutsky fired at least 73 blasts through his house early this morning. Many of them went through the back wall, hitting duplexes next door. He kept police at bay for four hours, then surrendered, saying he saw no reason why he couldn't do it. Koutsky was booked for inves-

tigation of reckless shooting. A police sergeant described the house as 'totally ventilated.'"

What possessed the writer to ask us a question he himself doesn't begin to answer? The script raises several other questions the writer doesn't address: Did police fire any shots? What prompted Koutsky to give up? Who *is* Roy Koutsky? An actor? (A bad actor?) Is he a newswriter "at liberty" (as they say in *Variety*), the victim of a *personnel surplus reduction* or *work force imbalance correction?* Was he shooting from inside? Did his shots penetrate the duplexes or just hit the outer walls? How much damage did he do? Is he the owner of the house? The sole occupant? Was he sober? Did he have problems? (He does now.) Has he a police record? Is he behind bars? Out on bond? Is he going to stay in his newly air-conditioned house or move? We don't want to know everything. But we do want to know more. The script should have been returned to the writer so he could give it another shot.

"The showdown at the Stick [jocktalk] . . . **Police called in to calm angry 49ers fans who showed up at Candlestick Park. They were there to collect ticket vouchers for the big playoff game. . . ."** Police *called in?* Did they phone the park and handle the trouble by phone? That's what it sounds like. All it needs is one more word, *were: "were* called in."

"A man with AIDS and a gun barricaded himself in a hospice on Twelfth Avenue in Los Angeles. The man is dead tonight. [That was like a video jump cut—an unnatural jump in the action. Between the first and second sentences, the man jumped from life to death without any cause, without any explanation.] **And as ___ ___ reports, police say it was that gun and not firepower from a police Swat team that took his life. . . ."** A script needn't proceed step-by-step chronologically; but it should proceed logically. And a writer shouldn't interrupt the narrative with the name of a reporter just to quote him quoting police.

Let's redo it: "A man with AIDS barricaded himself in a Los Angeles hospice today—with a gun. Police Swat teams surrounded the place, but before they could grab him, he fired and (feel the suspense growing?) shot himself dead. ____ _____ has the story:" Or "has more:"

The tease to that story had said, **"And a person with AIDS fires at police and keeps firing before turning the gun on himself."** A *person?* Why not *a man?* Or *an AIDS patient? Turning the gun on himself* is journalese. More to the point: *shooting himself.*

Don't shoot *yourself* in the foot with journalese. The *Reuters Handbook for Journalists* says journalese comprises clichés esteemed by journalists and often stems from their adopting the shorthand in headlines. The handbook lists examples it urges writers to avoid (and offers suitable choices): *"amid reports that . . . brace for a wave of violence . . . burgeoning* (growing) *. . . economic/fiscal woes . . . hit by fears that . . . in a bid to hammer out agreement . . . lash out . . . longtime foe . . . major* (big, large) *. . . massive* (big) *. . . oil-rich . . . rocked by . . . the statement came as . . ."*

More journalese jetsam and advice from the *BBC News & Current Affairs Stylebook and Editorial Guide:*

"Blaze. Classic journalese seldom used in spoken English. 'Fire' is nearly always better.

"Clash. Like *chaos,* it has been degraded by overuse.

"Crucial. Overused. Try 'important.'

"Daring escape. It's journalese. Also, if we say crimes are 'daring,' it might be taken to indicate approval or admiration.

"Daylight revealed the full extent of the damage. A tired way of getting from nighttime pictures to daytime pictures.

"Fighting for his life. Cliché, along with doctors 'fighting for the life of. . . .'

"Full-scale. As in a 'full-scale search.' It's a cliché. And what is the difference between a full-scale inquiry and an inquiry?

"**Gunned down.** Journalese and an ugly expression.

"**Gunshot wounds.** No. Say 'bullet wounds.' If a shotgun was used, they are 'shotgun wounds.'

"**Miracle/miraculously.** Leave it to God.

"**Only time will tell.** Aagh!

"**Rushed to (the) hospital.** A very silly cliché. Emergency patients are always taken there as quickly as possible.

"**Some.** As in 'some two hundred people.' Does it mean 200, or more, or at least 200, or nearly 200? It is imprecise.

"**Spark off/trigger.** Cliché.

"**Spell out.** Cliché.

"**Total.** Often it's fairly meaningless, as in 'total shutdown.'

"**Vowed.** Not used much in conversation. Try promised/threatened/predicted/said."

Several more examples of journalese listed in the *UPI Stylebook* include: *hosted* (held), *huddled* (met), *probe* (investigation) and *behind closed doors* (privately).

Now back to our look at broadcast scripts: "**A sell-out crowd showed up at the Sports Arena to see the Clips** [Clippers] **take on the great Chicago Bulls guard Michael Jordan. And they saw a great performance from that great Bulls guard John Paxson. . . .**" *Great, great, great?* Grating. Did that entire crowd really show up just to see Jordan? Bull!

"**John McEnroe in Big Chi to play tennis tomorrow. . . .**" *Big Chi?* Why would a sportscaster in a city even bigger than Chicago call it *Big Chi?* Have you ever heard that term used by anyone anywhere (except perhaps in Outer Podunk)?

"**One of Los Angeles' most pioneering woman passed away today. . . .**" *Most pioneering? Pioneer* is a noun and a verb, but no one can be *more* pioneering or *most* pioneering. *Passed away?* Undertakers, who call themselves morticians or funeral directors, may prefer *passed away.* And hospitals may prefer *expired* or *succumbed.* But newswriters say *died.* We do so because we shun euphemisms; we call things by their right names. We don't say someone was *dehired, decruited* or *deselected.* We say *fired.*

"A Shawnee day care center director today admitted firing an employee last month for drugging infants at the center." *Admitted?* One *admits* wrongdoing. From what we're told, it seems the director did right. The *writer* did wrong, though, by making the director's job description too long and unwieldy. Let's put *today* after the verb and defer *last month* to a later sentence. Better: "The director of a Shawnee day care center said today he had fired an employee for drugging infants." If the firing had been reported previously, we could say the director *confirmed* or *acknowledged* it.

"As most aviation buffs know, the military has been working for several years now [*now?*] **on development of an aircraft that's part helicopter, part turboprop. . . ."** Please don't tell us what some other people know. Tell us what *we* don't know.

". . . (Voice-over) The catapult launch of a high-speed jet from the deck of an aircraft carrier, the end result of many shipmates working in unison. . . ." *High-speed* jet? Ever hear of a *low-speed* jet? *End result* is a redundancy. *Working in unison? In unison* means corresponding exactly or uttering the same words or producing the same sounds at the same time. Sailors on a flight deck work *in unity.* They probably do nothing in unison, not even when they sing "The Navy Hymn."

Hear our plea, O editors, we beseech you. Come back. Please.

12

Be Your Own Editor

Every writer needs an editor, but every writer has to be his own editor. Seems contradictory, yet it's true. We all need editors. But before we turn in a script, we need to edit it ourselves. Rigorously.

One problem in editing our own copy is psychological: distancing ourselves from it. Somehow, we have to shut out any thought that we're performing surgery on ourselves. One way is to pretend that what we're examining is copy written by someone else, say, an intern. That way, we can give it an unflinching look. And correct it painlessly. And improve it considerably.

The problem with these broadcast scripts is they lacked writers and editors:

"Cleveland Council President Forbes says Cleveland can't afford to take a major step backward." Who *can?*

"Bay Area businesses are working short-staffed in many cases—as the flu season hits full stride. The flu is hitting hospitals especially hard . . . not too many patients, often not enough staff with nurses and physicians out with the flu. ____'s ___ _____ has the situation at just one Peninsula hospital."

Diagnosis: Confused. Is the writer saying *not enough staff* is out? Even if a comma is inserted after *staff,* the hospitals' problem is puzzling inasmuch as *not too many patients* have the flu. The intro to the reporter is also ailing. To say a reporter *has the situation* says next to nothing. And says it feebly. *Situation* is almost always pointless. When a reporter speaks of "an emergency situation" instead of "an emergency," you wonder, "How did we get into this situation?" (George Carlin says: "We *know* it's a situation. *Everything* is a situation.") Better: The reporter "has the story at a Peninsula hospital" or "So-and-so reports from a Peninsula hospital." If a writer persists in using *situation,* perhaps he should write a Situation Wanted.

Next patient: **"In case you haven't figured it out, the 1980s were hotter than normal. Weather experts say last year was the warmest in the record books, but the scientists say they can't be sure if the warming trend is part of the greenhouse effect."** So where's the news? Record heat is not something we can "figure out." If last year *is* the warmest on record, we don't need to quote "weather experts." When we use a term like *greenhouse effect,* we should add a few words of explanation. If something is worth mentioning, it's worth making understandable. The broadcast journalist Eric Sevareid said, Never underestimate the intelligence of your listeners and never overestimate their information. But what's the point of the story? Why is it being broadcast at all?

"The largest tankers on the Great Lakes are only one-third the size of the Exxon Valdez. That's only one reason why shipping experts say what happened in Alaska could never happen here. A spokesman for the Lake Carriers Association says the bottom of the Great Lakes is sand and gravel, nothing hard enough to rip a hole in an oil tanker. Besides, Great Lakes tankers have a double hull . . . not a single hull like the Exxon Valdez."

The first sentence may be true, but that's no reason for saying, in the next sentence, a huge oil spill could *never* occur in the Great Lakes. If two tankers collided, oil *could* spill anywhere. Or if a tanker ran aground on rocks—and the Lakes do have some rocky shores and rocky bottoms—we could have another gusher. In the last sentence, we finally see a valid reason for thinking the

Great Lakes may never suffer from a huge spill: lake tankers have double hulls. But the writer buried that point, or sank it. As for *reason why* in the script's second sentence, no need for *why*.

Better: "Experts say an oil spill like the one in Alaska could not occur in the Great Lakes. One reason: tankers on the Lakes have double hulls. The ship that caused the Alaskan spill, the Exxon Valdez, has only one hull."

A writer needn't be a maritime expert. We're expected to deal with many subjects every day, and Lord knows, we're knowledgeable about only one or two, if any. The writer of that script should have applied logic and common sense and more thought to what he was writing. Verdict: Not exxonerated.

"In the Malibu fire, arson is under investigation." Investigators are trying to determine whether the fire was caused by arson, but arson itself is not being investigated.

"It's been a long month of protest for Barbara Brenner of Whatcom County. For the past four weeks, Brenner has camped out in front of the Capitol building in Olympia—trying to send a message about her objections to a trash incinerator near her home. [Send a message to a trash incinerator? Trash it. *Trying to send a message about her objections = protesting.* A capitol *is* a building. So if she's living in front of it, she must be camping out.] **"Finally, today, Brenner got her chance to communicate her protest in person to Governor Gardner— and ____ _____ was there."**

Stronger: "The woman camped at the state capitol for four weeks has finally been allowed to talk to the governor."

"A lawsuit charging that Dayton school children are being harmed by forced busing has been dealt a blow. The Ohio Second District Court of Appeals in Dayton dismissed the appeal because it wasn't filed in time. A lower court earlier rejected the suit, which was filed by a Dayton School Board member and four

others." *Dealt a blow?* The appellate court threw out the appeal, so *dealt a blow* falls short. It was a knockout punch.

"Cobb County police are investigating a suspicious death at the River Bend Apartments on Akerskill Road. The victim has been identified as 47-year-old Marcia Thomas. She was a cab driver with the Victory Cab Company. . . ." *Has been identified as* is wordy. As long as she *was* identified, presumably by police or a relative, the writer need only say, "The victim was 47-year-old Marcia Thomas." Or: "The victim was Marcia Thomas. She was 47 years old."

"Erasing racism is on the minds of Cleveland city officials." They's what they *say.* We never know what's on someone else's mind. And *erasing racism* is a strange, unfamiliar phrase that shouldn't be on any writer's mind.

Whatever goes through your mind as you read this broadcast script, much too much went through the writer's mind—undigested:

"A former treasurer of Mahnomen County, Minnesota, has pleaded guilty to a charge of felony theft. [Delete *a charge of.*] **48-year-old Sandra Quale today entered the plea at an omnibus hearing in District Court.** [If you don't know what an *omnibus hearing* is, you're not alone. *I* never heard of it—and I can't even find it in a law dictionary. *Today* should not precede the verb. And in what town is the court?]

"Quale pleaded guilty to stealing just over 33-thousand dollars [we round off numbers; *just over* is wordy and seems to minimize the theft] **from the county from November, 1988, through September, 1990. She stole money from cash funds in the treasurer's office.** [What else *could* be stolen from *cash funds* other than money? Wrappers? Rubber bands?] **Special prosecutor Wayne Swanson said Quale took money from the funds and covered the theft by using incoming state dollars to make up the loss.**

[Let's make a fresh start: "A former treasurer of Mahnomen County, Minnesota, has pleaded guilty to stealing 33-thousand dollars from the treasurer's office. 48-year-old Sandra Quale admitted taking the money in cash over two years while she was treasurer. Special Prosecutor Wayne Swanson told the court, in (name of town), that she covered the thefts with incoming revenues."] **District Judge Russell Anderson ordered a pre-sentence investigation. Sentencing is scheduled November fifth.** [Better: "District Judge Russell Anderson ordered a pre-sentence investigation and set sentencing for November fifth."]

"The maximum penalty for felony theft is ten years in prison and a 20-thousand-dollar fine. But Minnesota sentencing guidelines recommend imprisonment of one year and a day, with a presumptive stay of execution. [*Presumptive stay of execution?* Is she on death row? Whatever that legal term means, the script can do without it. Better: "She faces up to ten years in prison and a 20-thousand-dollar fine. But state guidelines for felony theft recommend a year and a day."] **As a condition of probation, the guidelines recommend serving up to eight months of local time.** [Is *local time* time in a local lockup?] **Quale remains free on her own recognizance. She has resigned as treasurer and withdrawn from the November sixth election, but her name will still appear on the ballot.** [Don't raise a question you don't answer: If she receives the majority of votes, will she return to office? The next sentence might fill the bill: "Even if she gets the most votes, the law bars a felon from taking office."]

Another offender, this from major-market television:

"He was known as 'Pops.' [Starting a story with a pronoun is poor practice. Besides, "Pops" is no more distinctive than "Moms."] **Will Jamerson died on Sunday from an infection of the heart and lungs.** [People die *of* an ailment, not *from* it.] **Officially, he was not the world's**

oldest man [Tell us what he *was,* not what he was not.] **because he didn't have the birth certificate to prove it.** [*Officially?* Who in the world is the arbiter of longevity?] **That was destroyed in an Oklahoma fire back in 1873.** [Perhaps "Pops" told people that, but is it true?] **But by any measure, Jamerson deserves membership in the Old Timers Hall of Fame.** [Jamerson died, so *deserves* should be *deserved.* Why did he *deserve* it, except for his undocumented longevity? Especially in a hall of fame that doesn't exist?] **When he died, he was 117 years old."** Why didn't the writer tell us in the first breath that Jamerson was that old? Or said to be that old? Why did the writer start with a pronoun, depriving the listeners of any idea to whom he was referring? What was Jamerson's occupation? Or, at his age, preoccupation? Was he married? Any children? Where did he die? Boston? Was he the first "Boston Pops"?

"'He's a moose.' [When I hear a story start with a pronoun, I wonder whether I missed a lead-in.] **That's how the head of the newborn nursery at Newark's Beth Israel Hospital describes little Raymond Anthony Wegreznek** [No middle names or initials, please. This ran in another state, so there was no need for any name.] **... Actually, he's not little at all.** [Don't take time to describe him as little and then say he's not little.] **The bundle of joy** [cliché] **weighed in at 14 pounds, 10 ounces when he was born** [*weighed in ... when he was born:* redundant] **... He was over 24 inches long ... So big that his mother, Yolanda Wegreznek of Linden had to have a Caesarean. The baby couldn't fit below her pelvic bones.** [We don't go into clinical details.] **Mrs. Wegreznek says her new son looks like 'a little football player.' Both are to be discharged from the hospital today."** *Discharged* is hospitalese. In conversation, we'd say they're *getting out* of the hospital or *going home.* If they have a discharge, they ought to *stay* in the hospital.

Next: **"'It all started at a 5-thousand-watt radio station in San Diego.'** [A listener wouldn't necessarily recognize this opening line as a quotation—or misquotation. The original, oft-quoted line mentions Fresno, not San Diego. But perhaps the writer wanted to round it off to what he thought was the nearest major market.] **Those were the words used by actor Ted Knight as pompous TV anchor Ted Baxter on the Mary Tyler Moore Show, one of the top comedy shows of the 1970s. But it all ended for Knight** [today] **at the age of 62. The actor, who also starred in. . . ."** We never open with a quotation and then identify the speaker. We put the speaker before the speech. But that's not the news. The news is, "The actor Ted Knight is dead." Or "The actor Ted Knight has died."

Another entry in the weepstakes, this, too, from major-market news:

"A French justice minister [they have only one justice minister, so *a* should be *the*] **calls it** [what's the antecedent of *it?*] **a public relations ploy. But the lawyer for the convicted Nazi war criminal Klaus Barbie says his client has been stricken with cancer of the blood and needs special treatment. . . ."** The writer starts by telling us what someone called something without even identifying the something. The script was written for a late newscast, so perhaps the French minister's reaction is the latest development in a story 12 hours old. If that's the case, the story should be rewritten: "A French official dismisses the latest move by Nazi war criminal Klaus Barbie as a public relations ploy. Barbie's lawyer says Barbie. . . ." If the minister's reaction ran in the first wire story along with the first word of Barbie's purported illness, it would be better to start the script by presenting the lawyer's assertion and then the official's response. The best newsroom policy: action before reaction.

Here's the first part of another TV script:

"Relieved officials of the Simi Valley School District got a break. [Are residents of the Valley called Simians?] **A 2-million-dollar warehouse fire** [is that a $2 million warehouse or a $2 million fire?] **did not destroy valuable student records.** [Voice-over] **The fire swept**

through the district's only storage facility early this morning [better: *early today*] **... leaving parts of the building charred and smoldering. The warehouse contained books, supplies, student records and food** [better: "food, books, supplies and student records." Why? Series usually proceed from the shortest item to the longest, or from the oldest to the newest, or from the least important to the most important] **for the 27 schools in the district. Officials say despite the huge losses ... the show will go on."**

That script, too, was written for a late newscast. News of the fire was O.B.E. (overtaken by events): discovery that the records were not destroyed, so that may well be the lead. But the writer of the script did a clumsy job. Better: "Though a fire ravaged a warehouse for the Simi Valley School District today, student records are safe." As for the last line in the excerpt, *The show will go on,* that line should never have gone on. Perhaps because the writer was so close to Hollywood, he might have thought there's no biz except show biz. But that fire was no show-stopper. What was going on in the editor's mind? Or did the script sail right through—in one eye and out the other?

They say an unsung hero is a hoagie that lacks a press agent. But newsrooms do have unsung heroes, and often they're editors. With sharp eyes, strong writing skills, keen news judgment and bulging mental data banks, *good* editors salvage many a script. And if any of them had been on the job, they could have saved these next broadcast scripts:

"Four people have died in the crash of a small plane near Thief River Falls, in northwestern Minnesota. The plane was reported missing last night. The wreckage was found this morning. [Better: "A small plane has crashed near Thief River Falls, in northwestern Minnesota, and all four people aboard have been killed."]

"The victims are identified as Morris Steiger, Bruce Steiger, Brad Steiger and Dennis Halstrom, all of the Thief River Falls area. [If they have been identified positively, there's no need to say *identified as.* Better: "The victims *were. . . .*" Were the three Steigers related? You could probably find out with one phone call. According to a script from another station, Morris Steiger was the father of the other two Steigers and the founder of the Steiger Tractor Company.] **No ages available at this time.** [Why take time to draw attention to what you don't know? And so high up in the story?]

"The Pennington County Sheriff's Department says the men were returning to Thief River Falls when the twin-engine Piper Cub went down in a farm field some ten miles southeast of Thief River Falls last night. [Mayday! Mayday! A Piper Cub has only *one* engine. Better: "The sheriff (or sheriff's office) of Pennington County says the men were returning to Thief River Falls last night when their single-engine plane crashed on a farm about ten miles southeast of town."]

"Officials say the plane severed a telegraph line belonging to the Soo Line railroad and struck a railroad enbankment before coming to a stop. The cause of the crash is still under investigation." Why take time to tell us who owns the telegraph line? Better: "The plane cut a telegraph line, slammed into a railroad embankment and skidded to a stop. Investigators are trying to determine the <u>cause</u> of the crash." Another accident:

"Halifax police are investigating an early morning car-pedestrian accident near the city's common. Police say a teenage boy was riding along Quinpool Road when he was hit by a car around 9:30 this morning. He was taken to [a] **hospital by ambulance and treated for leg and shoulder injuries. No charges have been laid."** Help! Help! If the boy was riding, how could he have been in a car-*pedestrian* accident? *What* was the boy riding? A bike? A motorbike? A motorcycle? A skateboard? And how old is the teen? Thirteen? Nineteen? Is he a schoolboy? A busboy? A delivery boy? By late afternoon, when the story was written, the newsroom should have obtained all this information. What were the boy's injuries—bruises, fractures? There's no need to say he was taken away in an ambulance; that's how most injured people are taken away. We assume he didn't walk—or cycle. If, on the other hand, the car that struck him also took him to the hospital, that might be worth mentioning. Was the boy on the wrong side of the road? Was the car speeding? Who's the motorist? A banker? An anchor?

Another script from Canada: **"A major Canadian bank has broken the 10 percent interest rate barrier for the first time in three years.** [This could mean the rate has fallen below 10 percent or has climbed past 10 percent. And that's not a *barrier.*] **The pace-setter in interest-rate declines, the Bank of Montreal today chopped its prime rate a quarter point to 9.75 percent.** [Rates are *cut,* not *chopped.* Instead of *nine-point-seven five,* it's better to say *nine and three-quarters.*] **It's the third time in 10 days the Bank of Montreal has lowered its prime. It's the first time since March 1988 that a major bank has offered a single-digit prime."** The last sentence repeats the first. Judgment: the writer is not ready for the time called prime.

Network television: **"Like Los Angeles, the victim's family here** [New York City] **will sue for what their attorney says is part of a national pattern of abuse.** [What's abused is the English language! The prepositional phrase *like Los Angeles* modifies the subject of the sentence, *the victim's family,* and the family is not at all like Los Angeles. (Is anything?) Perhaps this is what the correspondent meant: "As in Los Angeles, the family of an alleged victim is suing the city for (specifics). . . . The family's lawyer says the alleged police misconduct is part of a national pattern." Someone can sue for an abuse, but no one can sue for what is said to be part of a national pattern.] **Like L.A., demonstrations have already begun denouncing police brutality.** [Like the first sentence in the excerpt, this sentence is ungrammatical: Demonstrations can't be like L.A. And wouldn't it be better to speak of *demonstrators?*] **If convicted, the five men face 15 years to life in jail . . ."** No one ever spends 15 years in jail, except a guard. Felons, sentenced to more than a year and a day, go to *prison.*

Before that part of the script, the correspondent had said: **"A police investigation** [in New York City] **later concluded that the officers had done nothing wrong, and today they pleaded not guilty to charges their attorney blasted as ludicrous and obscene, adding that the victim was, quote, a maniac."** Attorneys may argue forcefully, but writers shouldn't describe them as "blasting" anyone or anything. Only terrorists *blast* people. Or punks with boom-boxes. The excerpt from the script also points up the needlessness of the word *quote:* If *quote* didn't appear in the script, *maniac* would still mean *maniac.* So what does *quote* do for *maniac?* Answer: what a sadist does to a masochist: nothing.

Let's look at this lead:

"Police in Wisconsin say one of the most hazardous times for drunk driving in that state [*in that state* = *there*] **is from 11 a-m to one p-m.** Sounds as though that time is hazardous for drunk drivers themselves, the time they are most likely to crash or to be caught. Better: "State police [the script's second sentence identified them as state police] in Wisconsin say chances are high that you'll run across a drunk driver there—or be run into by a drunk—between eleven A-M and one P-M."

Apparently, Wisconsin needs more police to patrol highways, and broadcast news needs more editors to police writers' pathways and shortcuts.

Pretend you're an editor, and see what you'd do with the following scripts. If you *are* an editor, don't pretend. Edit. And whether you're a writer or an editor, don't become a target of T.S. Eliot's jibe: "Some editors are failed writers, but so are most writers."

"**News in this past hour from Moscow . . . . . that Gorbachev is willing to leave the Pacific . . . . . if America will leave the Philippines. The Soviet leader promises to abandon its naval base in Vietnam . . . . . only if America will leave our military outposts in the Philippines. The base the Russians use in Vietnam . . . . . was built by the U.S. Navy during the Vietnam war. It's the largest warm-weather port that the Soviets operate out of their country.**" It's a jumble out there. One problem is repetition. The writer says Gorby is willing to *leave the Pacific* if the Yanks will leave the Philippines. Twice, the writer says it. Twice.

That script was broadcast by an all-news station, so there's no need to start the story—or *any* story—with the word "news." Nor is there any need to use all those periods (unless you can get 'em wholesale). One period, or stop sign, is enough to get me to stop. If the writer wants the newscaster to pause, he can use a comma. But punctuation was the least of that writer's problems:

1. Gorbachev can't *leave the Pacific.* He has naval bases on the Pacific at Vladivostok and Sovetskaya Gavan, both in the U.S.S.R.

2. *The Soviet leader* promises to abandon *its* naval base? Should be *his.*

3. *Our military outposts?* Since when do *we* have bases? Our country has bases, but *we* don't.

4. The former U.S. base, Cam Ranh Bay, was built *for* the Navy, not *by* the Navy.

5. The largest warm-weather port they operate out of *their* country? Vietnam is not a part of the U. S. S. R. (Ever hear of Sovietnam?) Maybe the writer meant it's the largest such port *outside* their country.

6. A port doesn't operate *out of* anywhere. But a fleet operates out of a port.

We can see that the writer should bone up on geography, history and writing. His strong points seem to be in typing ellipses. An ordinary ellipsis consists of three periods to indicate an omission in text—or four periods to indicate that the end of quoted material has been trimmed. But *five* periods? A small point, perhaps. But a script is made up of countless small points. To see how a mass of points can form a coherent whole, look at paintings by pointilists. "Trifles make perfection," said Michelangelo, "but perfection is no trifle." He wasn't a pointilist, but he made the point.

"It was bound to happen. There are kid jugglers, kid actors, kid singers, but no kid stand-up comedians— until this weekend. Our family reporter, _____ _____, is here with a look at kid humor." Forget the *kid* stuff. *Kid* is acceptable in some scripts, but not in that script. Not the way it's used there. We hear about child actors, but not *kid* actors. What does *It was bound to happen* mean? Predestination? And what makes us believe there was never a juvenile stand-up comedian until this last weekend? Weren't there any two days ago? How do we know one never worked for Barnum? Or Ziegfeld? Or Letterperson?

"Cold weather always brings fires . . . and today it brought a bunch of them. . . ." *Always?* Cold weather does not *bring* or cause fires. Fires are started by sparks, chemicals, overheating or Boy Scouts. Just kindling. I mean kidding. More fires may occur in winter because people use faulty heaters or use them improperly. And firefighters face icy or snowy streets, frozen pumps or hoses and harsh winds. Finally: grapes come in bunches—not fires.

"It should come as no surprise that the U.S. Forest Service is running out of money." Aren't we all? If something comes as no surprise, why take time to tell us it's no surprise? When I tune in a newscast, I'm hoping for surprises. I don't like a newscaster to tell me that what I'm about to hear should come as no surprise.

"It's early September, and that means life choices for most seven-year-olds revolve around which color play-dough to bring to school. We said most seven-year-olds, because the one _____ _____ met tonight in Des Moines is busy reading scripts for his part in the new Dick Van Dyke series. Bill O'Sullivan has gone and

is going places." *Life choices?* One of those trendy terms that spread across the land like a blight. But seven-year-olds don't make *life choices* or most kinds of choices. Choosing is part of living, so *choice* by itself does the job. Kill *life*. (*Life choice* sounds like another trendy term, *lifestyle.*) Most seven-year-olds don't carry Play-Doh to school. And if any do, they *take* it there, not *bring* it. The last sentence of the script has a problem. The word *places* is needed after *gone:* "has gone places and is going places." But even so, the sentence doesn't go anyplace.

   "Hawkins says there is no description of the suspect . . . but police suspect he may have tried to rape the young girl." The antecedent of *he* is unclear. Do police suspect Hawkins of rape? Also: the sentence is a *non sequitur,* a statement that does not follow logically from what precedes it. Police suspect the culprit might have tried to rape the girl, but *not* despite the lack of a description. The girl had already been described as a seven-year-old, so *young* is superfluous. And please don't use a word (*suspect*) twice in one sentence in different senses, in this case once as a noun, once as a verb.

   "An accident or a murder. . . . . Sea World officials are not sure. . . . But a killer whale is dead in San Diego. During yesterday's performance . . . Witnesses say Kandu and Shamu collided at high speed. . . ." Better: "Two whales at Sea World collided today, and one was killed." For a second-day lead on that story, I need more time, maybe a month. Whales can kill, but only a human can murder or be murdered. (The same logic bars our referring to a *killer storm.*) Shamu on you.

   "A kinder, gentler Ohio is the goal of United Way of Ohio, according to testimony before a state senate finance subcommittee." Please send *kinder, gentler* to Sun City. Those adjectives have been overworked and deserve a long rest. And kindly don't hang attribution on the end of a sentence. When attribution is needed, broadcast style calls for putting attribution *before* assertion.

   Just pretend you're a broadcast newswriter.

We may not want to cast the first stone at Little Rock, but let's listen as an anchor there starts an evening newscast:

"Last night was a violent one in Little Rock . . . Ten minutes after the city's twentieth murder of the year, yet another shooting left [better: *"has* left"] **a man barely clinging to life.** [That's not the way to lead a newscast. At 5:30 p.m., *last night* seems like ages ago. And no need for *yet*—at least not yet.]

"Good evening, and thanks for joining us. [Why thank listeners? They should thank *us.* Look what we give them: news. Free. (Not *for free.*)]

"Shortly after five o'clock this morning [,] **police arrived at Tenth and Park streets to find 31-year-old Ray Anthony Smith lying in a pool of blood in the street.** [Police didn't arrive *to* find Smith in the street. They arrived *and* found him. Who *is* Smith anyway? A butcher? A baker? A brewer? How does he rate a middle name? Ordinarily, broadcast newswriters skip middle names or initials unless someone is regularly identified that way (Harriet Beecher Stowe, James Earl Jones, Andrew Lloyd Webber). Or unless the absence of middle names or initials might cause confusion. Supper time is an especially poor time to talk about blood. Further, the script proceeds on the wrong foot—*flatfoot*edly. The news is not that police arrived at an intersection, so let's not start by talking about *them.* Any time police *don't* arrive, you have a story. The news is that a man has been shot and may end up adding to the city's murder list.

"Smith had suffered a shotgun blast in the chest. Although no suspects are in custody [this suggests that police have not yet arrested people whose identity they know], **authorities** [if *authorities* means *police,* say so] **believe the shooting stemmed from an argument between Smith and another man and woman.** [Why do they believe that? Were there witnesses? If so, was the shooter the man or the woman?]

"Minutes after finding Smith's body [Smith was still alive, so police found *him,* not his body], **police were called to the Pines Apartments on Baseline Road, where a drug deal had apparently turned violent.** [*Apparently?* Obviously!] **36-year-old Tracy Buchanan told police he shot 19-year-old Michael Hardiman during** [better: *in*] **an argument over a narcotics buy.** [Who was the seller? Who was the buyer?] **Hardiman remains in serious condition. Buchanan will be arraigned on battery charges in the morning.**

"Meanwhile [purge that word from your vocabulary], **police say they are following up suspect leads** [*"Suspect* leads"? Doesn't even sound like cop-shop talk. More like chop-talk.] **in yesterday's brutal** [in contrast to *gentle?*] **double murder on East Sixth Street. John Wallace and Glen Myers were both found dead of multiple gunshot wounds.** [No need for *both* or *multiple.*] **There was no sign of forced entry or robbery.** [Who were the victims? Friends? Relatives? Partners? Were they shot in a shack, a shed, a shanty, a chateau?] **Authorities say they've been given a couple of names** [of witnesses? bad guys? bad gals?]**, but have issued no warrants.** When the writer said *authorities,* he probably meant *police.* But police don't issue warrants; judges do.

Then, at 6 p.m.: **"Little Rock police are looking for a robber who made off with a Metropolitan Bank branch automatic teller machine early this morning."** [The news is not that police are looking for someone. The news is that someone stole an automatic teller machine from a bank. That *is* unusual. So the story should start by reporting the action, not the reaction. And *today* is better than *this morning:* it's shorter.] **The robber used a wrecker to rip the machine free** [an unneeded word] **from its foundation at the bank on Baseline Road about 4:30 this morning** [better: 4:30 A-M]**. Witnesses reported seeing the machine dangling behind the wrecker as it was being driven south on Chicot Road. There's no**

word on how much cash was taken in the heist." A heist is a robbery. Although it was a rip-off, or rip-out, the thief who broke the bank is not a robber. A robber uses force or the threat of force against a *person*. Perhaps he's a burglar. And, if caught, a bungler. Better: "No word on how much cash he got away with."

Another script there: **"Things are getting back to normal in Chicago one week after that devastating flooding incident.** [The best things in life, as they say, are not things. And *flooding incident* is a wordy way to say *flood*. Most of the time, *incident* is a hollow word. Often, we hear of a "shooting incident." It's a shooting. Period. Better: "One week after Chicago's downtown flood, the city is returning to normal."] **Offices are open again, but they don't have heat. And basements are still water-logged. A tunnel leak that flooded much of the downtown Loop** [the site should have been mentioned much earlier] **has been sealed, but it could take another two weeks to drain the 50-mile tunnel system."** [Better: "could take two *more* weeks to drain. . . ."]

The next script in that newscast:

"Staying with business . . . Citibank is breaking new ground in the credit card category. [That transition—*Staying with business*—deserves no credit at all. Also: *category* is unneeded. Better: "new ground in credit cards."] **It's offering customers the option of having their photograph on their credit cards.** [Better: "The bank is offering to put customers' photos on their credit cards."] **It's part of Citibank's program to provide its cardmembers the greatest possible protection against fraud."** Sounds like bank-talk.

And: **"Here's one of those items that goes in the 'So what's new?' department.** [If the writer thinks it's not new or newsy, why use it?] **Was there any other choice? Most anyone can answer the question, 'Who's the best basketball player in this universe?' Well, Michael Jordan has been named the N-B-A's most**

valuable player for the 1991–1992 season . . . Surprise, surprise, surprise." Sounds like an acute attack of the cutes. Why mock your own story? (Leave it to me.)

All of which brings us to a crucial question: whether it's 5:30 p.m. or 10 p.m., do you know where *your* editor is?

13

Verbless Sentences

Verbless sentences. Any good for newscasts? Sometimes, yes; most times, no. A network example:

"In Tucson, Arizona, jury selection today in the U. S. government's controversial case against 11 people, featuring federal evidence from undercover informants."

How come no verb? Writer afraid to be verbose? Short of time? Verbless sentences, where appropriate, should be brief. The subject, *jury selection, deserves* a verb. A verb moves a sentence. What *about* jury selection? Was it begun today? Resumed? Completed? What *took place? Featuring,* a participle, acts as an adjective, not a verb.

Why start with a place-name? Every story occurs somewhere. A place-name doesn't arrest listeners. When listeners in Maine hear a story begin, "In Tucson," do they drop their cribbage boards and listen up? And when a story starts "In Maine," do listeners in Tucson freeze? (Would you introduce news about an orbiting shuttle with "In outer space today"?)

The place-name in that script *is* important, but it's probably the least interesting element. It should be used, though, before the end of the sentence, preferably near the top. Also: after saying it's a U. S. government case, calling the evidence *federal* is redundant. The informants were probably going to *testify,* so "testimony" is better than *evidence. Controversial?* Superfluous. Much of what we write about is controversial. If it weren't, we might not be

99

writing about it. Writers often insert *controversy* or *controversial* in the belief it sparks up a story.

Try this: "Jury selection began today in Tucson, Arizona, for 11 people being tried by the government for. . . ." Or: "Eleven people went on trial in Tucson, Arizona, today for allegedly. . . ."

This one-sentence script, whose subject lacks a verb, also comes from a network: **"A two-to-one federal appeals court ruling in Washington today that thousands of Japanese-Americans who were put into detention camps during World War Two do have a right to sue the U. S. government for compensation."**

Why start with the vote count before telling us what the vote was about? Whether it's two-to-one or three-to-none, the ruling carries the same weight. Did the court sit in D.C. or Washington state? Probably D.C., but who can tell? Further, the writer buried a good verb in the noun *ruling.*

Better: "A U-S appeals court ruled today that thousands of Japanese-Americans held in camps during World War Two do have a right to sue the U-S government for reparations. The court, in Washington, D-C, voted two to one."

Another piece of work from a network: **"In Kansas City, Missouri, today a guilty verdict in the federal trial of five alleged organized-crime mob leaders, charges that they skimmed two million dollars off the top of untaxed gambling proceeds from two casinos in Las Vegas. Each of the five convicted on eight counts. Each could receive up to 40 years in jail and $80,000 fine."** That's exactly how the transcript goes, without *an* before *$80,000.*

Why so many numbers in the script—seven in 20 seconds? Why the number of counts? Every indictment has counts, from one upward. Unless the number is significant, it's not worth using. Newspapers may carry the number because print reporters often work like vacuum cleaners, sweeping up every crumb, and, when assigned to write long articles, they use every last speck. Some reporters can't bear to waste anything. Or they're unsure of their news judgment and figure that totality assures safety. That way, they protect themselves from an editor who just might ask, "How come you didn't mention the number of counts?"

The first sentence in the script has four strikes against it: it starts with a place-name, it uses *today* before telling us what the story is about, it tells the story poorly, and it has a main clause that lacks a verb. (If *today* were a grabber, newspapers would use it in headlines every day.)

As soon as listeners hear the subject, *verdict,* they expect a verb. Instead, they hear *charges,* which turns out to be not a verb but a plural noun. And why does the script deliver the verdict before reporting who's on trial for what?

Organized-crime mob leaders? Ditch *organized-crime. Organized crime* and the *mob* are synonomous, so *mob leaders* does the job. When defendants are found guilty, they are no longer *alleged* criminals. They are certified criminals. Has a mobster ever sued a news organization because it called him a leader—without prefacing that word with *alleged?* And sued after being convicted?

Not until the last sentence of the script do we find a subject with a verb, but even that sentence needs work. No one gets 40 years in *jail;* that's where people are held for trial, serve time for minor crimes (misdemeanors), or wait for transportation to prison for committing major crimes (felonies). Nor do defendants *receive* fines. They're ordered to *pay* fines. For a mobster, an $80,000 fine is small change, not at all comparable to time in the slammer. So that fine is not worth reporting in a brief script.

Let's rewrite the script: "Five mob bosses were convicted today of skimming cash from casino gambling receipts in Las Vegas. A federal court jury [?] in Kansas City, Missouri, found them guilty of stealing two-million dollars. The five men face up to 40 years in prison."

Writing a verbless sentence isn't a criminal act; but those we've just examined violate good sense *and* good grammar. It *is* acceptable, sometimes desirable, to write an incomplete sentence, one which lacks a subject or a finite verb (a verb with a tense). An incomplete sentence or sentence fragment may be a one-word sentence ("Hello"), a phrase ("Now the news") or a dependent clause ("Until we meet again"). Fragments like these pop up in conversation, sometimes as verbal bridges. And can be used in newscasts to make a point compactly and emphatically; but they should be used deliberately—and sparingly.

14

"Tennis-Ball Writing"

One splotch can mar a portrait. And one wrong word can mar a script. Can you spot the wrong words in these scripts?

"A former court employee in Bay County has won a district court settlement and interest totalling 75-hundred dollars. Delores Glaza had worked for the county court system for nearly 40 years. She sued when the county refused to pay her for 125 accumulated sick days that she had not used. The jury also ordered reimbursement of some 25-hundred dollars in attorney fees. The case was heard by visiting Judge Joel Mills of West Branch. Bay County Circuit Judge Eugene Penzien testified during the two-day trial that no record of such an agreement to pay for unused sick days could be found. The county is expected to appeal."

The wrong word is *settlement*. The word the writer should have used is *judgment*. A settlement is a compromise by opponents in a civil suit; settlement ends the need for a judge or jury to resolve the issue. If there had been a settlement, the jury would not have entered any orders. And there'd be no appeal. Too bad the writer didn't know the meaning of the legal terms, and too bad an editor didn't halt the proceedings.

When you report about the courts, are you ever guilty of "tennis-ball writing"? The term is used by Louis D. Boccardi, president of The Associated Press, in his examination of this wire story: "WASHINGTON—The U.S. Court of Appeals agreed Wednesday to review a lower

103

court order that found the Nuclear Regulatory Commission in contempt of court for violating an order to hold
open budget meetings." Boccardi observes: "The problem
here is that we treat the reader's mind like a tennis ball
to be whacked back and forth across the net. Agreed to review. Bam! Contempt of court. Bam! For violating an order.
Bam! To hold open meetings. Bam! You can almost see the
ball flying back and forth. It's just too much. You cure it by
just stepping back and asking yourself, 'What really happened here?' This happened: 'WASHINGTON—The U.S.
Court of Appeals agreed Wednesday to review a contempt
finding against the Nuclear Regulatory Commission for
holding a closed meeting.'" Boccardi's comments are found
in a slim book crammed with good advice, *The Associated
Press Guide to News Writing* by René J. Cappon.

Next: **"The heavily traveled 41st Street bridge
began coming down today, leaving motorists to take
sometimes torturous detours."** *Torturous* means "causing great pain." The word intended is *tortuous,* which
means "twisting" or "circuitous."

Another script: **"The tiny space community of
Titusville is being bombarded with millions of people,
all hoping for a glimpse of the shuttle launch."** Unless a
circus is firing volleys of human cannonballs, Titusville is
not being bombarded by people. The writer probably
meant *overrun by.*

**"The Virginia Southern Christian Leadership Con-
ference is throwing a blockbuster at Governor Baliles
because of an appearance he has scheduled for this
evening."** A blockbuster is a bomb dropped by a plane, a
bomb so powerful it can destroy an entire city block. No
one *throws* blockbusters.

**"Well, _____, as I said on Monday, I think I'll main-
tain the position that it's pretty difficult to assess public
reaction to that story because it's hard to get deeply
enough into the public conscience to know what it's
doing."** [The wrong word is *conscience.* The anchor meant
consciousness. He should have been conscientious—and
coherent. How deeply that anchor tried to dig can be seen

in his next sentence.] **"I took the subway a couple** [should be followed by *of*] **times this week, rode a bus a few times this week, monitored telephone calls around the newsroom trying to get a feeling of what the public is feeling about all this, and I'd have to maintain my position that the public doesn't seem terribly interested."** No wrong words, just wrong methods. How about finding a few facts instead of fooling with *feeling?* In its round-about ramble, the script is sophomoric and soporific.

More scripts with wrong words:

"After all, the political system is not known for awarding those who preach austerity and sacrifice." *Awarding* should be *rewarding*.

"Atlanta-based D'Lites is sprouting up all across the country, serving healthy food fast." People try to stay healthy by eating food that's *healthful*.

"If your pet pooch turns his nose up at run-of-the-mill dog food, you might have a gourmand on your hands. ___ ___ has a solution for owners of finnicky pets." A *gourmand* is someone who eats heartily, sometimes gluttonously. The right word is *gourmet*.

"The company in Florida acted because two teachers became nauseous yesterday after drinking a Coke product from a vending machine." *Nauseous* means "causing nausea." Supposedly, the teachers became *nauseated*.

"The United States continues to put the pinch on Panamian strongman Manuel Noriega." Not *pinch* but *squeeze*.

"A frightening flight tonight for a Navy A-6-E Navy jet stationed at Whidbey Island." Personnel are *stationed;* planes are *based*. And *Navy* twice?

"It's all happening in a town named after the anti-royalist renegade who kicked the British out for good, or so he thought." Washington, D.C., was named *for*—not *after*—the general. (Geo. Wash. a renegade? Well, yes, if you're writing for the BBC.)

"Young ladies brandishing feather pompoms have been rehearsing all week in the broiling sun, and

the painters, sweepers and carpenters are sprucing up a city scarred by war and deprivation." Pom-poms are automatic, rapid-firing weapons, like certain anti-aircraft guns. The word needed here is *pom-pon,* which is a flower or ornamental puff. Instead of *ladies,* the preferred word is *women.* Ladies are wives of lords. (Heard about the maid who answered a help-wanted ad and asked the house-holder, "Are you the woman who advertised for a cleaning lady?") War may scar cities, but does deprivation cause scars?

"Wall Street was not wildly enthused about the agreement. . . ." Careful writers are unenthusiastic about *enthuse,* a back-formation of *enthusiasm. The Harper Dictionary of Contemporary Usage* asked its panel of 166 consultants whether they would approve of this statement: "The critics enthused over the new play." For use even in casual speech, 76 percent said no. When one panelist, Charles Kuralt, was asked whether he'd use *enthuse* that way, he replied: "Lord, no. A terrible word."

"The chief justice of the New Jersey Supreme Court wants the media to censor itself in pre-trial reporting." *Media* is plural for the Latin *medium,* so *itself* should be *themselves.*

"The airline accuses the union of wrongly staging a two-day wildcat strike." *Wrongly* means "incorrectly"; the word needed is *wrongfully,* which means "unlawfully."

If you spotted all the wrong words, take the rest of the column off. If you didn't spot the wrong words, your vocabulary could use enrichment. Words are a writer's currency, and you can't go anywhere short of funds. So get acquainted with a word-bank (we call it a dictionary), and don't let words fail you. Find the right word.

Mark Twain said: "A powerful agent is the right word: it lights the reader's way and makes it plain. A close approximation to it will answer, and much traveling is done in a well-enough fashion by its help, but we do not welcome it and rejoice in it as we do when the right word blazes out at us."

15

Writing Tune-ups

Time for a spring tune-up! A writing tune-up. You don't need to repair to a writing academy. Why not do it yourself, in the privacy of your own place—at your own pace?

This is going to be a micro-mini-tune-up, but it is a tune-up. Just read the following wire story and rewrite it into a 20-second broadcast script for a noon newscast in Middletown, U.S.A. Take your time. But no overtime.

What's important in writing the script isn't speed, and it isn't in being the first on your block—or the first to show up Block. What does matter? News judgment, story-telling skill, and the application of broadcast writing rules. Please keep this tune-up confidential: don't let anyone else see it, and don't mail it to me. After you've written your script, read the rest of this column to see what I've said about the wire copy and how I rewrote it. Not that mine is the one true version. There *is* no one true version. Several versions may be acceptable. One that is usable is mine—at least it should be. Ready or not, here's the wire story:

NORFOLK, VA. (AP)—Three sailors and 38 non-nuclear missilies on the aircraft carrier USS Dwight D. Eisenhower were washed overboard during exercises early today, the Navy said. Two sailors were rescued and one was missing.

Lt. Cmdr. Steve Burnett said that the 18 Sparrow and 20 Sidewinder missiles went down in deep water and that the air-to-air missiles pose no risk.

"They were not nuclear-powered. They were not armed," said another spokesman, Senior Chief Petty Officer Cindy Adams. "Therefore, they're harmless."

It was the third serious Navy accident in as many days. [Don't shift from an ordinal number—*third,* which refers to order—to an implied cardinal number. Correct: "It was the third serious Navy accident in *three* days."]

On Sunday [this story moved on a Tuesday], a student pilot crashed while trying to land on the carrier Lexington in the Gulf of Mexico, killing him and four people on ship [*on ship* should be *on the ship* or *on board*] On Monday, a pilot accidentally dropped a bomb on the guided missile cruiser USS Reeves in the Indian Ocean, injuring five sailors. [That paragraph has too many prepositions: five *ons* and two *ins.* That means the graf needs overhaul.]

In today's accident, the sailors were moving gear from the flight deck to the hangar deck when a wave washed them overboard about 90 miles southeast of Cape Hatteras, N.C., he said.

Burnett said two of the sailors were rescued at 2:15 a.m. and were treated by the ship's medical personnel. One was reported in critical but stable condition, the other in good condition. The names of the sailors were withheld.

Burnett said helicopters from a squadron in Jacksonville, Fla., took part in the search for the third sailor.

By far the worst Navy accident this year was the explosion in a turret of the USS Iowa in April. The blast killed 47 sailors.

Stop! Don't pass Go until you've written *your* script.

All right, resume speed. The first thing to do when picking up a piece of wire copy is examine the dateline, the place where the basic information was obtained. Listeners can't see the dateline, so it's incumbent on the broadcast writer to make sure that a place-name is inserted. There are exceptions: when writing about the President, for example, you don't need to say he spoke in Washington. But if he spoke out of town, a place-name is essential. In the story we're working on, the dateline, Norfolk, is irrelevant. (Though Groucho said, "Irrelevant never forgets.") Norfolk is the headquarters of the Atlantic fleet and probably where the Navy spokesmen spoke, but the action occurred elsewhere. So we have to say where.

The A.P. story starts by equating men and missiles, but they aren't created equal. Missiles are replaced easily; lives are irreplaceable. No tears will be shed over lost missiles, so I wouldn't mention missing men and missiles in the same breath. The best rule is: people before property. Usually. If a factory burns down and one man is hurt, we don't lead with the man who's hurt. Oddly, the wire copy doesn't mention *man* or *men*. Why not? All the dramatis personae were men. No women were aboard; only recently have women been assigned to the Eisenhower. (Would you shout, "Person overboard"?)

The wire copy says one sailor *was* still missing. When we deal with a case like that, we convert the past tense to the present. We can feel comfortable with "*is* missing" because when he's found or declared lost at sea, the wires will tell us promptly. Unless *they're* at sea.

The quotation attributed to a petty officer, that the missiles were not nuclear-powered, is pointless. Missiles aren't nuclear-powered, and air-to-air missiles, which planes fire at other planes, aren't nuclear-tipped. If you want to say the missiles pose no risk, attribute the information—and it requires attribution—to the Navy. Though the names of the spokeswoman (a chief petty officer) and the spokesman (an officer) may be appropriate for a wire story, for us the names are meaningless. And we wouldn't attribute anything to a *spokesperson,* an ungainly and unneeded word. And we can skip the first name and middle initial of the ship. After all, could the Eisenhower be confused with another carrier named the *Mamie* Eisenhower? (Skip middle intials, except for people whose middle initials are as close to them as birthmarks: Susan B. Anthony, Alfred E. Neuman and Edward R. Murrow.)

Were the men and the missiles struck by the same wave? Because the wire story doesn't say so, we can't say so—unless we phone the Navy and find out. The wire says the names of the sailors were withheld. No point in our repeating that. It's routine, and it doesn't tell our listeners anything. Even if the Navy did release the names, we wouldn't use them, unless we were writing for a station in Norfolk or one of the sailors came from our town. (Please don't say *our town* unless you're writing about Thornton Wilder.)

Here's my version:

"Three sailors on a U-S aircraft carrier were washed overboard just after midnight. Two of them have been rescued, but one man is still missing.

"The sailors had been moving equipment on the U-S-S Eisenhower when a wave swept them into the Atlantic, 90 miles off North Carolina. Also swept overboard were 38 aircraft missiles. It was the Navy's third serious accident in three days."

How did you do on the tune-up? Are you out of tune? (Am *I?*) If you find you *are* in tune, you should be able to make all your copy sing. If not, please stay tuned—and get in tune.

"Any fool can write," a sage once said, "but it takes wisdom to know when to erase."

Not only does it take sense and experience to know what to cut out, but also what to *leave* out. When we get a wire story laden with details, we're put to the test: which facts to omit. And, after we write, which words to delete.

We always face this test of sifting, selecting and discarding when we write a story. But the more we write, the less difficult the test. Even if we're better than we think we are, or worse than we fear, we can improve our skills with a tune-up. And it can be done with a self-administered exercise. You might call it "Hone Alone."

If you did well on our last tune-up, here's a chance to make it two straight. If you flubbed the last one, here's a chance to redeem yourself. Read this Associated Press story and convert it into a 20-second script:

WASHINGTON—Bits of metal, a medicine bottle cap and parts of a woman's shoe prove that Amelia Earhart landed on a remote Pacific island and later died there, probably from thirst [a person dies *of* something], an investigator claimed Monday [the day this story moved on the "A" wire].

"We have recovered artifacts that conclusively prove this case," said Richard Gillespie, executive director of the International Group for Historic Aircraft Recovery. "The facts are there. The case is solved." [Every few years, another investigator provides a new solution.]

Ms. Earhart [*Ms.* probably would have made Miss Earhart bridle] and her navigator, Fred Noonan, disappeared in the South Pacific on July 2, 1937, while on a flight from New Guinea to Howland Island. They were on the final portion [a *portion* is a share; better: *part* or *leg*] of an attempt to fly around the world near the equator [*portion of an attempt* won't fly].

Neither the flyers nor their Lockheed Electra were [correct: *was.* When *neither . . . nor* joins compound subjects, the verb agrees in number with the noun that's closer. Such conflicts can be awkward, so it's usually best to rewrite] found in an air and sea search mounted by the U.S. Navy. [Better: "A search by the U.S. Navy—by air and sea—did not find the flyers or their Lockheed Electra."] Later, reports surfaced that Earhart had been captured by the Japanese and died a prisoner. This has never been proven [not *proven: proved*], however, and the fate of Earhart has been the subject of numerous books. ["Is life fair?" a comic asked after a recent plane crash in Libya. "They search for Amelia Earhart for half a century, but they find Yasser Arafat in half an hour."]

At a news conference Monday, Gillespie said he has solved the 55-year-old [no need for *old*] mystery. [Didn't he already solve it in the second paragraph?]

He said his research shows that after Earhart and Noonan failed to find Howland Island, they came upon a small atoll, then called Gardner Island and now called Nikumaroro, and landed there on a dry tidal flat during low tide.

Radio distress signals were heard from the vicinity of the island for three days but then stopped, Gillespie said.

He also said that [no need for *that*] a massive storm north of Nikumaroro generated waves that washed the Electra from the tidal flat and dropped the airplane [delete the last three words] over the edge of a coral reef into 2,000 feet of water.

This is why, he said, that when Navy planes flew over the island a few days later there was no sign of the Electra. [Better: "That's why there was no sign of the Electra when Navy planes flew over the island a few days later, he said."]

Nikumaroro, then uninhabited, had no fresh water supply. Gillespie said he believes Earhart and Noonan depended on rainwater to survive, but the local [*the* and *local* are unneeded] rainfall was only about 1 ½ inches a year. The pair [people don't come in pairs, not even *au pairs*] probably died from [*of*] thirst, he said.

Gillespie said his organization visited Nikumaroro last October and discovered several artifacts they had not found in a 1989 visit to the island.

He said expert analysis of a piece of aircraft aluminum, a length of copper wire, parts of a woman's size 9 shoe and a bottle cap from a medicine bottle [to avoid *bottle* fatigue, can the first *bottle*] uncovered nothing that would disprove his contention that Earhart and Noonan died on Nikumaroro. [Are these items the *artifacts* in the preceding paragraph?]

"We're very confident that the Amelia Earhart case is solved," said Gillespie. [That's the *third* time he solved it.] The artifacts, he said, "form circumstantial evidence in such an overwhelming way as to make them conclusive." [Talk about threepeats!]

Among the claims:

A 23-by-19-inch piece of aircraft aluminum was found washed up on the island. Gillespie claimed it came from an undersection that had been repaired at the Lockheed plant in California after Earhart crash-landed in Hawaii months earlier. The piece was examined for TIGHAR by Joe Epperson, a National Transportation Safety Board metallurgist, who said the metal "was consistent" with what is known about the repairs made to the aircraft."

Epperson also examined a piece of copper antenna wire attached to the metal and he said it matched antenna wire from the same era.

Parts of a shoe sole found on the island were identified as from a woman's size 9 blucher-style Oxford by officials of the Cat's Paw division of the Biltrite Corp. It was from the left shoe and included a replacement heel, said Gillespie. Enlargements of photos of Earhart taken during the attempt to fly around the world show her wearing this type of shoe, he said, and even confirm that she had had the left heel replaced. [Fifteen months after the wire copy moved, an article in the *Sunday Times of London* said, "Earhart took size six shoes."]

A metal medicine bottle cap was identified by Warner-Lambert Co. officials as a type of cap used for stomach medicine in 1937 by the William R. Warner Co. Gillespie said Earhart was known to suffer from stomach problems.

Peter Wolf, a Warner-Lambert spokesman, said a company official who examined the lid [why shift from *cap* to *lid?*] briefly said it was of a type used until the 1950s. The William R. Warner Co. later became part of Warner-Lambert. Wolf said printing on the top of the lid was easily legible.

"It really didn't look like it had been weathered for 50 years," said Wolf. [This raises a question: Had the cap somehow been protected from the elements or had it been planted there?]

Gillespie said his non-profit organization has spent $750,000 on two expeditions to Nikumaroro in search of Earhart's plane, and now plans to return.

During the earlier trip, the TIGHAR team discovered an aluminum navigator's map case. Both trips were financed by donations and loans. Asked if he was seeking more donations for a third trip, Gillespie noted: "It's got to come from somewhere."

End of story. Glory! Should be *said,* not *noted.* The observation that money has *to come from somewhere* goes nowhere. Quotations should be used only when they advance a story, when they add color or when they illuminate character. The remark about money is not novel, interesting or worth repeating.

Now, it's *your* turn. Please rewrite the wire story into a 20-second script. Do it for the 5 o'clock news in Anytown, U.S.A. Go.

As soon as you're done, or undone, proceed to my version. There is no one true version, one that's acceptable everywhere by everyone. My version is just that, mine, one man's way of rewriting the wire story. But this one man has made so many mistakes over the years that he has drained most of them from his system. (He hopes.) So by now—after all his angst, *agita* and O.J.T. (on-the-job training)—his version should at least be usable:

"A new theory about the pioneer aviator Amelia Earhart, who vanished in the far Pacific 55 years ago. Now an investigator says Miss Earhart—on a round-the-world flight—landed on a tiny Pacific island and died there, probably of thirst.

"The investigator, Richard Gillespie, says he found debris that proves her adventure came to an end on what was called Gardner Island, now Nikumaroro."

If you think your script is better, please send it to me. If the judge concurs, yours will be reprinted in this column. If the judge disagrees, yours *may* be reprinted, but if so, your name will not be used. The decision of the judge is final. Yes, I'm the judge, and though my law be fudge, I'll never, never budge. (W.S. Gilbert can bear no grudge.)

This writing tune-up may not make you a sage or even a sagacious writer, but perhaps it'll make you a better eraser.

The free-for-all to rewrite the Amelia Earhart wire story brought in entries from across the country. The winner is a man who *needs*—and deserves—an introduction. He's a reporter for WPTV, Palm Beach, Florida, and his name is Matt Sczesny. His script:

"An international researcher says he has solved the mystery of aviation pioneer Amelia Earhart.

"Richard Gillespie says his discovery of bits of metal, a bottle cap and parts of a woman's size nine shoe prove that Earhart died on the South Pacific island now known as Nikumaroro. [I didn't use the shoe size in my script. But I wouldn't go to the mat over it.]

"Earhart's plane disappeared 55 years ago as she attempted to fly around the world."

Runner-up: Doug Esser, state broadcast editor at The Associated Press, Seattle:

"A researcher says pioneer aviators Amelia Earhart and Fred Noonan died 55 years ago on a tiny Pacific island after they left New Guinea.

"Richard Gillespie says parts of a woman's size nine shoe and a medicine bottle cap found on the island probably belonged to Earhart. He says the plane was lost in the Pacific, and Noonan and Earhart apparently died of thirst."

I left out Noonan in my version because he's a minor character. The more names you use, the more you diffuse the focus. The fewer names, the better. And the star of that story is Amelia Earhart. Noonan is a bit player. She's so widely known that the Library of Congress lists 78 books about her. The number of books on Noonan: 0. (The latest book about her, *Lost Star*, published in 1994, revives, and reinforces, the contention that she had been on an intelligence mission for the U.S. government and was captured by the Japanese.)

Although I did identify the researcher, Gillespie, in my script, I think we could get along without using his name. (Our listeners never heard of him, and they don't need to clog their brains with the name.)

Sczesny, Esser and I all picked up the source copy's reference to Miss Earhart's dying of thirst, but one reader objects to my saying *died of thirst*. Laurie Stein, a producer for JTN News, Los Angeles, writes:

"I have found a flaw in your Amelia Earhart script! [Why did she plunge that exclamation point into my psyche?]

"You wrote, 'Now an investigator says Miss Earhart—on a round-the-world flight—landed on a tiny Pacific island and died there, probably of thirst.' According to Los Angeles physician Joseph Gorek, people can die of dehydration but not of thirst. Thirst is simply a desire, not a cause of death. We might casually say Miss Earhart must have been 'dying of thirst' if she was stranded on that tiny island in the middle of nowhere, but her *cause of death* would have been dehydration."

Sounds plausible, but I wanted a second opinion. So I consulted Dr. Julia Ashenhurst, a Chicago physician. She concurred with Dr. Gorek. What they say makes sense. I guess they're technically right, apparently (he says grudgingly). But what's right for a doctor in filling out a death certificate may not always be right for a writer preparing a broadcast script. *Dehydration* is a word you and I know, but what about our listeners? Is it a "broadcast word"? Is it one used in everyday conversation (outside hospitals), one that almost every listener knows instantly? I plucked the phrase *died of thirst* from the wire copy without giving it a second thought. But now that I'm pushed to think about it, perhaps I'd write that she *died of lack of water*. Perhaps. What would *you* do? (My editor says I should accept *dehydration* and pipe down.)

Another sharp-eyed, sharp-eared reader, Ray Weiss of New York City, reports hearing this on radio: "The phrase 'long-term parking' took on new meaning this morning when Port Authority police found a body in the trunk of a car in the long-term parking lot at Kennedy Airport." That body may be parked for an eternity, Ray says, so the line *is* clever, though of questionable taste. Good for a barroom, not a newsroom.

Reader response to the self-tests in recent months indicates a thirst for more tune-ups. So here's another AP story to rewrite for air:

Anaheim, Calif.—Add one more injustice to life's unfairness: Short people of both sexes are more likely to suffer heart attacks, researchers say.

"The taller you are, the less is your risk of heart attack," said Dr. Patricia Hebert, who presented a study at the American Heart Association's scientific sessions Tuesday [today]. The study was conducted by Hebert and colleagues from the Physicians' Health Study at Brigham and Women's Hospital in Boston.

For every extra inch of height, she found, people's heart attack risk goes down 3 percentage points. This means that someone 5-foot-10 is 9 percent less likely than someone 5-foot-7 to suffer a heart attack. In the study, men under 5-foot-7 had about 70 percent more heart attacks than those over 6-foot-1.

Just why this is so is unclear. However, short people might be at higher risk because their blood vessels are skinnier, so they are more prone to becoming clogged. Researchers cautioned that just being tall is no guarantee of escaping heart trouble and recommended exercise and watching cholesterol for all.

While the Boston study is the largest to examine the question, several smaller reviews also have found suggestions of an association between shortness and heart disease. Among these is one that found a similar link in women.

"These findings appear to be generalizable to women as well as men," Hebert said.

Your assignment: write a 25-second script and send it to me. If it's a winner, I'll use your name. Otherwise, no name, no blame.

Stop. Don't read past this point, unless you've already written your script, don't want to, or don't dare. Here's mine:

"A new study says the people more likely to get heart attacks are short. That applies, apparently, to men and women. In the study, men under five-foot-seven had about 70 percent more heart attacks than those over six-one.

"The study was done at a Boston hospital. But researchers warn that being tall is no guarantee of escaping heart trouble—and urge people to exercise and watch their cholesterol."

Don't delay. Act today. Limited-time offer. In case of tie, duplicate prizes will be withheld.

Reader response to the challenge to rewrite a wire story about the risk of heart attacks was heartwarming.

"First," as a few anchors say (or the equally inane "We begin with"): a personal note. The winner, it turns out, is a former student of mine, Mark Cariker. He took my class in broadcast newswriting, but that shouldn't disqualify, penalize or stigmatize him. His script:

"A new medical study says the shorter you are, the greater your risk of a heart attack. According to researchers at a Boston hospital, every extra inch of height slightly lowers your risk. They say taller people have bigger blood vessels that are less prone to clogging. But if you're short, don't lose heart—they say it's the inches around your waist that still count the most."

Suggestion: Remove *medical* and *according to,* start the second sentence with *researchers* and, after *hospital,* insert *say.*

Runner-up: Nelson Burg, news director of WNEM-TV, Saginaw, Michigan. His opening line: "If you're built like a basketball player, chances are you will live longer than if you're built like a jockey." He's off to a fast start because he managed to distance himself from the source copy and write an imaginative line. I don't know whether it's medically sound, but it sure sounds good.

Another entry began, "Height may be even more of a blessing than once thought." Who ever said height is a blessing? The long and short of it is, it may or may not be.

Here's another: "A Boston study indicates that short people are more likely to suffer heart attacks than the tall." Boston *should* be mentioned but not so soon. *Boston* is not what makes the story interesting. Only a few listeners, on hearing *Boston* or *Austin,* are going to turn up the volume. In a note accompanying his script, the writer said that identifying the hospital where the research was done forestalls phone calls from listeners looking for more information. (*Forestall?* Picking up on my use of that word, Doug Esser, state broadcast editor for The AP in Seattle, asks slyly, "Isn't that an aircraft carrier?")

If you were writing in Boston, mention of the hospital would be natural. Inasmuch as this story isn't about a *cure*—a word to be used with great care—nor a *treatment,* there is no need to identify the hospital. Usually (a prudent word in writing about writing—usually), it's best not to identify an out-of-town hospital. Or even a hospital in your own town. Unless your town is so small the newspaper lists hospital admissions. Or unless you want listeners to send get-well cards.

One more entry: "New research shows a person's height might be an indicator of their risk of heart attack. Dr. Patricia Hebert and colleagues at. . . ." Person is singular, so it must—must! must! must!—take a singular possessive: either *his* or *her.* If you don't want to use *his* or *her,* or are reluctant to combine them in *his or her* (which sounds like someone straining to cover all bases and biases), try another approach: "New research shows people's height may be an indicator of their risk of heart attack." The writer of that entry could have avoided any conflict by deleting *their* before *risk.* The next flaw is the writer's use of the doctor's name; in that script, there's no need for any names. As for the other entries, let's not get into name-calling.

"Failure is normal and instructive," says the writing coach Donald Murray. "From failures, we see ways to achieve success." And as Plato might say, the unexamined script is not worth rewriting. Let's examine this flop and rewrite it. Try turning it into a 20-second script and send it to me. The exercise will do you good.

Here's the flawed original (calling it flawed is like calling Vlad the Impaler impolite), as broadcast in New York City:

"Most of the nation's worst nuclear reactors have been designed by General Electric, according to a

report released today. [Broadcasters should never hang attribution at the end of a sentence. Remember the rule: attribution precedes assertion. Also, the lead lacks a source. Is it a government report? A report by disinterested—and distinguished—scientists? A report by a partisan with a mission?] **Details from __ ___:** [Who wants *details?* Better: "__ ___ has more." Or "has the story."]

"**While** [better: *although; while* is best used to mean *during*] **General Electric has designed only a third of the nation's nuclear reactors, those reactors account for 70 percent of Public Citizen's** [the listener can't see the capital P and capital C, so the name may sound like a mass movement rather than an advocacy group] **20 worst nuclear lemons.** [Sounds as though they're ticking time bombs or whatever the nuclear cliché is. Further, no one would ever say *70 percent of 20;* make it *14.* Do the math for listeners.] **The news** [*news?* it's an assertion by someone with an agenda] **was delivered to G-E Chairman John Welch by the consumer group's director of the Critical Mass Energy Project Bill Magavern.** [Bill Magavern's title needs to be shortened or deleted, and his name should be left out. Consider the poor listener.]

"**Public Citizen says it used 11 safety, performance and economic criteria in its study** [so what the first sentence called *worst,* we now learn, doesn't mean "most likely to blow up—or melt down"], **and in his letter, Magavern said his group wants Congress to investigate the reactors' safety.**

"**Based in Fairfield, Connecticut** [who cares where? G.E. is everywhere], **G-E says its reactors have proven** [*proved!*] **their safety through 30 years of operation worldwide and that regulators in numerous countries, including the U.S., Germany, Switzerland and Japan, have endorsed the reactors' safety and its** [*their!*] **containment system in reviews** [no need for *in reviews*]. **G-E nuclear energy spokeswoman Lynn Wallis** [no need for title and name; *G-E* suffices] **says that** [no need for *that,* at least not that *that*] **the group making the allegations**

opposes nuclear power and that their statement needs to be taken in that context." And how! Where was the quality-control monitor—the editor—to make sure the script was straight, solid and sober? Where was the editor? Gone fission?

Entries in the challenge to rewrite the story about General Electric were generally good but not electrifying. Several started well, then lost power.

A few entries said Public Citizen blamed G.E. for designing 14 of the country's worst nuclear reactors but did not list the criteria. That lapse leaves the impression that at any moment those reactors might go sky-high.

The best rewrite was submitted by Keith Acree, a producer at WGHP-TV, High Point, North Carolina:

"The watchdog group 'Public Citizen' says General Electric designed 14 of the nation's 20 worst nuclear reactors.

"The group says it considered safety, performance and economic factors in creating its bad reactor list—and it wants Congress to investigate. [*Factor* is a much-misused word. It means "an agent or cause that contributes to a certain result." I'd say, "The group says that in making its list it considered safety, performance and economics. And it wants Congress to investigate."]

"G-E says its reactors are safe. It also points out that 'Public Citizen' is a group opposed to nuclear power." I'd say, "G-E says its reactors are safe—and that 'Public Citizen" opposes nuclear power."

Honorable mention: Susan Ashline, Veryl Bohn, Doug Esser, Morgan Holm, Cameron Knowles, Todd Morgano and Jim Pratt.

Almost everyone else will get a "late" or an "incomplete."

16

A Second Look

Every script needs a second look, but these broadcast scripts seem to be first drafts never given a second thought, perhaps not even a second's thought:

"Drugs, sex, vandalism and littering were the complaints lodged against West High School students at last night's Waterloo School Board meeting."

If you start a story with a list before setting it up properly, you make the story difficult, if not impossible, to follow. We aren't used to hearing sentences that start with a list and go from bottom to top. You would present a recipe with a preface: "This is a recipe for. . . ." You would not start by rattling off a list of ingredients. Better: "People who live near West High School complain that students have [committed various acts]. Neighbors told the Waterloo School Board last night that. . . ." Or "Students at West High School have allegedly [done this, that or the other thing]. People who live near the school told the Waterloo School Board last night that. . . ."

Drugs and *sex,* those words in themselves, are not offenses. Acts, yes; words, no. Further, the introductory items slide downhill by ending with an act that is anti-social but not on the same level. It's like saying that a suspect has been charged with rape, murder and mopery with intent to gawk.

"It's that time of year again. The Benton Franklin County Fair opens in Kennewick this morning for a five-day run."

It's that time of year again is a dreary way to start a story. It sounds as though whatever follows is going to be ho-hum: "It's that time of year again: Tomorrow is National Mosquito Abatement Day."

"Inmates who commandeered two wings of the Oklahoma State Penitentiary in McAlester say seven guards will be harmed if any attempt is made to storm the buildings." *Commandeer* is best reserved for a take-over of property by police or military. If possible, put the *if* clause before the consequence clause: "Inmates who took over two wings of the Oklahoma state prison in McAlester say that if anyone tries to storm the buildings, the seven guards they're holding will be hurt." That plays fair with listeners by telling them up-front that it would happen only *if.* And it puts the emphasis where it should be: on *hurt.*

"NASA witnesses wrangled in public today over whether the space shuttle's reusable solid rocket boosters had a built-in safety problem. Privately, ____ News has been told of just-raised new safety questions about the shuttle's newest rocket boosters to come off the assembly line and possible safety problems at the shuttle's brand-new launch pad in California. [If the anchor has something else new—other than *new, newest* and *brand-new,* he should make that his lead.] **Also, ____ News has been told that NASA now may be investigating the possibility there were booster rocket close calls in midair on previous shuttle missions. . . ."**

Told *privately?* What does that mean? Reporters get much of their information in private conversations, not at public events and news conferences. (Even when they don't generate much news, we don't call them *press conferences.* Reason: Many listeners think *press* refers to newspapers.)

And what does this mean: "____ News has been told"? Told by whom? The director of the FBI? A disgruntled engineer? A little bird? Is the informant someone in a position to know, and is he correct? How do we listeners know? The frequently used "sources say" tells us nothing. It says only, "We heard somewhere."

Did "___ News" try to learn whether what it was told was true, or did they just serve as a conveyor belt and move unsubstantiated material along to us as is?

How would witnesses wrangle? Wrangle with one another? Officials holding a hearing may wrangle with a witness, and lawyers may wrangle with a witness, but have you heard of two witnesses' wrangling with each other? (Usually, the only witness permitted in a court or hearing room is the witness who's testifying at that time.) The testimony of two witnesses may conflict, but that's not wrangling.

The last sentence of the script was written by a master of huffing and puffing. That sentence also begins with "___ News has been told," apparently a gimmick intended to lend "artistic verisimilitude to an otherwise bald and unconvincing narrative," as William S. Gilbert (Sullivan's Gilbert) put it. I don't doubt that "___ News" has been told something by someone. But if you accept whatever you're told and turn around and tell the world without a clue as to who said it, you ought to be working on a turnip truck.

Another network script: **"Confirmed word tonight that the I-R-S says it will take action against 750-thousand Americans who have defaulted on student and government loans totaling one-point-six billion dollars."**

Confirmed word is an odd way to start a story. Those two words suggest that some of what the newscaster delivers is *un*confirmed, so he's trying to make it seem that what he's about to say is solid. When a story *is* confirmed—and shouldn't *all* stories be confirmed?—it's best to tell the story without fanfare: "The I-R-S says. . . ." If, on the other hand, a previous story said the I-R-S *reportedly* was taking action, this might work: "The I-R-S now confirms that. . . ."

Another network script:

"Here at home, the Commerce Department re-ported today that its chief measure of future economic activity, the Index of Leading Indicators, rose a modest two-tenths of one percent in April. Though modest, the analysts said that the increase suggests continued economic growth and no recession this year."

Here at home? Does the anchor live in a studio? Wouldn't a listener in Seattle be unsettled by first hearing *Here at home* and then finding out the story comes from 2,400 miles away?

At the beginning of the second sentence in the script, *modest* is a dangling modifier. The writer wants to say the rise was modest, but, as the script tells it, the adjective modifies *analysts*. (To paraphrase Churchill's remark about a rival, The writer has a lot to be modest about.)

"Just a few days of campaigning left, and emotions are running high, whether you're for the incumbent, the opposition or no election at all."

Emotions are running high, mixed emotions and *emotional rollercoaster* should be sent to the Retirement Home for Impoverished Clichés—one home whose <u>occupants</u> should be condemned.

Some scripts read as though the writers never gave them a second glance and their editors never gave them a single second. So let's give these scripts a second look:

"A pretty pickle for officers and enlisted person-nel alike at the Orlando National [should be *Naval*] **Training Center in Florida. The drill instructors** [should be *company commanders; drill instructor* is a term used by Marines] **have been bawling out the wrong man, getting the wrong guy up in the middle of the night for guard duty, and such like.** [*Such like?* No like! It's ungrammatical. Sounds like Valley Girl prattle.] **"The prob-lem lies with the McLanaghan brothers . . . John, Gene,**

**and Tony. Officials believe the 6-foot-1, 18-year-old sib-
lings** [*siblings?* not a broadcast word] **are the first triplets**
[if they're triplets, they must be siblings] **to go through
the facility** [*base;* why use the pretentious *facility,* a euphemism for rest room, also a euphemism] **since it was
founded** [*commissioned*] **in 1968. Nevertheless, the
brass has agreed to let them stay together through
their basic training."**

If anyone's in a pickle, it's the triplets. They're the
guys left with a sour taste. Few officers and enlisted personnel among the 17,000 on the base would ever run
across them.

Nevertheless = even so. That implies that if they
weren't the first triplets at the base, they'd be allowed to
stay together. Chances are, they enlisted on condition
they stay together. But who can say for sure whether
they're the first triplets on the base? And who cares
whether they're the first?

Better: "Three sailors at the Naval Training Center in Orlando, Florida, have a problem: they're brothers—
triplets. Because they look alike, they're mistaken for one
another. Sometimes the wrong one gets bawled out. And
in the middle of the night, the wrong one is awakened for
guard duty. The McLanaghans—John, Gene and Tony—
come from _____, and are 18 years old. Despite the
confusion, the Navy is letting them stay together through
boot camp."

That original script was broadcast by a network.
Yes, a network. So was this one:

**"A ferry boat capsized and sank in the Philip-
pines. There were 200 people on board. Three were
rescued. The rest are missing and feared drowned."**

This script is usable—it *was* used. But it should be
strengthened. Usually, the key word or words in a sentence should be placed at the end. The key word in the
lead is *sank;* in mid-sentence, it's submerged.

By saying *the rest,* the script forces listeners to mentally rewind and subtract 3 from 200. That's distracting.

The writer should do the work and calculate the number of casualties.

Better: "A ferry in the Philippines overturned today and sank. About 200 people are missing—and feared dead. But three people were saved."

Finishing a sentence with a one-syllable word that ends with certain consonants—for example, *d* and *k*—generally gives it a sock. The script would have an even stronger kick if it turns out the skipper was *dead drunk*.

Why did I substitute *overturned* for *capsized?* Some listeners may not know what *capsized* means. (Do you know your *cap size?*) *Overturned* precludes any doubts. No need to call it a *ferry boat;* a ferry *is* a boat. Yes, *ferry* is a sound-alike. But even a *half*-listener is highly unlikely to think that a fairy has done a handspring.

Another network script: **"P-T-L founder Jim Bakker said today he'd try to buy back the P-T-L ministry if it is liquidated** [*sold*] **in bankruptcy court. Bakker, in a surprise visit** [who cares whether he showed up unexpectedly?] **to the Heritage U-S-A theme park** [where is it?], **said, quote, "Every piece of ministry that comes up for sale, I will try to restore to the people it was meant for." Asked how he would try to do that, Bakker said, "I have a lot of friends." P-T-L is currently in bankruptcy court, up to 130-million dollars in debt."**

The use of the words *quote, unquote, close quote* and *end quote* in newscasts has been assailed by experts for almost 50 years. They say those words are heavy-handed, old-fashioned, not conversational, have a staccato sound, tend to interrupt the listener's thought, direct attention to themselves, and are shunned by skillful writers. (End of lecture.)

Unless a quotation is so dramatic, so significant or so extraordinary that it should be used word for word, a writer can usually boil it down and tell it more clearly and crisply than the speaker did. And a writer who uses "I" in a quotation is taking a risk: the newscaster who delivers the script may seem to be referring to himself.

Currently is unnecessary. *Is* conveys the sense that whatever is going on is taking place right now, at this very moment.

Let's work on it: "The T-V evangelist Jim Bakker says that if a court sells his P-T-L ministry, he'll try to buy it back. On a visit to his Heritage U-S-A theme park near Charlotte, North Carolina today, he said he'd try to return every part of his ministry to what he called "the people it was meant for." P-T-L is in bankruptcy court— in debt up to 130-million dollars. How would he pay for P-T-L? Bakker said he has "a lot of friends." (Would you call a Bakker scam there a *Charlotte ruse?*)

As with those other scripts, no one took a good second look. Which is one reason so many newspeople are in a pickle.

17

Thou Shalt Not Scare Listeners

Let's add a new commandment to our clipboards, bulletin boards and cranial gourds: Thou shalt not scare listeners.

The creation of this commandment (not by the Great Creator but by a lowly scribe) is prompted by a spate of scripts that probably scared some listeners. Perhaps even scared some away:

"This is a very complicated and confusing financial story." That first sentence of a story about a complex fraud is neither arresting nor inviting. Why begin a script with a turn-off?

Many stories that we're called on to write are a tortuous tangle of facts. And we have to apply every bit of our mental horsepower. But we shouldn't rush to announce that we're baffled or buffaloed (even when we are).

"The world doesn't want to hear about labor pains," the pitcher Johnny Sain used to say, "it only wants to see the baby."

Would an experienced singer ever preface a song by telling us how she spent years struggling to develop her voice and had a sleepless night and has a sore wrist and is trying to chase down her lost car keys (if not a few lost chords)? Can you imagine her inflicting those problems on us?

Her job, no matter what she has been through, is to sing. The writer's job, no matter how complex or scary the story, is to simplify and clarify—not *scare*ify.

Here are some more violations of that new commandment: Thou shalt not scare listeners:

"If you feel good about your children eating in school cafeterias, think twice. [Not only scary, but also tainted by preaching.] **When health inspectors visited the Leon County school district's kitchen, that** [should be *which*] **stores and serves food for 17 schools, they found moldy cheese, damaged canned goods and bug-infested pasta. An investigation is under way to determine whether the bad food was shipped to the kitchen or spoiled in the warehouse. Twenty-two cases of macaroni had to be thrown away because it** [should be *they*] **had beetles or weevils in it** [*them*]. **So maybe you had better think about brown-bagging your kid's lunches."** The best policy is: Speak no weevil. And the writer should stick to facts, not editorialize.

Let's bag it and try again: "Health inspectors say they've found trouble in the Leon County schools' main kitchen: canned goods damaged, cheese moldy and pasta infested by bugs. The kitchen stores and serves food for 17 schools. The inspectors are trying to find out whether the bad food had been shipped from a processor or had spoiled in the warehouse. Or did it go bad after it reached the kitchen? Among the problems: 22 cases of macaroni had to be thrown out because of infestation by beetles or weevils." Only nine words shorter than the original but more palatable.

A local lead-in (in its entirety): **"It's a place where we like to take our children. For years, playgrounds have been the place where kids can have fun and stay out of trouble. But there's some new information about them that will scare you. __ __ is in the newsroom with more."** *Me* scared about playgrounds? What scares me is a newsroom that *wants* to scare me.

Another scary story from another city:

"How does the thought of 10 percent ground bones and other meat remnants in hot dogs, sausage or bologna sound to you? That will be the case if the

Department of Agriculture has its way. . . ." How can a writer ask a question, then say, "That will be the case"? *What* will be the case? And what's the percentage now? More than 10 percent? Less than 10 percent? What is a *meat remnant?* Would 10 percent ground bones and the other ingredients be harmful?

Another script: **"Listen up, or this story will drive you crazy.** [Why tell listeners to listen? If people aren't already listening, how can they hear a newscaster tell them to listen? Besides, newswriters are not in the business of telling people what to do.] **The city's planning on closing off some Manhattan streets for pedestrians to have all to themselves. ___ ___ has this report on where the city is giving people on foot the right of way. . . ."** Despite the warning in the first sentence of the script, listeners who don't listen are not going to be driven crazy, especially by that story. The reporter goes on to tell which streets will be closed to motorists, so perhaps a few drivers trapped in traffic might be driven crazy. But who'd notice in Madhattan?

Still another: **"The library board is considering boosting the cost of a library card for non-residents from five to fifteen dollars. . . . Before becoming unnecessarily alarmed, all people living in Erie County are, for library purposes, considered to be** [delete *to be*] **residents."** *Unnecessarily* alarmed? In contrast to *necessarily* alarmed? Alarmed about a card fee?

Two painless pointers (no need to alarm readers): In presenting a price increase like that one, it's better not to say "from five to fifteen dollars." That wording suggests the possibility of several levels according to a cardholder's distance from the library: perhaps $10 for those who live more than 10 miles away, $15 for those beyond 30 miles. So it's better to say the cost of a card might be increased "to 15 dollars, from 5 dollars." Or instead of *boosting the cost of a library card,* try "*tripling* the cost of a library card—to 15 dollars." Also, in news scripts, we don't use dollar signs or any other symbols. We spell out everything. We abbreviate nothing. In a few instances, for organizations that are widely known, we can use initials the first time we mention them: A-F-L-C-I-O, C-I-A, F-B-I and N-double-A-C-P.

Many scripts are scary for another reason: They've been put on the air untouched, it seems, by human hand—or mind. A national newscast:

"A mortar bomb killed seven young people while they were playing chess and riding their bicycles last night in Sarajevo." Playing chess *and* riding their bikes? The place-name should be near the top, not at the end. Yes, mortars bombard a place, but they fire shells, not *bombs*.

Another item from a national newscast (in its entirety):

"One boss makes his female employes raise the flag in the pouring rain. [Shocking!] **Another follows the motto 'People are animals."** [Shameful!] **But the title of 'Worst Boss in the Nation' this year goes to the boss who requires employees taking time for a funeral to return with an obituary.** [Disgraceful! How dare he ask for proof! In fact, neither an obit nor a death notice is proof of death; you can clip them from a newspaper without attending the funeral.] **The worker who nominated that boss wins an all-expense-paid trip to Hawaii, and needs it."** That's silly; how does the writer know the worker needed a trip to Hawaii? Who sponsored that contest? Who cares? Who sponsored that writer, editor (if any) and anchor? And they call that news? Now *that*'s scary!

A broadcast script gets the fisheye:

"A thumb that was found earlier this month in a six-and-a-half pound mackinaw has been identified. [Identified as a thumb? Everything that has happened so far this month was *earlier* this month, so *earlier* is uninformative. Perhaps *a week ago,* or *ten days ago,* or *early this month.*]

"According to Sweetwater County Coroner Mike Vase, the thumb belongs to 32-year-old Robert Lindsey of Green River. Vase says Lindsey was boating on Flaming Gorge last July when Lindsey was involved in a prop accident. [Avoid *involve;* the sentence works without it.] Vase says Lindsey apparently went into the water in front of the boat to help some other [no need for *other*] people that [*who*] had fallen in, and the [*his*] boat apparently went over the top of Lindsey, and that's when Lindsey lost his thumb.

"Vase says the thumb was in the water for 202 days [do the math for listeners and make it "almost seven months"] when it was found in a fish Feb. 13th. Vase says his office was able to identify the thumb through several different tests [delete *different*]. Vase says [that] when Lindsey heard about the thumb, he contacted his office. [Then what?] Vase says the thumb's skin outline is similar to Lindsey's hand. [Whaaat?] Also, Vase says the bone structure from [*of*] the thumb is similar to Lindsey's. Vase says the size of the bone structure is the same as Lindsey's. [Huh?]

"The coroner says he feels very comfortable that the thumb belongs to Lindsey. [It's easy for *him* to be comfortable.] He says his office could do a fourth test, D-N-A. However, because of the current information, a D-N-A test would be a waste of the taxpayers' money. [And all this detail is a waste of listeners' time.] Vase says a D-N-A test on the thumb would cost about 12-hundred dollars. [So?]

"Vase says the chances of finding the thumb is [*are*] phenomenal. [The chances are *infinitesimal.*] He says when you take into account the chances of catching a fish, catching the fish with the thumb in its stomach, opening the stomach, and with 'catch and release' [did the fisherman ignore a conservation measure?], finding the thumb is phenomenal. Sounds phenomenally repetitious. But for Coroner Vase, the script is phenomenally flattering: he's mentioned 11 times. So is Lindsey. Though the winner hands down, with 13 mentions, is Thumb. (The writer was all thumbs. But, at least, he didn't call the thumb-bearing fish a fingerling.)

How would you rewrite that script? Or would you toss it back? Let's give it a try:

"Here's a true fish story: Almost seven months ago, a Green River man lost his thumb in a boating accident. Now a fisherman has found the thumb—in a fish. Last July, 32-year-old Robert Lindsey jumped off his boat on Flaming Gorge to help some people who had fallen into the water. Lindsey's boat came so close to him, the propeller sliced off his thumb. Even so, he was able to save the people in the water."

The last two sentences depend on whatever the facts are. Which reminds us: writing is writing reporting. That insight by journalism professor Mel Mencher merits honorable mention. Reporting is largely fact-finding; you have to get the facts, organize them and set them down effectively. There is no substitute for good reporting no matter how well you write. As journalism professor Curtis MacDougall put it, the most important step in communication is obtaining something worth comunicating.

A script shouldn't raise questions it doesn't answer. If that script had mentioned a boating accident without telling us Lindsey had tried to help some people, then the script wouldn't have raised any questions. But by introducing the people in the water, the script was obligated to tell us who they were and what happened to them. How many were there? Two? Twenty? Did they fall off a boat? *His* boat? A pier? A barge? A ledge? Did Lindsey rescue them despite his injury? *Before* his injury? Did they drown?

And to end the rewrite: "Sweetwater County Coroner Mike Vase says tests show the thumb was Lindsey's. Lindsey says. . . ."

Besides being wordy, the original script has some holes: Where was the fish caught? What's Lindsey's occupation? Is he right-handed? Was it his right thumb? (Did he say with a sob, "Now they'll call me Lefty"?)

Let's look at another script:

"The smiling maestro of 'Champagne Music,' who entered several million homes every Saturday night for more than 30 years, is dead. [If information in a long "who" clause or any long subordinate clause is essential, give it a sentence of its own. Most performers on television smile, so smiling is not worth mentioning.]

"Lawrence Welk passed away at his Santa Monica, California, home last night. [People don't *pass, pass on, pass away, expire,* or *succumb.* People *die.* Let's try this: "The bandleader Lawrence Welk is dead." Or "has died."] When you say someone died in his *California home,* you suggest he has another home, or homes, elsewhere. *Maestro* fits Toscanini. But Welk?]

"The German-accented bandleader toured the country for 25 years without making much of an impression in the music business. But when he appeared on a Los Angeles television station in 19-51, Welk found his fame." [*Found his fame?* Lose it! Same for *German-accented.* Would you say Churchill was *English-accented?* Or Scarlett O'Hara *southern-accented?* Also: delete *in the music business.*]

"He accompanied his musicians with an accordion and danced a graceful waltz with his 'Champagne Lady' vocalist. [Better: "waltzed gracefully." A "vocalist" is nothing but a singer with an extra syllable. *His 'Champagne Lady' vocalist* isn't conversational. Better: "his singer, known as the 'Champagne Lady.'" Did Welk dance with her and play the accordion at the same time?]

"In recent days, Welk struggled with pneumonia. He was 89." That doesn't say he died of pneumonia. Did he? Maybe the wire copy didn't carry the cause of death, so the script dealt with the gap by mentioning pneumonia. When you first heard about Welk's death, didn't you wonder, "What happened? What did he die of?"

If the perpetrators of those scripts want to write their way to network, it'll take time and work. Hard work. According to Jacques Barzun, "Simple English is no one's mother tongue. It has to be worked for."

18

Don't Make a Long Story Too Short

Brief is good, but too brief begets *"Good grief!"* **"A California scientist says inhaling polluted air might speed the growth of certain types of cancers. He bases his conclusions on lab tests with tumorous mice."** That's the whole script. But far from the whole story. Not that we want to hear the whole story. If the story matters (and if it doesn't, why use it?), we'd like to know a little about the scientist: not necessarily his (or her) name or specialty but his affiliation and a fact or two that would give him credibility. Yet his findings—judging from that skimpy script—are hardly new or interesting. To say that breathing polluted air *might* cause trouble is about as newsworthy as saying that bathing in the Ganges *might* make you sick. When you say something *might,* you leave open the possibility that it might *not.* And *might* leads to another question: *might* is the past tense of *may,* and, in another sense, *might* suggests a probability that's even weaker than *may.* Did the writer of the script use *might* to mean the probability is small, even slight? If so, the story is even flimsier. As E. B. White remarked: "When you say something, be sure you have said it. The chances of your having said it are only fair."

Let's sharpen the focus of our microscope: *tumorous?* Ever heard the word? Most people haven't. Listeners can probably deduce its meaning from the context. But *tumorous* is certainly not conversational, except, perhaps, among mousekeepers. Did the mice already have tumors, or did the polluted air cause the tumors? What were the pollutants? Was the foul air the kind that blankets Los Angeles? How did the findings become known? A medical journal? Who sponsored the research? Is the scientist reputable? A scientist at all? Or did the writer use the label indiscriminately? Without knowing something about the scientist's credentials and research, we could easily infer that breathing polluted air might just as easily *not* speed the growth of certain cancers—at least among mice. If the findings are solid and based on tests with humans, the story could have great relevance to us. Otherwise, it's just filler or padding. Without dismissing the "scientist" or his work, I get the feeling that the more the newswriter might tell us, though, the less we'd care to hear about any of it. After all, are we men or mice?

Another underdone brief: **"Good news from the state highway patrol, at least less bad news than expected. There were only nine highway deaths in North Carolina this holiday weekend, half the number predicted."** For nine families, the news is neither good nor bad; it's catastrophic. *Only* nine deaths? *Only* is a qualifier to be used with caution, and usually it's highly inappropriate with deaths. *Who* predicted the number of deaths? Not that I care. Nor care to hear *any* predictions. But without identification of the predictor, I don't know whether it was the police who came up with the prediction or a disinterested group. Most media predictions never come to pass. In 1975, a federal agency predicted that by 1985 U-S traffic deaths would zoom from 44,525 to 72,300. The fact is, they fell to 43,825.

The National Safety Council, for one, has given up predicting traffic deaths. And newscasts should quit carrying predictions and focus on reporting what *has* happened, not what may never happen. Did you ever hear of this prediction by a U.S. senator in 1930: "There is as much chance of repealing the 18th Amendment [Prohibition] as there is for a humming-bird to fly to the planet

Mars with the Washington Monument tied to its tail"? (Even if you don't remember that prediction, let's drink to it!) A 19th century American humorist, Josh Billings, warned: "Don't ever prophesy; for if you prophesy wrong, nobody will forget it; and if you prophesy right, nobody will remember it."

Good news—bad news quips should be left for stand-up comedians. The newscaster could just as easily have begun that script: "We have good news and bad news. The bad news is, we have no good news. The good news is, we have no more bad news."

Another brief: **"Employees of savings and loans around Springfield are attending seminars this week on how to handle themselves if their banks** [S&Ls are not banks] **are robbed. The seminars are being conducted by Springfield Police Chief Terry Knowles."** The story sounds like an item for bulletin boards—at S&Ls. Why would listeners care about the seminars? Even if they were told when and where the sessions were being held, they couldn't attend. And the script doesn't tell them anything worth knowing. Now, if the station has time and resources, a reporter could use that item as a stepping-stone to a legitimate story. What is the chief's advice to the employees? What should listeners do if *they* happen to be at the scene of a robbery? Why are the seminars being held? Has there been a recent string of hold-ups at S&Ls and banks? (Brecht might have asked: Is it a greater crime to rob an S&L or own one? Which brings to mind the S&L operator who wailed, "Twelve people out of 260 million convict me, and they call that justice.")

Another all-too-brief: **"Sources tell ____ News** [needs *that*] **Bob Price, a long-time part-owner of Reliable Chevrolet, has sold his interest in the business to a Kansas City dealership owner. The sources say Price will KEEP his part of another dealership, Reliable Toyota."** Let's scrap that stuff about "Sources tell us." Most of our information comes from someone's telling us something. But *we* aren't important; what we find out *is*. Are the sources Reliable? Who are the sources? Price himself? A rival? The buyer? A mischief-maker? Any confirmation from anyone? Why did Price sell? How much did he get? How much did he make or lose on the sale? How big was his interest in the Chevy shop? Seventy-five percent? Five percent? The buyer's name? Does any of it matter, except to a few listeners? Is it news at all?

If the story is true and worth using—on the basis of that script, we can't tell—let's write it right: "A part-owner of Reliable Chevrolet, Bob Price, has sold his stake. He sold it to a Kansas City dealer. . . ."

Yes, too brief is bad; terse is worse. So let's see to it that our scripts don't leave questions or listeners dangling. Newsrooms shouldn't get rid of the beef, just the fat.

Good scripts are usually brief and brisk. But some are so lean they leave listeners in limbo. Though we don't want to add fat to a script, this one needs some brawn: **"President Bush is in excellent health, aside from some trouble with his left eye . . . Doctors say he's showing signs of glaucoma . . . He's now on medication."**

The President may be in good shape, but the script isn't. Who pronounced the President healthy, the newscaster? If the source is a physician—or anyone other than the newscaster—the assertion needs attribution. And when attribution is needed, attribution precedes assertion.

The *is* at the beginning of the script is un-newsy. It doesn't tell us whether Mr. Bush has been healthy for a lifetime or only since lunchtime. News is what's new. News is change. News is the unusual. But news is not what's standpat or old hat. We wouldn't write that 260 million Americans slept well through the night. But we would write about someone whose sleep was shattered when his home blew up or burned down. If the President has been well all along, the news is the discovery of trouble:

"President Bush has developed an eye problem. After his annual physical today, doctors said his left eye shows signs of glaucoma, a disease that can cause loss of vision. So they prescribed medicine and said that otherwise his health is excellent." The rewrite starts without attribution because the White House's disclosure of the problem can be considered an admission against interests (as they say in court), not a self-serving statement. So it's safe, at least in a story like this, to lead without a source. Do you think the White House would announce falsely that the President has a physical problem? The original broadcast script, reprinted in its entirety, is 25 words; mine is 41. Longer, yes, but stronger. At least in my eyes.

Another script that's too lean: **"Lawmakers from 42 nations passed a resolution today calling for a global commitment to halve** [not a broadcast word] **pollutants over 20 years** [awkwardly placed] **that are believed to contribute to global warming. The vote marks the end of a three-day environmental conference in Washington."**

Was the United States one of the 42 nations? What effect, if any, is the resolution likely to have on U. S. laws? What is its likely effect on global warming? What does global warming mean to *us?* ("Think globally, act locally.") Could the polar icecaps melt and flood our attics? Is the threat of warming real? We don't have time to answer all those questions, but if we had more facts, we'd be able to write a better story. (And we'd have a head start if the conference had called itself Emission Impossible.)

Let's rewrite the script: "Lawmakers from 42 nations passed a resolution today calling for international commitment to cut by half pollutants believed to contribute to global warming. The cutback would take 20 years. The resolution came at the end of a three-day environmental conference in Washington, D-C."

The most objectionable element in the original script, which moved on a news agency's broadcast wire, is the use of *halve*. Most listeners would probably hear of a "commitment to *have* pollutants." Which is an example of the perils of not first reading our copy aloud to ourselves—carefully. And of not being alert to homophones, words that sound alike but are spelled differently and have different meanings. (Homonyms also sound alike and have different meanings, but they're spelled alike.) Why didn't a wire editor catch *halve?* (One supervisor who did, Lee Hall, then news director of WSB, Atlanta, kindly sent me his haul. Where I come from, that writer's misstep would have had an editor's vowels in an uproar. And the *writer* would catch it—from the editor.)

The most frequently used homophones in newscasts are probably *their/there/they're* and *cite/sight/site;* careful writers try to avoid *cite* and *site.* There are many other three-way homophones. And Bill Owen of ABC even points out some four-way homophones: *cents/cense/scents/sense; oar/o'er/or/ore; palate/palette/pallet/pallette;* and *right/rite/wright/write.* Then there are *psychic* and *sidekick.* Several of those words are so uncommon they pose no problem. But—along with that old sound-alike trap: *a tax on* and *attacks on*—they remind us that as we tap on our keyboards, we should not only watch our words but also tune in with our inner ear.

Let's look at another scanty script: **"Sabrina Gallon of Queens was as surprised as anyone to find out that a nude photograph of her appeared in Hustler magazine back in October of 1983 . . . Turns out, say the courts** [*courts?*], **that her ex-boyfriend sent in the photo with a forged consent form . . . Gallon has been awarded 30-thousand dollars since Hustler never checked the authenticity of the form."**

The first sentence of the script is not new, and it may not even be true. How do we know she was surprised? That's what *she* says now. The only surprise in the script is that the news, such as it is, is in the last sentence.

That script needs fleshing out: Who *is* Sabrina Gallon? A novice in a nunnery? A sergeant of gunnery? A purveyor of punnery? We don't need her résumé, but we do want to know who she is. And let's not start a script with the name of an unknown.

Let's redo it: "A Queens woman has won a 30-thousand-dollar judgment from Hustler magazine for running a nude photo of her—without permission. A Federal judge in [place-name] made the award to Sabrina Gallon, a _____. The court found that a former boy-friend had sent in her photo with a forged consent. And that the magazine hadn't verified it." (However you rate the rewrite, at least it doesn't call *Hustler* the grossest national product.)

As a rule, lean is good. Short words. Short sentences. Short stories. But in our effort to make a long story short, let's not short our listeners.

19

Dial 911 for Help

They say you're never too old to learn new mistakes. And if you're never too young to unlearn old mistakes, a look at this script might help youngsters *and* oldsters. Let's look at it bit by bit in slo-mo:

"A 23-year-old Platteville woman will spend three weeks in Grant County jail after she was found guilty on one count of drug trafficking last week in Grant County Circuit Court.

[A peck of problems:

[The abrupt shift in tense, from the future (*will spend*) to the past (*was found*) is grammatically inconsistent.

[What's after *after* should come before.

[*Last week* is worse in an opening sentence than *yesterday*.

[The woman's age *should* be used, but not in the first breath. Everyone has an age. Nothing distinctive about hers. It doesn't merit prominence. If she were 11 or 99, that might be another story.

[How can the writer say the woman *will* spend three weeks in jail? Maybe she won't spend even one night in jail. Maybe she will appeal and maybe her conviction will be overturned. Or maybe the judge will have a change of heart and commute her sentence. Maybe she'll kill herself or be killed by another inmate. Or escape. Or drop dead.

[*One count?* Counts seldom count.

144

[The end of that sentence suggests she was trafficking in the court itself.

[*Grant County* shouldn't be mentioned twice, not even for a repeat offender.]

Now for the second sentence of that script: **"R__ P___ of Platteville is charged in connection with an incident two years ago in which she reportedy sold 25 dollars' worth of cocaine to an undercover agent.** [*Charged* and *reportedly* were proper when she was arrested, but now that she's convicted, those words are outdated. Don't you want to know her occupation? Also, the first sentence has already identified her as a resident of Platteville (a Platte*villain?*)]

"According to the criminal complaint, the incident occurred in August of 1989 at a party in the township of Platteville. [Platteville again? And no need to refer to the complaint. The judge has now ruled that she did make the sale at the party. Also: The second sentence said *two years ago,* so the month and year are redundant.]

"The undercover agent witnessed P___ sell small bags of a white, powdery substance to several individuals, and he asked her if he could get in on the deal. [*Witnessed = saw. White, powdery substance = white powder. Individuals = people.* Save *individual* for *individual rights.*]

"After P___ sold a package to the agent, he took it to the residence of Grant County Sheriff Deputy Robert Floerke, where it was later tested and identified as a controlled substance. [*Residence = home.* No need for *Grant County.* No need for *later.* It couldn't have been earlier. Better: "where a test identified it as cocaine."]

"In court last week, Judge George Curry found P___ guilty on one count of selling a controlled substance. [*In court* is repetitious. Where else would he have made a finding?]

"He ordered her to serve three weeks in Grant County jail, ordered that P___ serve 30 hours' community service and pay 203 dollars in witness fees. [*Serve*

. . . serve . . . service? No. Better: "He sentenced her to three weeks in jail and 30 hours' community service. And he ordered her to pay 203 dollars in witness fees." No need for *Grant County* again.]

"P___ is currently serving one week of the jail sentence. She will serve another week beginning October 4th, 1992, and October 4th, 1993." Better: "She has started her first week in jail, but her second week is not scheduled until next October, and her third week a year later." Isn't her jail sentence odd? And worth a quick explanation?

The writer might have avoided that muddle if he'd taken time to think the story through before starting. The story was already a few days old (the defendant was convicted *and* sentenced on the same day), so spending a few more minutes on it wouldn't have hurt.

One way to get a grip on a story is to assume it's the biggest story of the day: try to visualize the banner across the front page of the local paper. Which few words would the banner use to summarize the story?

Another way: Pretend you're dialing 911 and telling the story to an operator. Gotta make it fast. And simple. The originator of that method is Eileen Fredman Solomon, who teaches at Lindenwood College in St. Charles, Missouri. She says that if you think about reporting a story to 911, you are forced to condense the essence into the quintessence. Sure, compression is harder than expansion. That's why broadcast newswriters are paid those telephone-number salaries.

So let's phone 911: "Platteville woman convicted of selling cocaine. Got three weeks in jail. One week now, one next October, one a year later. And she must do 30 hours' community service. Sold coke to people at a party, including undercover agent." The 911 approach may not provide the precise words for the lead, but it can come close. It makes clear what the story is all about and requires you to crystallize your thinking.

"911" can also help you write tight. Keep in mind what Professor Solomon tells her students when she wants to inspire brevity: "God created heaven and earth in 10 words."

From start to finish, each word in a script must work, and if your start is bad, you'll come to a bad end. With that in mind, how would you rewrite—or edit—this network news script? Or would you pass it along as is? Or turn it into confetti?

"The U-S Navy had to shoot down one of its own planes today over the Mediterranean, a carrier-based E-two-C Hawkeye. The Hawkeye is an early warning plane. In today's incident, a Hawkeye from the carrier Forrestal caught fire while supporting allied relief efforts for the Kurds in northern Iraq. The five-member crew bailed out 40 miles from Cyprus, but the Grumman-built plane kept going. A Navy attack aircraft shot the Hawkeye down for what the Navy called safety reasons."

What about the crew? People are more important than property. Did the crew survive? If they bailed out near Cyprus, an island, they probably landed in the drink. Were they rescued by a ship, a chopper, or what? If they had been killed or lost at sea, the writer surely would have told us. But as it is, the question is left hanging. Were any of the crew burned in the fire? Were any hurt while bailing out? Or hurt when they hit the water—or the ground?

"In *today*'s incident"? What other day are we writing about?

The script refers to "the five-member crew," not the "five-man crew." Yet, according to the Pentagon, they all *are* men. So why not say so? The attribution at the end of the script suggests there might have been a reason other than safety for the shoot-down. Perhaps the Navy didn't want the plane and its electronic gear to fall into the hands of unfriendlies.

And why start the script with the outcome instead of building up the story dramatically? Let's rewrite it:

"A U-S Navy plane caught fire over the Mediterranean today, and the five-man crew bailed out. Navy helicopters rescued them—unhurt—from the sea near Cyprus. But the burning plane, an E-two-C Hawkeye, kept going. So for safety—or security—a Navy fighter plane shot it down." Original: 79 words; rewrite: 47. Shorter, sharper, stronger. If I had been told to write five more seconds, I'd add, "The Hawkeye had been on early-warning duty supporting Allied relief work for the Kurds in northern Iraq."

The original script mentions *carrier* twice, when once would suffice; the rewrite doesn't mention it at all. Whether the Hawkeye was land-based or carrier-based is unimportant. So is the name of the carrier (unless the carrier is Typhoid Mary).

The rewrite omits "Grumman-built." The name of the builder is immaterial, unless the Navy alleges faulty construction or there's another compelling reason. Stacks of newspaper and magazine stories, books, movies and documentaries have told us about the Titanic, but can you identify the ship's builder? Who cares?

How would you handle this local television script? **"The L-A-P-D was called to a Reseda neighborhood early this morning after a teenager tried to fuse an explosive at a friend's house and it blew up in his right hand, creating** [better: *causing*] **an explosion so loud it woke up neighbors four blocks away and blew a hole in the sidewalk. Neighbors say Chris Sterling, a 19-year-old resident** [of where?]**, was seen staggering down the block from the neighbor's house, crying for help."**

The script lurches off on the wrong foot. And the first sentence is far too long: 53 words. Police are called, or sent, to just about every crime that's reported, so the calling of police, or their dispatch or arrival, is not news. If police *refuse* to go or can't find the crime scene, then you have a story. But after all, or *before* all, this story is not about police. Here, they're only supporting players. The main character is the punk who was working on an explosive. Shouldn't we be told promptly what became of him? If he survived, what's his condition? If neighbors say he *was seen,* they're probably the ones who saw him. So it would be preferable to say, "Neighbors say he staggered." Let's turn our spotlight on him and use information supplied later in the script to rewrite it:

"A young man in Reseda was working on an explosive early today when it blew up—and tore off parts of his right hand. The blast was so loud it woke up people four blocks away. Doctors say he's in serious but stable condition. . . ." (His lawyer may try to win a jury's sympathy by calling him a "teen," but he's close to adulthood—if not yet an adult hood.)

After two neighbors speak on camera, the original script resumes with voice-over:

"The bomb squad evacuated the area, searched the friend's garage [*Whose* friend? By now, listeners might well have forgotten about the bomb-maker.] **and detonated remaining explosives** [type? amount?] **in a containment chamber. Police found fragments of the boy's hand up to 70 feet away from** [no need for *away*] **where the explosion took place. Chris Sterling was taken to the Northridge Medical Facility, where doctors say he's in serious but stable condition.** [No need to identify the hospital unless we want listeners to send flowers.] **Police say they are still trying to find out where exactly** [*where* alone does the job] **the explosives came from and how Chris** [don't call a bomber by his first name] **and his friend** [doesn't he—or she—have a name?] **were able to get a hold of them."** *Get* alone does the job.

What were those two characters doing with explosives? Any charges filed against them? Although they're responsible for their own bomb's going off, it's the editor who's to blame for letting this bomb go on the air.

20

No Headlinese, Please

Ever think of scripts as racehorses? Some run smoothly and swiftly. They're winners. Some move ineptly. They're also-rans. With more effort, some may make it. But before they finish, many will falter.

Train your binoculars on these entries and see how you'd size 'em up:

"In the Bronx, precipitation delaying the Yanks-Red Sox game."

Precipitation? In the Bronx? No thonx. We call it *rain.*

"Mother Nature's great watering system is drenching the Eastern plains tonight."

What the writer means is, "It's raining." Why drag *Mother Nature* into it? She's overworked and too weather-beaten for the news. So are other time-worn personifications: Jack Frost, Father Time, Lady Luck, the Grim Reaper and Old Man Winter.

Another big-city television script: **"One of the nation's most prominent homeless advocates was found hanged to death in a Washington, D.C., shelter."** *Hanged to death?* If someone's hanged, he *is* dead. *Hanged to death* is a redundancy, like *smothered to death* or *strangled to death.*

Homeless advocate sounds like an advocate who is homeless, instead of an advocate *for* the homeless. *Homeless advocate,* like too much broadcast newswriting, has the clang of "headlinese." That's what *The Random House*

Dictionary for Writers and Readers, calls the space-saving jargon of poor print-headline writing, "characterized by piled-up nouns, clipped words or abbreviations, commas instead of conjunctions, and sometimes a stark cluster of monosyllables." And why try to pump up the script by calling Mitchell Snyder *one of the nation's most prominent?* Better: *A leading advocate* (or *champion*) *of the homeless.*

Another station: **"Those who knew Snyder were stunned and saddened."** In reporting a death, why say friends and neighbors are shocked or saddened? Would they be pleased? Why take time to report the predictable—and often self-evident?

Same script: **"Snyder struggled for years to gain recognition of the homeless problems in the country."** *Homeless problems?* Problems in need of homes? The writer means: problems *of* the homeless. *In the country?* Most of the homeless are in the cities. Better: "in *this* country."

Another script: **"Some pretty strong words today from the president of Iraq. Saddam Hussein says his nation has sophisticated chemical weapons. . . ."** His words are not at all *pretty.* Strike *pretty.* Without it, the sentence is stronger. Which is why Strunk and White urge us to avoid qualifiers (*very, little, pretty, rather*): "These are the leeches that infest the pond of prose, sucking the blood of words."

Network television: **"The picture above the desk is of his father, who was a public school inspector under the Czar, and really pretty well-to-do."** *Two* useless qualifiers: *really* and *pretty.* Better: "The picture above the desk is of his father, who inspected public schools under the Czar and was well-to-do."

Same script: **"But it was in December, 1922, that Lenin came to the office, felt weak—he'd already had one stroke. The clock on the wall says it all. Lenin left this office at 8:15 for the last time."** *Says it all* says nothing. The clock doesn't tell us Lenin was leaving his office for the last time. And it doesn't tell us *why* Lenin left. And it doesn't tell us whether that was the last day of his life. The script goes on to say that for the next ten months he spent most of his time in his bedroom recuperating and then went to his home in Gorky for more rest. He died there, 13 months after his last day at the office. What does the office clock say about all this? What does it tell us about a question Lenin asked: "Why should freedom of speech and freedom of the press be allowed?" What does it tell us about his ruthless use of force and terror? For all this—and more—the clock strikes out.

One of Lenin's favorite pieces of music was identified by a correspondent in that segment as "Beethoven's 'Pathetique' Symphony." Beethoven wrote a "Pathetique" sonata and Tchaikovsky wrote a "Pathetique" symphony, but Beethoven never wrote a "Pathetique" symphony.

Later, a correspondent asked the Soviet Union's current prime minister: **"You'll think I'm obsessed with the subject, but would you say, then, that President Gorbachev** [the interviewee] **and this government is in no political danger?"** Don't use a singular verb (*is*) for a plural subject (Gorbachev *and* the government). In one short question, the interviewer manages to combine a mouthful of how-*not*-to's: Don't tell the interviewee what he thinks. Don't disparage your question or yourself. Don't suggest an answer. Don't ask a question that can be answered with a yes or no. Better: "How politically secure—or insecure—are President Gorbachev and this government?"

From local TV: **"Here's a story about boys and girls and their dogs.** [Voice-over] **They're not fancy pets. But they're lovable just the same. And they were all showcased, kind of, at a pet show for the average dog in Springfield, Missouri. More than 100 kids and canines participated,** [that comma should be a period] **some did tricks, others just did whatever they wanted to. And there wasn't any grand prize, just the kind of rewards you get when you see kids and their dogs having a good time."**

Any story starting with *Here's a story about* or *This is the story of* plods a path so well worn that it has become a rut. What does *showcased, kind of,* mean? That *kind of* is substandard; the second *kind of,* in the last sentence of the script, should be *kinds of.*

Instead of telling us what the pets are not, the script should tell us what they are. Implying that only fancy pets are lovable is absurd. What is an *average dog?* Why shift from *dogs* to *canines?* When the writer cuts his eyeteeth in journalism, he'll realize that the dog that does best is a plain old dog. After just one go-round, we see that none of those entries makes it to the winner's circle. For them, alas, the pound.

21

One-Word Openers

Pow! *Wham! Bam!*

Slam-bang language in the comics doesn't hurt anyone, but must we jolt our listeners like that?

A recent example from local radio: **"Guilty! That's the verdict from a Boulder County jury after a strangulation death. We get the details from. . . ."**

And from network television: **"Indicted! The federal government comes down hard on Eastern Airlines."** The anchor opened the newscast by reading that headline over a videotape showing the inside of a hangar and an Eastern jet.

Guilty is an adjective, and the verb, *indicted,* serves there as an adjective. What makes sentences sing—and singe—are nouns and verbs, concrete nouns and vigorous verbs. But adjectives, like spices, should be used gingerly.

Confused! That's what I am by one-word leads. Why? Conversational, they're not. People don't talk that way. And people don't listen that way. Our ears are accustomed to the standard speech pattern among English-speaking people: subject-verb-object, S-V-O. Ever hear a comedian start a joke with a punch line? He'd be laughed off the stage.

People usually start conversations with a subject, then go on to a verb: "Don dropped dead." No one would tell you: "Dead. That's what Don is." Our ears—and minds—aren't used to hearing people blurt out one-word openers, like scare headlines in tabloids. But some newscasters do it daily. And nightly.

154

You can say this for one-word leads: They're easy to write. And they spare a writer the effort of thinking through a good, engaging lead. One-word-lead fanciers can easily store a batch of sock-'em leads so they're on tap for any eventuality:

"Shot! That's what a bank robber was today."

"Smashed! That's what a school bus was today. The driver, too."

"Laughing. That's what S—and—L owners are doing all the way to the bank."

"Miss America. That's what we hope enemy bombs do."

Backing into a story is unnatural: **"A rifle and a handgun. That's what the sheriff of Jacksonville, Florida, says James Pew had with him when he walked into a G-M-A-C office today and started shooting. Eight people died. . . ."** Better: "Eight people were shot dead." Still better: "He shot eight people dead."

Another overwrought—and underthought—lead: **"When you're dead, you're dead.** [If you heard an anchor say that, would you nod in agreement and marvel: 'How perceptive! I never had thought death through to its logical conclusion: once dead, always dead'?] **And I don't need a funeral.** [Would you wonder, why would a vibrant young newscaster need a funeral? And would you say to yourself, 'That's the kind of clear thinking you gotta admire'?] **"With that, Brewers manager Tom Trebelhorn decided not to appeal the five-game suspension that the American League office handed down today."** People don't talk that way. People don't start speaking with a quotation and then back into who said it. And broadcast newswriters who know their craft don't put attribution *after* a quotation. Further, it wasn't *with that* that Trebelhorn decided not to appeal.

Let's redo it: "The American League suspended Milwaukee Brewers Manager Tom Trebelhorn and eight players today for fighting. Their brawl broke out last night in the Brewers' game against the Seattle Mariners. . . ." The active voice works there, with the American League taking the action. But when the person—or people—who were the target of the action are more important than the agent taking the action, the passive is usually better: "Milwaukee Brewers Manager Tom Trebelhorn and eight players have been suspended for fighting. The American League took the action because of the brawl last night in the Brewers' game against the Seattle Mariners. . . ."

While we're at it, let's go back to that network script near the top. After that in-your-ear opening **"Indicted!"** and a fast sentence, the anchor said:

"Good evening. For the first time tonight, a U-S airline, Eastern Airlines, is charged with crimes . . . crimes that may have put passengers at risk. As we reported here last night, ten of Eastern's managers and supervisors were charged as well. The indictment says. . . ."

What makes the story news is that an airline has been indicted. Not that it's a first. Even if it were the second time, or the fifth time, it would still be big news. *For the first time* in the lead of a story delays delivery of the news. A writer has an opportunity to say an event is the first of its kind—if that's significant, and if it *is* the first. But first he should tell what happened. Even if the firstness is worth mentioning, it's not worth mentioning first. Who'd write, "For the first time, two jumbo jets collided, and. . . ."?

Further, *for the first time tonight* is ambiguous. Does it imply that another airline may be charged before midnight? And what does *tonight* add? Also, the sentence lacks an action verb. *Is charged* expresses no action, no change in status, which is what news is all about. You can write *is charged* about someone charged a year ago.

As we reported here last night raises questions: If a newscaster reported a story last night, why is he reporting it again tonight—at the top? And why is he telling us he already told us? For viewers who were *not* watching last night, that line doesn't help. And it doesn't help viewers who *were* watching last night and remember the story. And it sure doesn't help those who have forgotten. Even if everyone who's watching remembers last night's story, tonight's harking back to last night doesn't move the story ahead a jot. The apparent purpose of that line in the script is self-promotion. Keep your hands on the keyboard and off your own back. Instead of wasting everyone's time on that, staff members should have made sure their information was correct. In fact, those indicted were *nine* managers and supervisors, not ten.

The ombudsman for the *Kansas City Star and Times,* Donald D. Jones, said, "Errors of fact do more to undermine the trust and confidence of readers than any other sin we commit. A city editor I know used to say, 'A story is only as good as the dumbest error in it.'"

22

Looking for Trouble

The trouble with many scripts is that the writer doesn't take enough trouble, and the anchor doesn't trouble over them at all. As a result, many scripts raise far more questions than they answer.

A recent radio script: **"The doors are open . . . and it's business as usual at the Sizzler restaurant in Melville on Route 110 today.** [Why are you telling us this? News is the *un*usual. And linking verbs (*are, is*) don't express action, only inaction.] **"This after an elderly man accidentally hit the gas pedal and rammed his car in reverse into the side of the restaurant . . .** [*This after?* Most *after*thoughts should be rethought—and re-written.] **"Three people were hurt—all with minor injuries . . . The driver of the car, 78-year-old Meir Lupovici, was not hurt. Nor were his wife and another passenger.** [Who *was* hurt? Were the three people eating? Arriving? Leaving? Loitering? Who *is* Lupovici? Where does he live? Is he retired? From what? Had he and his passengers just eaten at the Sizzler? Is he licensed? Insured? Did police ticket him? Had he been taking medicine? Was he allowed to drive home after the accident? Was he able to?]

The script continues: **"Police say Lupovici—after hitting the building—then put the car into drive and hit another building.** [*Which* other building? Anyone there hurt? How far is the second place from the Sizzler? What caused him to hit another building? So far, he's hitting two for two. What was the damage to the Sizzler? Just charred at the edges?] **"The folks at Sizzler tell us they thought a bomb had gone off when the car hit.** [*Which* folks? The folks working there or the folks eating there? For that story, *folks* may be too folksy.] **"The restaurant re-opened just a few hours after the accident last night . . . and they're open today."** We heard it was open in the opening line, so we don't need a second helping.

The first sentence of the script is weak, even for a second-day lead. So let's redo it: "The Sizzler restaurant in Melville has re-opened. Last night, a motorist accidentally hit the building, and the place closed for several hours." Better yet: "Police are trying to figure out how a motorist hit a Melville restaurant and then struck another building."

The same radio station also carried this item: **"Burger King going the celebrity route with its salad dressings.** [Shouldn't the newscaster get a dressing down for writing a lead without a verb? A sentence fragment (a subject without a verb) is sometimes acceptable, even desirable, but that lead goes nowhere. *Going* is a participle. It's an adjective, not a verb. If the writer had added the auxiliary verb *is* to help make it *is going,* he'd have a verb with a tense. But he still wouldn't have a story.] **It will use Paul Newman's Own Dressings in coming weeks. No word on whether Newman will do commercials for Burger King."** So what?

Another script: **"A young Cuban refugee is safely on shore in Miami after drifting in the Atlantic for five days. 16-year-old Isbert Castro was found clinging to an inner tube off the Florida coast. He floated all the way from Cuba . . . a distance of about 250 miles. Rescuers are now looking for the young man's brother-in-law, who also set off from Cuba on an inner tube."** *Is* in the first sentence does nothing. Does nothing but raise questions: has the lad been on shore for an hour? A day? A week? His name raises still another question: is he related to Fidel? A rule in newswriting is not to raise questions you don't answer. We can't always follow the rule because we can't always get the answers, but, chances are, the writer knew the answers to those questions. Or he could have phoned the wire service that moved the story and asked. Good writing requires good reporting. Not necessarily fact-finding on the scene but an ability to spot gaps in a story—and fill them. Or at least write around them. Smoothly. That script was broadcast 750 miles from Miami, so there's no need to identify the refugee. Who found him? How far from shore? At least the writer didn't say the refugee was washed up.

Let's redo the script with an action verb: "A young Cuban has escaped to Florida on an inner tube. The Coast Guard [a guess] rescued the 16-year-old boy from the Atlantic, off Miami [another guess]. His brother-in-law had also set out on an inner tube from Cuba, 250 miles from Florida, and now a search is on for <u>him</u>."

The next script raises other questions. It's reprinted in a manual that a broadcast journalism teacher gives his college students. The manual calls it "an actual television script" written by a network correspondent for a newscast. Here is the first segment: **"In the last few weeks, the streets of Port-au-Prince has** [*has* they?] **become a bold, sometimes violent forum for political expression in Haiti. The country's Communist Party, along with other groups, have called for the resignation of the current military government . . . the national governing council."**

The first error in the script (apparently retyped from the original) is the use of a singular verb, *has,* when the subject is the plural *streets.* The second error is the use of a plural verb, *have,* with a singular subject, *Communist Party.* Though *Party* is followed by *other groups,* we need to apply this grammatical rule: an intervening phrase—*along with, accompanied by, as well as, in addition to, including, joined by, no less than* or *together with*— is not part of the subject, so the subject remains singular.

Elsewhere, the script says: **"In the political turmoil, dozens of factions have rushed in to gain ground.**

Because of Haiti ties to the U-S, even [do we even need *even?*] **anti-American sentiments are being openly expressed.**" *Haiti* is wrong. It should be either *Haitian* or the more readily understood *Haiti's.* And the sentence would be stronger with the key word, *openly,* put at the end. But are Haiti's ties the reason such sentiments are expressed openly?

Were the errors in subject-verb agreement made by the network correspondent or by someone who retyped the script? In either case, why didn't the teacher, a former networker himself, catch the errors and fix them? Or point them out?

And why aren't people in newsrooms taking the trouble to ask more questions? Not that we go looking for trouble, but why should *we* have to ask all those questions?

23

As You *Like* It?

Time to change our *like* style? If we use *like* and *as* interchangeably, it *is* time. *Like* and *as* are not interchangeable. *Like* can't be slipped into a gap in a sentence, like a wild card. Unlikely as it may seem, a recent newsroom printout shows how one reporter fell flat on his interface:

"Mayor Daley finally got tired of all the embarrassing stories about how easy it is for people to sneak into the supposedly secure areas of O'Hare airport, *like* where the planes are. So Daley hired a security expert. . . ."

Careful writers no like. *Like* is not a conjunction. But it *is* acceptable as a preposition when it introduces a noun or pronoun *not* followed by a verb: "She writes like a dream." And *like* is O.K. when the verb is merely implied: "He takes to running like a fish to water." But in "He eats like it's going out of style," replace *like* with *as if.*

When used as a preposition, *like* means *similar to* and should be followed by an object, either a noun or a pronoun. In that script, *like* is followed by *where,* an adverb. (*Like where* is that kind of writing put on the air? I'll never tell the name of the city. And I won't identify the O&O.) One way to spot trouble: if you use *like* as a preposition, you should be able to substitute *similar to* and make it work. If you can't, then *like* is wrong.

Better: ". . . secure areas of O'Hare airport, *including those* where the planes are." But *are* is a linking verb and expresses no action. Let's give the sentence a lift by activating the end: ". . . including those where planes [no need for *the*] come and go."

When *like* is used as a verb, it's a transitive verb, so it must be followed by an object. Which means that the first sentence in the third paragraph, "Careful writers no like," is no go. (Of course, if you write for Tonto, that's another story.)

Like and *as if* are not interchangeable, either. But there are a few exceptions, idiomatic phrases: "They shopped like crazy." *Crazy* is an adjective, so theoretically the sentence should read, "They shopped *as if* they were crazy." *Like crazy* is an idiom, so we get dispensation— but we can't ordinarily justify sloppy usage by saying it's conversational.

"*Like* has long been widely misused by the illiterate," Strunk and White say in *The Elements of Style;* "lately it has been taken up by the knowing and the well-informed, who find it catchy, or liberating, and use it as though they were slumming. If every word or device that achieved currency were immediately authenticated, simply on the ground of popularity, the language would be as chaotic as a ball game with no foul lines."

Although illiterates and the *like*-minded seem to groove on *like,* some uncertain writers shy away from it even when *like* is all right. They've been warned so often to watch out for *like* they figure that if they don't use it at all, they can't goof. So they write, "He drives a car *such as* this." Or they write, "She keeps a dictionary handy, *as do* most writers." But in both sentences, *like* is proper *and* preferable.

Another comment on that script: Instead of telling the story in a simple, straightforward style, the reporter implies that the mayor acted—*finally*—because he got tired of negative stories. How can a reporter know *why* the mayor acted? Did the mayor blurt out, "I finally got tired of all the embarrassing stories"? Perhaps the mayor acted as soon as he realized that security at O'Hare was inadequate. So it's best to stick to facts, unless you are an infallible mind reader.

On the same television newscast, another weak script: **"At this hour, a woman and two children are hospitalized, one in critical condition . . . after fire raged through their West Side apartment."** *Fire* is a far more arresting word than *at, this, hour, woman, children* or *hospitalized.* Or all of them put together.

At *no hour* do I start with a boxscore of dead and injured and work back to the cause. I set the stage and start with action. And I don't let a fire *rage* or *race.* At least not that one. Better: "A fire in a West Side apartment has injured four people—two children and their mothers. (We learn about the other mother later.) And one child is in critical condition."

Also, there's that feeble *are.* Have those people been hospitalized for an hour, a day, a week? Tens of thousands of people are hospitalized *at this hour.* The story was broadcast at least five hours after the fire, so *at this hour* sounds overheated.

The script resumes: "[Voice-over] **Fire officials say a 36-year-old woman suffered from** [delete *from*] **smoke inhalation. Her five-year-old daughter is in critical condition at Saint Anthony Hospital. Two-month-old Angie Gayton suffered from smoke inhalation and is in fair condition at University of Illinois Hospital. Her mother was treated at the scene. The blaze began around eleven this morning in the basement of the building. The cause of the fire has not yet been determined."**

The 36-year-old woman and the 2-month-old infant suffered smoke inhalation, but the script doesn't say how the 5-month-old child in critical condition was hurt.

The script shows no signs that any names were supered, so why did the writer use the name of the baby but no one else's? And why identify the hospitals? In a big city, there's usually no need to do so. The script's first sentence mentions only one apartment. Were the families living together?

Let's rewrite the last two sentences: "The fire started in the basement. [*Of the building* is understood; I'd skip the time: every fire starts at one time or another. And the time there is not significant.] No word on the cause." A verbless sentence, particularly at the end of a story, is unobjectionable. The new last sentence has several advantages: it's shorter, it ends with a one-syllable word, and I like it.

And like it or not, if those two scripts are worth doing at all, they are worth doing right.

24

Empty Vessels

Time is precious; talk is *not* cheap. And what drives up the bill are words that are empty. Not empty in themselves but empty in certain combinations. Let's look at some partial scripts to see how we can toss out the empties and save time:

"The cause [of a crash] **is still unknown, but we note that there was thick, icy fog at the time, and the outside temperature was about 60 below zero."** Which words add only time? *We note that, at the time* and *outside.* (Have you ever heard anyone mention the temperature *inside?*) Without those time-wasting words, the sentence reads: "The cause is still unknown, but there was thick, icy fog, and the temperature was about 60 below zero."

"In Kennebunkport, the town was buzzing with the arrival of Bush and the First Lady. Local bars were jammed." The needless word? *Local.* What other kinds of bars would a town have—*regional? National?* Better: "Kennebunkport was excited by the arrival of President and Missus Bush." Is bar-jamming the biggest deal in town? Isn't there anything else going on behind the Bushes? I'd avoid having a town *buzzing*—or chirping, or slurping. At least the writer didn't call it *Kennedybunkport.*

"The children and the driver were treated at a local hospital for cuts and bruises." There's that old thief of time, *local.* Where else would the injured be taken? If someone is taken elsewhere, that may be worth mentioning. Otherwise, we can assume the hospital *is* local. (Also, *local* police. There are no national or international police. There are state police, and we call them that. Otherwise, all police are local police. Another empty word: *area,* as in "*area* hospital." Used as an adjective, *area* is best left for "*area* code" and "*area* rug.")

"Cold temperatures mixed with rain caused some problems on Maine roads this morning." Couldn't listeners take that to mean only the *main* roads had problems. The needless words: *temperatures, mixed* and *some.* Stronger: "Rain and cold caused problems today on Maine's roads." As one old Mainer, E. B. White, says, "Omit needless words."

Another empty word we often hear tied in with rain is *activity,* as in "thunderstorm *activity.*" Although some weathermen seem to think *activity* brims with action, it's often empty. Also: "cloudy *conditions.*"

"Inmates at several Ontario jails are now threatening strike action. . . ." Another empty word, at least in this combination, is *action.* As for *now:* no need.

"Whether that sense of paralysis extends to international affairs is the big question being asked, and it's a question many feel cannot be answered except for a crisis situation. . . ." That script is network, but it needs work, especially on that empty word, *situation.* A crisis *is* "a crucial or decisive point or situation," so *situation* is superfluous. The script is woolly and wordy. *Who* is asking the *big question?* Who are the *many?* And how would a crisis—whatever the writer meant by that— answer the question?

"The elderly woman who was shot and killed in the incident will be buried today in Fairview." Empty words: *in the incident.* The script had already mentioned the shooting and the robbery twice, so *in the incident* adds nothing but time. We also hear daily (and nightly) about "the shooting *incident.*" "The shooting" suffices. Further, a shooting is hardly an incident; an incident is usually a minor event, say, a jostling on the bus.

"The Supreme Court of the Philippines has wrapped up hearings on the constitutionality of holding presidential elections in February . . . but has not issued its decision on the matter." Yes, *on the matter* is empty. Without *on the matter,* the network script means the same. If the court hasn't voted yet, we can say *decided* instead of *issued its decision,* and the sentence will be even stronger.

"The worst snow fell in Wisconsin, Iowa, Minnesota and the High Plains . . . with winds of 40 miles per hour and the temperatures tonight dropping below the zero mark." *Mark* is empty. "The *worst* snow"? Is it toxic? Perhaps the network writer meant "the *heaviest* snow." As for *per,* deposit it in a snowbank. *Per* is Latin, and Gilbert Millstein, the retired editor of "NBC Nightly News," says it should be used only <u>with</u> a Latin word, as in *per capita.* So make it "40 miles *an* hour." *Per day* and *per year* should be *a day* and *a year.*

"The Coast Guard said the 300-foot-long ship burst a hole in its hull." The empty word is *long.* The second problem with the network script: A ship doesn't *burst* a hole in its hull, unless it has an internal explosion. That ship *tore* a hole, *ripped* a hole, or *punched* a hole. Another network example:

"Chrysler management and union officials today continued round-the-clock meetings aimed at ending the seven-day-old strike." The empty word: *old. Today* should not precede the verb. Listeners assume they're hearing today's news, so inserting *today* so soon wastes time that could be used for a more interesting word. And *continued* is not one of them. If the writer can't find a new angle in a long-running story like this, she can write: "Chrysler and the union are still meeting round-the-clock to try to end the seven-day strike." That eliminates *continued,* turns the noun *meetings* into a verb, discards *today* and tightens the sentence.

"After July first, only their Maple Heights office will issue license transactions." Empty *and* redundant:

transactions. Issuing a license *is* a transaction. The office will issue licenses, period.

"Video lottery will soon become reality in the state of South Dakota." Empty: *the state of.* Would you say "I'm going to visit the *city* of Denver"? Another time-waster: "It took three months' *time.*" Or "a seven-day *period.*" And "The Dow Industrials closed up five points today—at the 36-12 *level.*" Also empty: "the *color* green." And: "The attacks were sexual *in nature.*"

"The Public Utilities Commission is in the process of deciding whether or not to reopen discussions on the purchase of power from Hydro Quebec." Empty: *in the process of.* The sentence means the same without it. *Whether* <u>means</u> *whether or not,* so *or not* should also be deleted. Also empty: *in order* as in "He went there *in order* to find work." Also: *of,* as in "He jumped out *of* the window.")

Be on the lookout for all those empty words and others that creep into our copy. When you're weighing a word, remember: If it's not necessary to leave it in, it *is* necessary to leave it out.

25

Thou Shalt Not Give Orders

Does it annoy you when people tell you what to do? Even when you're paid to take orders, do you like being told, "Do this," "Do that"? Do you? Probably not. Then why do you, or at least some of you, keep telling listeners what to do? (Yes, I do that, but it's my book. Right?)

You can see what it looks like, or sounds like, in this network voice-over: **"A chain reaction of tragic accidents today in the South Korean port city of Pusan. Look at this. A five-story building collapsed after its foundation was eroded by seawater, flooding in when a temporary dam gave way. . . ."**

Look at this? What a way to talk to viewers. They're already looking, aren't they? Let's not use the imperative unless it's imperative. If a tornado is bearing down on our town, I wouldn't mind a newscaster's telling me to go to my cellar—with celerity. Or if a newscaster learns that enemy missiles are on the way, I wouldn't beef if she tells me, "Take cover," "Head for the hills," or "Kiss your aspidastra good-bye." But otherwise, the imperative mood is best used by emperors, drill instructors, animal trainers— and writing coaches.

"Don't forget: Today marks another deadline. April 15th is the day all studded tires must be off all vehicles. . . ." The imperative may be acceptable for a few events if you use it judiciously: when it's time to file income taxes and when it's time to change the time. But convert *Don't forget* into a positive reminder: Remember.

A network anchor has told his audience: **"Listen to this."** Listen to *me,* Buster. Don't tell *me* what to do. When you offer me a newsy newscast—well-written, well-edited and well-delivered—I'll listen. Eagerly.

Another network contribution: **"Stay here with us."** Are our newscasts so lacking in interest and are we so lacking in confidence that we feel we have to beg people to stay tuned? What would you think of a writer who pleads, "Don't turn the page; stay with me"? What will an anchor say next? "Watch our news—or else!"

A local TV script: **"But watch the next play. Herschel Walker, no longer bothered by the presence of Tony Dorsett, races 54 yards for the score. . . ."** Why tell people who *are* watching to watch?

A related ailment shows up in the next script: **"The Pistons have to be feeling good about splitting in Los Angeles. The Lakers have to be concerned that should the home-court advantage hold up for the next three games, their bid for a repeat championship will be over."** *Have to be?* You have to be kidding. Please don't tell us what people *have to be.* And you started both sentences that way.

Local TV: **"Now take a look at the latest news on federal AIDS funding. According to the New York Times, there's a new move within the Administration for a lot more funding than. . . ."** How can we *look* at a "tell" story?

Another script: **"The figures are just one more reflection of how thoroughly drugs have infiltrated every level of society. Listen to this. In a three-year period, about 68-hundred people applied for city police jobs. Twenty percent of them showed traces of drugs in urinalysis, and another five percent came up bad during routine background checks. . . ."**

Listen to this, Mister (or Sister): Don't poke me in the eye, ear or chest. I'm already listening to your newscast, so what's the point of telling me to listen? If you hadn't started your story so ineptly, you would have caught my attention. Better: "The scope of the drug problem in _____ is underlined by newly released figures: in three years, 68-hundred people have applied for police jobs. Tests pointed to drug use in about 13-hundred of them—20 percent. And 350 more, five percent, were disqualified by background checks." *Scope* is a handy one-syllable word; it's not just a mouthwash. The next script comes from the same station, perhaps the same writer:

"If you own a G-M car, listen carefully. General Motors may want it back. The company is recalling 136-thousand. . . ."

Can you imagine any great practitioners of "the arts babblative and scribblative" telling us to listen carefully? Through the way professionals use their skills, we *want* to listen carefully. Besides the imperative, that script has other problems. Though it's a hard-news story, it starts with a weak word, *if*. Besides, many listeners who are not G-M owners may not bother to listen at all.

"Check bouncers, beware! A new federal law which goes into effect today will mean 'Ricochet City' for those who write checks one day, thinking they'll cover them with a deposit two days later. . . ." *Check bouncers* might be a suitable salutation for a closed-circuit broadcast in a prison. Singling out such a tiny segment of the population as *check bouncers* excludes other people— or reduces their interest. Or insults them. What, or where, is *Ricochet City?*

Another script: **"Delinquent fathers, beware! There is a new law in New York that will make it easier for ex-wives to collect child-support payments. . . ."** Delinquent newswriters, beware. Be aware that your job is to report the news, not issue warnings. That is imperative. Further, it's best to ditch *there is*. Better: "A new law in New York makes it easier for ex-wives to collect child-support payments. Governor Cuomo signed it into law today, and it allows employers to. . . ."

Still more: **"Get out your calculators. There's been another settlement in the Washington Public Power Supply System fraud case. . . ."** Let's not assume every listener has a calculator. But would any listener who scrambled to use one be able to follow your story? Anyway, as the script unfolded, listeners had nothing at all to calculate.

A network script: **"Mark it down as a possible future. It isn't just any contender for a House seat who can cause an instant nationwide stir just by announcing his name. . . ."** Mark down what? Why? What is *a possible future? Instant nationwide stir?* What's that? And how could a House candidate cause one? A person announces his candidacy, not his name.

Local: **"You're going to like this forecast."** Dear weatherman, please don't tell me what I'm going to like. I'll decide. And please don't come at me like a pushy pitchman ("Order one today").

"When we come back, ___ ___ will bring us a breathtaking look at Norway you don't want to miss." *Don't want to miss?* Sounds like a spiel from a carnival barker.

Let's stop telling listeners what to do—or think: Read my tips!

26

Hedge-Hopping

Arguably, the most enervating word that infects newsrooms these days is *arguably*.

A recent network documentary: **"The Navy justifies the whopping 43-million-dollar price tag for each plane by claiming that the F-14 can strike at up to six targets at once, over ranges in excess of 100 miles, using its million-dollar-a-shot Phoenix missiles. Sadly, that claim has yet to be proven, and the maintenance and reliability record of this super-high-tech aircraft has yet to meet the target set by the Navy 15 years ago. But from the pilot's point of view, it's the F-15 which is, arguably, the most complex of them all, because he alone commands the various engine, navigation, flight control, and weapons systems."**

Arguably, a trendy synonym for *debatably,* weakens whatever it touches because it's meaningless. Except for indisputable facts—and, now, even long-indisputable facts are being argued—almost every assertion is open to argument. Perhaps even that one. Instead of *arguably,* the writer could have called the F-15 *perhaps* the most complex. Or *possibly*—or, if true, *probably*—the most complex. Or *extremely* complex.

Inarguably, the script has other flaws. In the last sentence of the script, is it the pilot who says the F-15 is the most complex, and is he the one who says it's *arguably* so? Further, what's the antecedent of *he?* The script mentions the pilot's point of view, but the possessive *pilot's* cannot grammatically be the antecedent of *he.*

174

Other faults:

• In the first paragraph quoted from the script, *whopping* before an amount is subjective—and a cliché. Like a *staggering* 43-million. Or a *cool* million. Or a *measly* million. And *price tag = cost.*

• The first sentence quoted is overloaded with facts and figures: 43-million, F-14, six targets, 100 miles, million-dollar-a-shot. "A sure way to lose a listener," the *UPI Stylebook* says, "is to overemphasize statistics, percentages and technical detail."

• Unless *proven* is used as an adjective before a noun ("a proven remedy"), *proven* should be changed to *proved.*

• The second sentence can confuse listeners by using *target* in a different sense from *targets* in the first sentence.

• The writer piled up too many nouns-as-adjectives before the noun *systems.* As for *commands,* a better word is *controls.*

Whatever the asserted shortcomings of the Navy planes, that *script* is not airworthy.

Back to *arguably.* Even weaker uses of the adverb have surfaced recently. This from a journalism review: **"These days women can cover almost all the beats that used to be male preserves—especially at** *New York Newsday,* **the newest and arguably the most enterprising of New York City's tabloids."** The city has only two other tabloids, and as sure as P.M.s follow A.M.s, every tab would argue that *it* is the most enterprising.

Still weaker, this from a Manhattan magazine: "[A business executive] **orchestrated what arguably was one of the most cunning takeovers ever.**" Compounding the weakness of *arguably* is *one of the.* One of the 10 most cunning takeovers? One of the 50 most?

From major-market TV: **"The news is better than thought.** [My first thought: what's this all about?] **Ted Williams, arguably the greatest baseball player ever, is recuperating after suffering** [instead of *after suffering:*

from] **what is now being called a minor stroke this weekend.** [Voice-over] **The 75-year-old Hall of Famer is awake and alert, according to a hospital spokesman** [we don't hang attribution on the end of a sentence] **in Gainesville, Florida. Williams is the last player to hit over .400 in a season. We wish Ted a speedy recovery."** Why extend wishes to someone who can't see your program? Or even to someone who can? Unless you're trying to exude enough warmth to be able to work for the Welcome Wagon. Why did that writer latch onto *arguably?* Perhaps because it's in vogue. Perhaps because he wants to write a sentence that sounds stronger than facts allow. So he uses a weasel word that he thinks listeners don't notice. *Greatest baseball player* (no need for *ever*)? That *is* arguable. If anyone deserves the designation *greatest,* the sportswriter Bill Gleason says he'd nominate Aaron, Cobb, Gehrig, DiMaggio, Mantle, Mays or Ruth, not Williams. But let's not argue. We can't state everything with absolute certainty; some stories do need escape hatches. But these broadcast examples show how some loopholes can become laughable:

• **"He's an alleged attempted cop killer and suspected survivalist who allegedly fired eight shots at a Howard County policeman a month ago."** The script—which might be called an *alleged* script—could have been bulletproofed this way: "He allegedly tried to kill a Howard County policeman by firing eight shots at him. The suspect is also said to be a survivalist—someone preparing to survive a catastrophe."

• **"Relations between the U-S and the Soviet Union could get much better . . . or worse, possibly depending a great deal on today's events."** Talk about fearless forecasts.

• **"June is perhaps one of the best months to be in Chicago."** Chicago has only 12 months. Instead of *perhaps,* the writer could have said *usually.* Perhaps.

• **"Seven people were reportedly injured in a two-vehicle head-on collision near Marathon Satur-**

day. . . . **Authorities say** [the injured] **were taken to Buena Vista County Hospital. . . ."** *Reportedly* is unneeded. If we have confidence in our sources, we can go ahead and report the accident without qualification. Let's just say that people have been taken to a hospital and not attribute that sliver of news to amorphous *authorities*. And why call them authorities? What are they authorities *on?* Does the writer mean police? Sheriff's deputies? Hospital employees? Who? If possible, be specific. But don't list them all. Use your noggin: exercise news judgment. Better: "Two cars crashed head-on near Marathon, and seven people were hurt."

Another broadcast script illustrates the danger of a useful but often unneeded escape-hatch word—*apparently:*

"Traffic on northbound I-5 was slowed for some time [two minutes? two hours?] **tonight after a horse trailer overturned near. . . . The horse apparently became jumpy before the accident. A veterinarian on the scene says the horse jumping around** [should be *horse's*] **in the trailer apparently caused it to overturn. The horse was given a sedative but apparently suffered no serious injuries.** [A little better: "The horse apparently suffered no serious injuries but was given a sedative."] **The horse and trailer were apparently coming back from a horse show."** *Apparently* four times! Didn't anyone vet that copy? Apparently not.

Sure, we often write without enough information, so we need to qualify what we do know. But we must know how to hedge—with care. And where. Indisputably! Certainly not *arguably*.

27

Accentuate the Positive

A network evening newscast, lead story:

"No one yet knows why, but an earthen dam holding back an artificial lake high in the mountains of northern Italy gave way today. In 20 seconds, witnesses say, as many as 260 people in the valley below were dead under a roaring avalanche of mud, water and debris. __ __ is there."

No one yet knows why some writers accentuate the negative. Strunk and White say, in *The Elements of Style:* "Put statements in positive form. Make definite assertions." Listeners want to know what *is,* not what is *not.*

People don't start conversations or anecdotes by saying, "No one yet knows why." It's a fuzzy phrase you could slap on many stories: "No one yet knows why, but a burglar shot a bank robber." We can't interest listeners by trumpeting what we don't know.

The most important element in that broadcast script about the collapse of the dam is the deaths, but the deaths are buried in the middle of a sentence. Instead, the writer emphasized insignificant words. Better: "A dam in Italy's mountains collapsed today, and a torrent of water killed as many as 260 people."

Other network leads: **"We don't have details yet, but OPEC oil ministers have reached an agreement. . . ."** Don't start by telling us what you don't have. Tell us what you do have: "OPEC oil ministers have agreed to. . . ." Besides, who wants to hear *details?* Skip details. Tell us what's most important. *Details* is a dirty word, at least in my book. And this is my book.

"Long-time residents of Florida's Gulf coast are no strangers to hurricanes." Isn't it the hurricanes that aren't *strangers* to the residents? Better: "Long-time residents of Florida's Gulf coast are familiar with hurricanes." Or "Long-time residents of . . . know hurricanes well."

"There is one group of Americans, and it is not small, which has never had to worry much about its medical benefits. America's veterans have traditionally been entitled to free medical care. . . ." Although the literary device of litotes—expressing an affirmative by negating its opposite—is not bad in some print contexts, it's difficult on air, especially when coupled with another negative, *never.*

If that group is not small, it's large. In fact, the only vets entitled to free medical care, except for former POWs, are those in need or those with service-related conditions. But if the group is entitled to free care, as the script says, then saying members *never had to worry much* about care is incorrect. They would never have had to worry at all.

A local lead: **"There are no reports of damage or injury tonight following a strong earthquake near Los Angeles, possibly along the San Andreas fault."** That opener doesn't move. And *following* should be *after.* Better: "An earthquake has jarred Los Angeles, but no one is reported hurt. And there's no report of damage." Unless damage is huge and fatalities are few, the best policy in reporting accidents and disasters is: people before property.

Another non-starter: **"The figures are not yet complete, but the tentative death toll in Cameroon following the release of volcanic gases earlier this week, is at 15-hundred, with as many as 300 people hospitalized."** Figures are often incomplete, but the way to go is to start with what can be said for sure: "The toll in the volcanic gas release in the West African nation of Cameroon has now reached 15-hundred dead. And as many as 300 people are hospitalized." *Dead* is a good, strong word to end a sentence with. But don't try to work it into every story.

"We don't know how much money is missing from university funds [no need to proclaim what we don't know; the news is what we *do* know], **but since Sunday the chief accountant has been missing. That's the reason Virginia Union President Dallas Simons is ordering a full-scale investigation into financial irregularities at the university."** Better: "The chief accountant of Virginia Union is reported missing, so the university has ordered an investigation into alleged financial irregularities." Or if the accountant's absence had already been reported: "The disappearance of the chief accountant at Virginia Union has now prompted the university to order an investigation into alleged financial irregularities."

"Nobody wants to take the blame for 16-hundred deaths in the Philippines marine disaster." No volunteers to take the blame? What a shocker!

"On day two of the Detroit teachers' strike, teachers walking the picket line are no happier about the way things turned out than when they walked out yesterday. There are clutches of teachers gathered around Cody High School, and. . . ." *No happier?* On the second day of a strike, who'd expect strikers to be happier? *Clutches?* Only eggs and chicks come in clutches. Not teachers, even if they're clucks.

"Jurors in the trial of El Rukn leader Jeff Fort and four other gang members won't be seeing any movie footage of Clint Eastwood when trial resumes Monday. . . ." Nor will the jurors be seeing any footage of Pee-wee Herman. Better: "The judge in the trial of El Rukn leader Jeff Fort says the prosecutor cannot show jurors part of a Clint Eastwood movie."

"Nothing doing in the N-B-A playoffs tonight, but there are a couple [should be followed by *of*] **coaching changes to report."** News is a change in the status quo, not what's *not* doing. The writer should have led with the coaching changes. Or, if the facts warrant, try this: "The N-B-A playoffs resume tomorrow night, with all the finalists getting tonight off." Or: "The N-B-A finalists are getting the night off. The playoffs resume tomorrow night."

Those scripts were all DOA. But they can be revived without any *abracadaver.* It's easy to make them come alive. When you're tempted to write a negative lead, just say no. Or, if you're a Thoroughbred, just say neigh.

28

Can You Spot the Mistakes?

Twenty-and-a-half questions: Where do these network word-bites need work?

1. **"The new policy was an unexpected surprise, which may explain why it was announced in the midst of a holiday weekend."** *Unexpected* surprise? Ever hear of an *expected* surprise? *In the midst of?* Better: *on.*

2. **"That's what Jay Scharoff did; former chief of nuclear medicine, now chief honcho of his own pet shop."** A *honcho* is a chief, so *chief honcho* is redundundundant.

3. **"His veracity in such matters is always doubted, though, especially since he and his brother were overheard in a restaurant plotting plans to feign an injury to get out of a tournament."** The tenor of this commentary (and the baritone, too) was that a bad boy of tennis was up to no good. But no one *plots* plans—or *plans* plots.

4. **"Authorities were apparently led to the grave site by Irene Seale, who's accused of helping her husband, Arthur, kidnap Reso."** No need for *site; grave* suffices. And *site* is risky because it sounds like *sight* and *cite.* Better: "Agents went to the grave, apparently led there by Irene Seale. . . ."

5. **"This property, which sold for $1.5 million, is being completely razed except for the pool and tennis court."** No need for *completely. Raze* sounds the same as *raise.* Better: *torn down.*

6. **"Upon entering the country, U.S. Customs officials confiscated about a dozen RU-486 pills from this**

182

woman, who wanted only to be identified as Leona." Dangling modifier. *Upon entering the country* applies to the woman, not the customs agents. And a misplaced modifier: *only.* Better: "When this woman entered the country, U.S. customs agents confiscated about a dozen RU-486 pills from her. She wants to be identified only as Leona."

7. **"Then he started talking about a plan to export Alaska's most abundant natural resource, water, to 20-million thirsty Californians through a plastic pipeline that would lay on the bottom of the ocean like a giant garden hose."** That sentence seems as long as the pipeline, which would *lie* on the bottom.

8. **"With more than 12,000 Haitians at the U.S. Naval base at Guantanamo Bay, Cuba, the holding site for asylum-seekers is said to be filled to capacity."** *Filled to capacity* is a redundancy. If something is filled, then it's full. Which means it has reached its capacity. *Said to be* is weak: can't a network find out for sure?

9. **"The paperwork is a Byzantine labyrinth of forms."** *Maze* would do the job. *Byzantine labyrinth* is redundant. Besides, how many listeners know what *byzantine* means? Or *labyrinth?* Or both?

10. **"Across the state, the most draconian cuts ever in post-secondary education are, according to the educators, plowing under what has been one of the best public university systems in the world."** *Draconian?* How many listeners know the word? (How many writers do?) *Harsh* is better. *"Most draconian cuts ever in post-secondary education"?* Does the reporter know about all the cuts in post-secondary education? Does anyone know? The assertion about the cuts' being *draconian* needs attribution. The attribution now in that script applies only to the cuts *said* to be plowing under what's *said* to be a fine school system. *According to the educators:* no need for the definite article, *the,* unless the writer is referring to *all* educators.

11. **"But the anger here won't be quelled for long if the talk of change isn't followed with tangible action."**

Should be "followed *by*." *Tangible* means *touchable,* as in *tangible* assets. Perhaps the writer meant *visible* action. But there's no need for any modifier.

12. **". . . after a heavily armed gunman seized the local high school."** *Armed gunman* is redundant. Ever hear of an *unarmed* gunman? The script should have said "heavily armed man." Also: no need for *armed police* or *armed soldiers.* Ever heard of *unarmed* soldiers, except in the Salvation Army?

13. **". . . single moms still outnumber single fathers by a margin of 7 to 1."** It's not a margin; it's a ratio. Better: ". . . single mothers rearing children outnumber single fathers rearing children, seven to one."

14. **"This led the judge to not only sequester this jury but keep their identities secret."** The construction should be parallel, so *not only* should be coupled with *but also.* In addition: *jury* is a collective noun, like *group,* and takes a singular verb. Better: "This led the judge *not only* to sequester the jurors *but also* to keep their identities secret." Better yet: "This led the judge to sequester the jurors and keep identities secret."

15. **"And how would you like to be a marketing executive at Reebok this morning? Probably wouldn't want to be because the shoe company sunk 25-million dollars into an advertising campaign centered around Dan and Dave. . . ."** The campaign was centered *on* them. Nothing can be centered *around.* But it can *revolve around.* The past tense of *sink* is *sank,* not *sunk.* Likewise, the past tense of *shrink* is *shrank.* Caution: watch out for other irregular verbs—and other irregularities.

16. **"She helps them to reconcile their past history with their present imprisonment and to face the future."** *Past history* is redundant. Better: ". . . their past freedom with their present imprisonment. . . ."

17. **"And what kind of crimes did these older inmates commit?"** Correct: "*kinds* of crimes."

18. **"'You have a right to know what I'll do and where I stand.' That from Democratic presidential can-**

didate Bill Clinton today." If you heard that first sentence come from a newscaster, wouldn't you assume he was letting his hair down—or getting ready for a hearth-to-hearth? A basic rule of writing news for broadcast: never start a story with a quotation. Listeners can't see quotation marks. They rightly assume newscasters are voicing their own words, unless the newscasters make clear beforehand that they are quoting someone else. That's why broadcasters' rule is: attribution before assertion.

19. **"That's a savings of 10-million dollars in one year, not to mention young lives turned toward an honest living."** The word is *saving* (no final *s*). *Savings* are what you have in your bank. Or used to have.

20. **"Stay with us."** Isn't that how you talk to a dog? "Stay!" Please, dear anchor, don't issue commands. And please don't beg us to sit. Or fetch. Or roll over.

20½. **"His victims scoffed, saying that's just a fraction of the real number."** *Fraction* can be slippery. Any number less than 100 percent is a fraction: ⅒ is a fraction; so is ⁹⁄₁₀.

Though all those network excerpts were considered good enough to go on air, they remind us that "good enough" is seldom good enough.

More network word-bites that need more work—and more bite:

"There are few misfortunes that can befall a woman worse than being a woman in India." *There are* is weak, wordy and wasteful. Almost every sentence starting that way can be shortened—and strengthened. You can start a story many ways, but, with few exceptions, *there is, there are* or *it is* is not the way to go. They are all dead phrases. Forms of *to be,* like *is* and *are,* are linking verbs and express no action. Better: "Few misfortunes can befall someone worse than being a woman in India." Wouldn't that also apply to tourists? Better still: "A woman faces few fates worse than being born in

India." *Faces few fates* poses problems, so let's try again: "A girl born in India may face a dreadful life—or death." Writing takes work, and, as Beverly Sills, the opera singer, says, "There are no shortcuts to any place worth going."

"There are similar tales of misery that trail almost every child, every teen-ager, aimless and lawless in the streets." That sentence is easy to fix. Delete *there are* and *that:* "Similar tales of misery trail almost every child, every teen-ager, aimless and lawless in the streets."

"There has been a lot of attention lately on the high cost of prescription drugs in this country, but there are ways to save, as __ __ reports now in. . . ." Two *there are*s. Why say that a lot of attention has been paid to a subject? A lot of attention has been paid to a lot of subjects, and few of us care to hear still more about a lot of them. Don't we tune in to hear what we haven't heard about at all? Let's rewrite it: "Some prescription drugs may cost too much, but __ __ has found ways to save:"

"There was a whoop of delight from the anti-smoking advocates as the City Council clerk announced the vote." Better: "When the City Council clerk announced the vote, anti-smoking advocates whooped with delight." Why is the rewrite better? It puts the emphasis where it should be. In the original script, the highlight, *whoop of delight,* is trampled in the rush of words. Our rewrite puts it in the right place.

"Even if we assume a few retirements, there would be at least six conservative justices sitting there, so it's going to stay a basically conservative institution." There's too much *there* there: two in one sentence. Even in the middle of a sentence, or the middle of a script, *there are* is a strong candidate for replacement. *Therefore,* let's get rid of it right now: "Even if we assume a few retirements, at least six conservative justices remain, so the court is going to stay basically conservative." On further review, let's retire *basically.*

"Today's hearing marked the first chance for some of the principals at Empire to speak out on the

morass of allegations that have been leveled against the company in the past two months." *Morass?* More *what? Morass* isn't a broadcast word, the kind widely used and widely understood. How often do you use—or hear—it in conversation? The reporter said the Congressional hearing was the executives' first chance to speak out. Not so. They *chose* to wait until today. Better: "Several top executives at Empire responded publicly today to the charges against the company."

"Here at home tonight, a story rivaling any made-for-television movie. This one involves a respected chief judge of New York state's highest court. . . ." Here at whose home? What are listeners in Peoria and Pocatello to make of *here at home?* Not only is *here at home* a cliché, it's also unnecessary, inaccurate and disorienting. Is comparison to a made-for-TV movie intended as praise? Why compare the story to anything? Why not just tell the story without ballyhoo? Let it stand on its own.

"President Clinton won support today from U-N Secretary-General Boutros-Ghali for the planned U-S airdrop and insisted it will not send the United States down a slippery slope to further involvement." *Slippery slope* is so good at depicting a dangerous declivity that it has been traveled by every Tom, Dick and Mary, and they've worn it down into a ditch. Cliché-prone writers still stumble into it. Steer clear.

George Orwell, the English writer, said, "Never use a metaphor, simile, or other figure of speech which you are used to seeing in print." He died in 1950, before broadcast news took off, or he probably would have added, "or are used to hearing on air."

Orwell said: "Never use a long word when a short one will do. If it is possible to cut a word out, always cut it out. Never use a foreign phrase, a scientific word, or a jargon word if you can think of an everyday English equivalent. Break any of these rules sooner than say anything outright barbarous."

And Orwell advised: "A scrupulous writer, in every sentence that he writes, will ask himself at least four questions, thus: What am I trying to say? What words will express it? What image or idiom will make it clearer? Is this image fresh enough to have an effect? And he will probably ask himself two more: Could I put it more shortly? Have I said anything that is avoidably ugly?"

29

Perils of Polls, Pollsters and Polling

A network newscaster recently reported: "**If you've any doubt that the presidential political year has already begun, you should be at the big Republican powwow in Orlando, Florida, where there'll be a straw poll today. . . .**" One of the weakest words of tongue or pen is *if*. So why make a story iffy? And why the *you?* This is an election year, so I had no doubt whatsoever. But why should I be in Orlando? And for a straw poll? I don't give a rap about the results of a straw poll, let alone the hemidemisemi-pseudo news that a poll *will* be taken. So what?

That item, though, is a mere straw in the wind. During the coming weeks, the wind will be sweeping in the results of all sorts of polls—the subject of wire stories, press releases and newspaper stories. Broadcasters will use those polling results because they seem convenient, precise and late-breaking. But Rich Jaroslovsky writes in *Psychology Today*, "Because they rely heavily on statistics and numbers, polls convey an illusion of precision that is just that—an illusion."

Assuming you're having a slow news day (or a no-news day) and just can't say no, you should at least make sure that any poll you do report is presented properly. The findings must never be reported as absolute truths. Blanche Schleier tells her students at New York University: "Think of a poll as a snapshot of a constantly changing set of public feelings and beliefs. . . . Say a poll *suggests, estimates, predicts.* . . . Be sure to look at the survey's margin of error and consider how it may affect poll results. If a poll shows Candidate A with 48 percent . . . and Candidate B with 52 percent, and the margin of error is three to four [percentage points], one candidate is not 'leading' the other."

Professor Schleier, a former network producer, says when evaluating polls to determine their validity, broadcasters should keep these points in mind: "When was the poll taken? Opinions can change quickly in response to events, especially during election campaigns. Check to see [whether] poll results are dated. How were the interviews obtained? [By phone? In person?]

"How were the questions worded? They easily can be 'loaded' to achieve the desired result. . . . Even the *sequence* of questions should be considered. Small differences in . . . wording can cause big differences in results. How many in the sample didn't respond, said 'I don't know' or were undecided? A large number of undecided voters means . . . that the electorate is 'volatile,' and reliable estimates may be impossible."

Some other points to consider in sizing up a poll:

Who commissioned the poll? An interested party? (Do disinterested parties pay for polls?)

Who was surveyed? Eligible voters? "Likely" voters?

Were those questioned a true random sample?

How many people were interviewed?

Who were the interviewers—professionals or volunteers?

What was the margin of error?

Does the lead of the story you received accurately reflect the results of the poll?

Bad polls tend to drive out good polls, according to Humphrey Taylor, president and chief executive officer of Louis Harris and Associates. He lists several reasons:

"1. An unexpected poll finding is more suprising, and hence more 'newsworthy' than one that confirms what other polls also report. Bad (i.e., inaccurate) polls are more likely to be surprising and therefore more likely to be reported.

"2. Bad polls are cheaper than good polls. A survey of 600 people is less expensive than a survey of 1,250. A poll with very few questions is cheaper than one with more questions. High-quality sampling and interviewing cost more than poor quality. And so on. If the media report findings regardless of their quality, why spend money on better polls?

"3. One-day 'instant' polls are much less accurate than polls conducted over three or four days because of all the people they miss. But the media love them because they are the 'first with the news' about public reactions to events."

Taylor defends valid polls, and goes on to say (in *National Review* of October 19, 1992): "900-number straw polls are not polls. . . . Poll results are the answers to questions and are therefore critically dependent on the wording and, sometimes, on the order of the questions. . . . Opinion on most issues is more complicated than a yes/no to one or two questions. . . . Surveys of adults, registered voters, or likely voters will all yield different answers. . . . Focus groups are not polls. . . . Electronic town halls are not polls. . . . Candidates' polls are often misleading. Polls are leaked not to inform but to influence the media and the public. . . . If nobody cares about the quality of polling, cheap and dirty polls will surely drive out good ones."

A newsroom reference, *The Associated Press Stylebook and Libel Manual,* says: "Polls based on interviews on street corners, calling a 900-number or mailing coupons back from magazines may be good entertainment, but such polls have no validity. They should be avoided. In such unscientific pseudo-polls, the opinions come from people who 'select themselves' to participate. If such polls are reported for entertainment value, they must NEVER be portrayed as accurately reflecting public opinion and their failing must be highlighted." And the stylebook goes on to advise: "Do not exaggerate the poll results. . . . No matter how good the poll, no matter how wide the margin, the poll does NOT say one candidate will win an election. Polls can be wrong and the voters can change their mind before they cast their ballots."

The most important question about a poll: is it *news,* and is it worth reporting? Would even a first-rate poll serve any useful purpose, except for politicians, special interests—or producers in need of copy? Do your listeners trust polls? Do you? Do polls help people vote more intelligently? If a pollster says Candidate A is leading by five percentage points, how much attention do you and your listeners pay to that? Do you need to know which way the wind is blowing before deciding how to vote? No matter what polls find, broadcasters should remember that the only poll that counts is the one held in polling places (the first Tuesday after the first Monday in November).

Even pols were saying pooh to polls when two prominent pollsters, George Gallup and Louis Harris, surveyed voters on a hypothetical presidential race in 1975 and found themselves polls apart. Harris said that in his poll Senator Humphrey beat President Ford, 52% to 41%. But just a few days later, Gallup reported his poll found the reverse—Republican Ford beat Democrat Humphrey, 51% to 39%. The cause of the disparity: Harris polled "likely" voters; Gallup polled registered voters.

If "scientific" polls can raise doubts, how about their unscientific, ill-begotten offspring, the "man-in-the-street" interview? Too many stations spend too much time asking passersby, for instance, what they think of the governor's new tax plan. But too often the passerby hasn't heard of the plan, or hasn't thought about it, or has no basis for forming an opinion, at least not one worth listening to. If a reporter questions ten persons, and six oppose the tax proposal, three favor it, and one says he's undecided, chances are, the producer will simplify the results and present two "pros" and two "cons."

That editing conveys the impression that the public is evenly divided. Or the producer will choose the answers that are most amusing, lively or provocative. But before assuming that passersby (or hangers-on in the newsroom's favorite hangout) reflect public opinion, we should ponder: how many members of the public have opinions worth listening to?

A nadir in mindless questioning in "man-in-the-street" interviews was reached when the Inquiring Photographer of a New York City tabloid asked people during a recent heat wave, "Is it hot enough for you?" Surprise: no one, or at least no one quoted in the paper, said no.

And a low point in broadcast news was reached a few years ago when a network ran video of a colorful parade in San Francisco. After a one-man band passed, the correspondent asked an out-of-towner, "What do you think of him?" The reply, which *was* broadcast: "I don't know what to think of him. We just walked up."

Polls? Count me out.

30

You and *I*

A network anchor began a story with a bang: **"We're going to burn them with smoke, gas, fire and bullets. We will burn this house down.** [Newsroom frictions turning ugly?] **Threatening words . . . contained in a letter from the radical group. . . ."**

Oh, so those *aren't* the anchor's own threats. Why didn't he write it right and put attribution before assertion? That way we'd know at the outset who said what and to whom. All of which illustrates how dangerous it is to start a story with a quotation, especially with *we.*

Even when you attribute a quotation correctly, it's perilous to use *we,* as this network script shows: **"The U-P-I quotes a senior aide to Libyan leader Muammar Khadafy as saying Libya will attempt to assassinate President Reagan if the U-S attacks Libya. The aide is reported then to have said we have not sent anyone to kill him. . . ."** *We?* The writer should have paraphrased the aide and made it *they.*

Another word to avoid in scripts, especially in quoting someone, is *I.* How many times have you heard an anchor quote someone, perhaps your mayor, as saying, "I have to take off 25 pounds"? When the anchor quotes him directly, it sounds as though the mayor wants the *anchor* to take off the weight. Paraphrasing is usually the best way to deal with quotations, anyway, so the writer need only change *I* to *he*—and avoid *I*-trouble.

After the Achille Lauro hijacking, U.S. Navy jets intercepted an Egyptian plane carrying the culprits. A network newsman began his story: **"We had finally gotten it right. We had evened the score."** *We?* Sounds as though we've abandoned our journalistic neutrality and joined the fray. **"We had plucked them out of the sky,"** the newsman went on, **"and dropped them in** [*into*] **Sicily."** Sounds like cheerleading, by jingo.

"We all know," a local anchor said, **"we should never play cards with a man named Doc."** You can bet we all don't know that. Or that it's a line from the novelist Nelson Algren. And that he also said, "Never eat at any place called Mom's." Algren neglected to add: and never eat where a sign says "Eat." Or "Open." Or "Good Food."

And from a network anchor: **"The Russians, as we know, tend to think in terms of long-range strategy."** Do we know that? (I don't.) Even if Washington knows for sure how Moscow thinks, how many of the rest of us know that? Who knows?

A local anchor: **"Also this morning, you may have seen the glow of a fire around six forty-five. We understand that a main electric line from the Penelec substation at 20th and Greengarden broke and fell across the railroad tracks. . . ."** *We understand* seems like speculation or an interpretation of an observation. We'd better <u>know</u>. If the writer means *understand* in the sense of *know,* he has no need for *we.* He can just go ahead and present what occurred as fact, not what seems like supposition. Most listeners could not have seen the glow mentioned in the first sentence, so it's best to begin at the beginning: "A fire broke out near a Penelec substation this morning. It started when an electric line broke and fell across the railroad tracks. . . ."

A local radio anchor said in a newscast: **"Many of us have a fear or phobia over** [*about*] **riding horses. In Vassar this weekend, what may be a nightmare to horse lovers became a tragedy for 13-year-old Jesse**

Rodgers. Jesse was helping a family friend train horses at the Vassar Fairgrounds Saturday afternoon. While he was leading one of the animals, Jesse got tangled up in one of the reins. The horse bolted and dragged the boy for a considerable distance before the rein broke. Rodgers was taken to Caro Community Hospital, where the tragedy ended as he was pronounced dead."

If that weren't such a pathetic story (and, yes, a pathetic script), I'd say the writer took the long way around the barn. Building up to the last word, *dead,* a strong word, might have worked if the script were brief and brisk. I would have tried to put *dead* or *killed* at the end of my *first* sentence. And right after *dead,* I would have put a period.

The script is flawed in many ways: Our fears have nothing to do with the story, particularly any fears about *riding;* the victim was not riding. A phobia *is* a fear, so there's no need to use both words. Better yet, delete them. "Night*mare*" might strike some listeners as a pun, and this is no time for humor. And I wouldn't bring in *horse lovers;* they're like *us*—and not part of this story. Further, the *tragedy*—if that abused word can be dragged in here—didn't end when the boy died. Certainly not for family and friends. The writer James J. Kilpatrick reminds us *tragedy* is "too powerful a word to to be used in describing everyday misfortunes, accidents and deaths. Precisely employed, 'tragedy' involves some element of moral failure, some flaw in character, or some extraordinary combination of elements that produce a tragic consequence."

I hesitate to haul in Descartes *after* the horse. But I think, therefore I am going to think out loud: sloppy thinking leads to sloppy writing. Which leads to another dazzling insight: Clear writing requires clear thinking.

A network anchor said: **"The shuttle Discovery is waiting down there on the launchpad. We are due to blast off in a hour. We'll provide live coverage. . . ."** *We* are blasting off? *We?* Whee! Wow!

Whenever a newscaster says *we,* we have to wonder: To whom does *we* refer? Himself? Is he using the royal *we,* as in Queen Victoria's "We are not amused"? In using the imperial *we* to maintain an impersonal tone and avoid the personal *I,* he often sounds imperious. Or is he using the editorial *we* to express a collective view?

Another irksome example is the opening line of too many newscasts: **"We begin with. . . ."** Why waste time with those words when we know from the start, even before, that the first story the anchor reports is the one he's beginning with? Would you begin a conversation by saying, "First, I want to begin by asking, 'How are you?'" Or would you just go ahead and say, "How are you?"

Also thought-free is this opening: **"Our top story tonight is. . . ."** Somehow, I've figured out that the first story the anchor reads *is* the top story. How often does a newscast start with the next-to-the-top story?

We can lend a human touch to a story. But too many newspeople wind up sounding pretentious or presumptuous. When can we use *we* safely and sensibly? When it's natural, logical and unambiguous. But *we* seldom is, so it's usually best to leave *us* out.

You is a good word, but it can be bad news. The trouble with *you* is, it may not apply to most listeners. Or any listeners. Once in a while, *you* in a news script works. It lassoes listeners. It's direct, personal and conversational. Most scripts, though, would be better off without *you.* You'll see why in these broadcast examples:

"You would think the huge city plows wouldn't have much trouble getting around in the snow and ice. Well, one truck ran into a bit of trouble this morning. The driver of the truck was headed north on Zimmerman Road. Coming down the hill just before 38th Street, he tried to stop for the light when he hit ice, started to skid, hit a dry spot, then flipped over. Street department officials say this is the first time in at least 20 years some-

thing like this has happened. . . ." The writer should have buried *you* instead of burying the lead. *We*—and what *we*'d think—have nothing to with the news. The writer needn't tell us what he thinks we would think. If we thought about snowplows at all, we'd probably think they are having a hard time. As used in the second sentence, *well* doesn't work well. This is a hard-news story that needs a harder approach. The writer should first tell us the plow flipped over and what happened to the driver.

"Have you ever taken out the garbage and wondered whether you might soon run out of space in which to dump it? Well, according to a new study. . . ." I've taken out a lot of garbage in my day and night, but I admit I've never thought about its future. Perhaps it could be dumped in abandoned *well*s.

"You've heard us talk many times before about the increase in state police patrols on any holiday weekend. They're looking for speeders and drunk drivers. On the New Year's holiday, they're looking even harder. . . ." The opener is a downer. If we had heard that newscaster talk about something many times, we wouldn't care to hear about it again. When the writer says patrols are now looking *even harder,* should we infer that until now they hadn't been doing their best? Reminds me of newspaper writers scratching for a fourth-day lead in a big murder: "Police *intensified* their search today for. . . ."

"If you're a real fan of the Beatles or a number of other rock groups, then there's an auction under way in London you might be interested in. . . ." If I'm not a *real* fan, or even a fake fan, wouldn't the auction still be taking place? And wouldn't I still be interested? After all (or, to be precise, *before* all) the writer suggests that even *a real fan* might not be interested. We don't characterize stories as "interesting," and we certainly shouldn't tell listeners they *might* be interested. That's a turn-off, or a turn-elsewhere.

"Is your pet immunized against rabies? That's what Cook County animal control officials are urging

pet owners to do now that a case of rabies has been confirmed in the county. . . ." But what if a listener doesn't own a pet? If you ask a question in a lead, as Tim Wulfemeyer warns, you may not like the answer. The second sentence of the script is illogical: officials can be *asking* that question, but they can't be *urging* it.

"It's time to get your flu shots. The city's Health Department will be offering the innoculations free to those who are chronically ill or over the age of 65. . . ." Those are the groups for whom flu shots are recommended, but what about listeners who are not chronically ill or are under 65? Better: "It's time to find out whether you'd be wise to get a flu shot. And, if so, to get it. . . ."

"A fair-sized earthquake hit central California today, five-point-five on the Richter scale. No deaths or injuries, but you could feel the ground shake at the Diablo Canyon Nuclear Power Plant. . . ." That's a network script, written for listeners from sea to briny sea. On the East Coast, that quake would have to be more than *fair-sized* for me to feel it. (I'm not a Quaker.) The writer could put more power into the second sentence by building up to the key idea: "No deaths or injuries, but at the Diablo Canyon Nuclear Power Plant, the ground shook." Period. Stop.

"If you were to own a business leased from the School Board, the Park District or some other governmental body, chances are pretty good that you could get away with not paying your property taxes. . . ." Why turn a solid story into iffy, *you*ish mush? How many listeners own businesses or want to? And is the writer planting the idea in listeners' heads that if they owned a business leased from a government body, they could *get away* without paying taxes?

Now what do you think of this *you?*

"If you like to pay by check, but you sometimes lose track of your checking balance, this could make bounced checks less painful: the House of Delegates has passed a bill that would keep Maryland banks

from charging more than 15 dollars for returned checks. . . ." To my eyes, and ears, this *you* works—and well. Most listeners pay or receive checks and know something about checks. The writer took a legislative story and related it to us directly and appropriately.

How about this? **"Do you like to shop with coupons? A University of Northern Iowa home economist says coupon-crazy Iowans aren't saving as much as they think. . . ."** *You* fits because the question hits home, is short and simple, and can be answered instantly. But the second sentence loosens its grip on us by shifting from the second-person-singular *you* to the third-person-plural *Iowans.* The writer should have stuck with *you,* at least through that second sentence: "If so, a home economist at the University of Northern Iowa says you're not saving as much as you think." Moral: If the *you* fits. . . .

You can be most effective in soft-news stories—if *you* sounds natural, doesn't devalue the story, and applies to the vast majority of your listeners. But before using *you,* consider whether *you* is the best way to go and whether listeners will feel that you're talking to *them.* It's up to you.

31

Transitions

Meanwhile. Starting this ramble with *meanwhile* is odd, but no more so than most *meanwhile*s we hear in newscasts. What makes them odd? In most cases, *meanwhile* (and *meantime*) can be deleted without any loss, which would mean a gain. In the other cases, where a transition between stories *is* desirable, another kind of link is better. Sometimes, all that's needed is *and, but* or *another*. Or a transition based on a key word or idea embedded in the stories you're trying to meld.

For example, after a story about fighting in Ruritania, several transitions could lead the listener along: "Fighting also broke out in Fredonia," or "In nearby Fredonia, rebels surrounded the palace," or "But the fighting in Fredonia ended." Smooth flow is the way to go, but not all stories can be sewn together so that a newscast seems like a seamless narrative.

Use of *meanwhile* lets listeners see the stitches. And by directing attention to itself, *meanwhile* gives away our m.o. Transitions should be unnoticeable. A skillful cabinetmaker joins his panels neatly. Leaving the joints exposed is considered poor artisanship, and Ron Meador says bridging them with crude or clumsy devices "is like assembling fine furniture with roofing nails."

Another reason a careful writer avoids *meanwhile:* other careful writers have told him to. Also, because it evokes facetious undertones, as in the pornographer's "Meanwhile, back at the raunch."

201

On top of that, *meanwhile* is usually used incorrectly. *Meanwhile* means "in the intervening time" or "at the same time," but many newswriters use it without regard to two stories' time relationship. Here's a broadcast example: **"Meanwhile, tomorrow, a Maricopa County judge will decide if the governor's special assistant. . . ."** *Meanwhile tomorrow?* That's what the man-person said. At other times, in other places, other writers also man-handle *meanwhile*.

A network example: **"National leaders of the Assemblies of God gather in Springfield, Missouri, today to debate the future of TV evangelist Jimmy Swaggart. Meanwhile, a New Orleans TV station aired an interview last night with a woman who said she was the prostitute who. . . ."** *Meanwhile* last night? (Did that woman use any mean wiles?)

A local script uses three items (in separate paragraphs) and links them with two trite transitions:

"Your paycheck went farther [should be *further;* save *farther* for physical distance] **last year than in any year since 1961. Inflation in 1986 rose only one-point-one percent, thanks largely to a 60 percent drop in oil prices. That drop kept inflation from hovering around the four percent level.** All those numbers are numbing. The exact percentage is desirable in that story, but as the *Reuters Handbook for Journalists* says, "In everyday life, people think in fractions, not decimals. So in stories where mathematical precision is not essential, use *a quarter, a third, a half* rather than *25, 33, 50 percent,*" The gist of another Reuters suggestion: In a story that says 68 percent of Americans watched a certain event on television, it's better to write, "Two out of three Americans watched. . . ." And the percentage should be used later in the story. The next item in the cluster:

"Meanwhile, the stock market recorded its first decline of the New Year today. The Dow was down ten-and-a-half in heavy trading. [Better: "The stock market fell today—the first time this year. The Dow slid ten and a half points. Trading was heavy."]

"Speaking of falling numbers, ___ ___ has our chilly forecast for the rest of the week...."

Speaking of tortured transitions (and I just tortured one), here's a similar strained segue, from a network: **"The Soviets, as with much of the West, continue to watch the blood-drenching war in the Persian Gulf between Iran and Iraq.... Even as we speak, Iran confirms that its troops are massing again...."** *Even as we speak?* Unspeakable! What makes that transition so awful is its decrepitude and its inexactitude. When the anchor went on, at dinner-time, it was 3 a.m. in Iran, an unlikely time for any confirming.

Another network correspondent told of President Reagan's defense of a foreign ally, then also reached into the boneyard for a transition: **"On a domestic note, Mr. Reagan defended his embattled attorney general, Edwin Meese, and said many of his aides accused of ethics violations have been victims...."** No need for *on a domestic note*. The correspondent could have just said, "Mister Reagan also defended an old friend." The second *his* in the excerpt refers to Meese, but the writer intended to refer to the President's aides. *Embattled attorney general* is journalese, the *hack-speak* of too many writers. Likewise, "the besieged Bork" and "his much-troubled nomination." Those descriptions are labored and they're not good writing, not good news-speaking, not good journalism.

In an effort to tie unrelated stories together, a network anchor said, **"Wall Street and Big Oil are one thing, farm lands in the heartland another."** And writing a sensible transition is still another thing. Besides, aren't Wall Street and Big Oil *two* things? If you like to see unlike elements linked, try this imaginary transition: "Combat in the Persian Gulf is one thing, an increase in U-S postage another." Reminds me of a con man I used to know in Chicago. His breast pocket sprouted a handkerchief embroidered with "There's no business like God's business," tagged with "Daniel 3:13." One day, I told him I had searched the Book of Daniel but couldn't find the quotation. "I didn't say that's from the Bible," he replied huffily. "I said, 'There's no business like God's business.' That's all. 'Daniel 3:13' is something else." Many other broadcast transitions are also something else:

Closer to home. This seems silly after we hear a story from the Persian Gulf only to learn that the next locale is nowhere near the listener and not close to her home. Also disconcerting and unnecessary: *Back in this country.* If the story begins, "A federal grand jury in Detroit . . . ," even the most unsophisticated listener knows it comes from this country.

Elsewhere. Newscasts usually consist of stories from many places, so almost any story can be prefaced with *elsewhere.* As a transition, it's nowhere.

Here locally. A rip-roaring redundancy. Besides, where's *here?* In the studio?

Next. Should be nixed. A story that's next doesn't need that nexus.

On a lighter note. Usually used after a grim story, making the transition nonsensical. *On a much lighter note* is as senseless as *Much closer to home.*

On the diplomatic front. Avoid fronts unless you're writing about a war front, a weather front or a waterfront.

In sports. There's no chance that a listener would confuse a ball score with a consumer-price report. Or a stock market story with a science story.

In business, in science, in medicine, in foreign news, in international news, and all the other *ins* imaginable (and unimaginable) should be deposited *in the Dumpster.*

In related news. About as relevant as saying, *In unrelated news.* If the next story is related, there's no need to use those words. Find a natural connection and slide into it with everyday words—naturally.

In other news. Every story on a newscast differs from all others. If the first five minutes has been devoted to one big story, shift to the next story by going to a commercial. Or pausing. Or changing tone. Or changing camera. Or anchor. Or writer.

According to an able transition team, Arthur Wimer and Dale Brix, the best rule in thinking about a transition is to use word bridges when they seem helpful and logical and the words are not wasted. "Otherwise," they say in their *Workbook for Radio and TV News Editing and Writing,* "don't use [transitions] if they seem forced, illogical or awkward."

And finally only signals viewers to head for the fridge. Or the loo. Or the zorch (which sesquipedalian viewers call a zapper).

Meanwhile? Forget it.

32

"Remember, They're Only *Half*-Listening"

Ed Bliss, the editor of the "CBS Evening News with Walter Cronkite," used to tell his writers to think of the audience: "Remember, they're only *half*-listening." He told me often. Apparently, he thought *I* was only half-listening.

His reminder comes to mind when I riffle through a folder of scripts that suggest the writers were not thinking of listeners, or half-listeners, or perhaps not thinking at all.

Here are several broadcast examples: **"Former Camden county freeholder 55-year-old Peter Delgrandi was found shot to death several times** [sounds like overkill] **inside his Collingswood, New Jersey, home last night at 15 Harding Terrace. Detectives rushed to the scene shortly after eleven last night and found Delgrandi** [should be *Delgrandi's body*], **a former Republican leader. Delgrandi's murder is being treated as a homicide."** On the basis of the facts presented, and that was the entire script, how can the writer call it murder? And if police regard it as murder, then of course they'll treat it as homicide. A murder *is* homicide. Why use *found* twice? Why does a big-city station broadcast an out-of-town address?

Now that we've shot that script full of holes, let's try a better lead, with a few assumptions, for the next 'cast: "A former Camden county freeholder, Peter Delgrandi, has been shot dead. He was shot in his home in Collingswood late last night, and police call it murder. . . ."

206

"When a young man died last year from injuries suffered in a polo match in Oak Brook, it was a little-known tragedy [there's that tragically overworked word again] **outside those people who follow the sport. Polo is not, after all, one of the major mass-appeal sports. . . ."** Is there a *minor* mass-appeal sport? Even if there is, polo isn't one of them. Better: "The death of a player in a polo match at Oak Brook last year was not widely known outside his family, except to polo fans."

"The handshakes have been exchanged between White House and Congressional deficit-bashers, confirming the eleventh-hour agreement to slash the federal red ink by 30 billion dollars this year, 45 billion next." Possible subjects for that sentence are many—but *handshakes?* And can ink be slashed? But why would *bashers* turn *slashers? Deficit-bashers* should have been killed by copy-busters.

"No First Lady, American or Soviet, ever had a busier, more visible day. While her husband and President Reagan were behind closed doors, Raisa Gorbachev toured Reykjavik in a motorcade of presidential proportions." Some First Ladies have had extremely busy and visible days: Nancy Reagan on the day she became First Lady, Pat Nixon on the day her husband quit the White House, Jacqueline Kennedy on the day her husband was murdered. How can anyone tell who was the busiest and most visible? Which points up a lesson: Never should writers lead with "No one ever." No, never? Well, hardly ever. *Behind closed doors?* Where else would the two First Gentlemen confer? In an open lobby? An open field?

"No one can answer why the video taping of the Monday night Bay City Commission wasn't aired on Bresnan Cable. . . ." Almost certainly, someone *could* tell why. From the rest of the script, it's clear the writer meant he couldn't find anyone who could or would explain.

**"There is some bold new thinking in North Camden, and it surrounds the idea of a safe zone. That's what parents want around the Holy Name school." How do you *surround* an idea? *Surround . . . around?*

"It could only happen here. After a nationwide search, a Cleveland school superintendent was picked, put in office, fired after 10 months and then paid off with 300-thousand dollars in taxpayers' money." It can't happen *only* there. It happens elsewhere, too. Mistaken logic and misplaced modifier. Correct English: "It could happen only here."

"Apparently, French officials had the chance to arrest the man who supposedly masterminded last year's Mideast T-W-A hijacking, but chose not to, hoping not to upset delicate negotiations involving the French hostages in Lebanon." Too sketchy. Too many qualifiers (*apparently, supposedly*). Too many *not to*'s too close.

"Since Joe Frolio retired from the Omaha Public Power District 10 years ago, money isn't as plentiful as it once was." The money supply is more plentiful than ever. The problem is, Joe thinks he's not getting his share.

"Profit-taking late in the day forced investors to give back some of yesterday's gains." How can someone who profits be compelled to give back gains? And to whom would the investors give them back? Another thoughtless line on stock market reports: "Gainers trounced losers." Since when do market *gainers* and *losers* face off? The writer could say, "Gainers *outnumbered* losers," or "Gainers *led* losers."

"Gusty winds off Cape Canaveral have temporarily suspended efforts to salvage debris from the shuttle Challenger." *People* suspend efforts. Winds caused the suspension of efforts. Winds themselves don't suspend anything, except kites.

"The surgeon general also announced [insert *that*] the General Services Administration must enforce a smoking policy at all federal buildings by July first." What does the writer mean? That the way to get rid of those abstainers is to smoke 'em out?

"Following yesterday's substantial decline of the dollar in Japan and as the dollar falls a little on overseas markets today, the Reagan administration continues to warn that further declines could be harmful, but the White House is not saying what action will be taken to stop the greenback's fall." Forget the greenback; stop the decline in newswriting. For starters, the writer began writing before he's ready. He hasn't decided what the news is, so he weaves in several strands. Like a squid squirting ink, the writer starts with *following*. That's confusing because *following* can mean "after" or "pursuing." He clouds the waters further with his next word, *yesterday's*, which yanks listeners back to the previous day. Then, *substantial*. Why use a three-syllable word when a one-syllable word, *steep*, does the job? (Mark Twain said, "I never write 'metropolis' for seven cents when I can get the same . . . for 'city.'") He winds up with a 49-word swamp that would leave listeners in deep goo. The news is that the Administration says the slide in the dollar could cause harm, but it isn't saying what Washington will do to try to stop the slide.

And here's a Golden Oldie from a network newscast: **"After his secession in Katanga—a secession which bled the United Nations and the Congo white— he came back from exile a year ago. . . ."** Bled the Congo *white?* Didn't the reporter and his bosses first read the script aloud to themselves—carefully—before airing it? Wasn't anyone listening to what was being said—not just *half*-listening?

33

News Is Not Us

"Let's never forget," a reporter says in the movie *Broadcast News, "we're* the real story." In real life, some newspeople do think *they're* the story. But here's news for them: they're *not!* The real story is the news, not the newsman.

A newsroom climate that lets reporters insinuate themselves into stories, or encourages them to do so, fosters the view that newspeople are newsmakers. Too many of us think we're not only the messengers but also an important part of the message.

For example, the opening lines of these broadcast scripts:

"Carrollton police tell us one person was injured during a car chase overnight." We don't know whether it was a Chevy chase, but *us* is out of place. *Us* deserves no place at all. Whatever police tell us may be news, but their telling us is not news.

"As we've been reporting [sounds as though we're about to get old news], **Wall Street is reeling after stocks plummeted more than 500 points today."** *We* should stay in the background. If we've been reporting it, why report that we've been reporting it? Sure, news of Wall Street's plunge deserved reporting in every newscast that day, but it needed updating to make it fresh. The assertion that Wall Street is *reeling* is reaction, not action. As a late-day script, this is a little better: "The Dow-Jones 500-point plunge today has left Wall Street reeling."

210

"It was a full-fledged media event that brought every TV station in the state to northwest Nebraska today. The occasion was the announcement by former Republican state chairman Kermit Brashear that he is officially joining a crowded Republican race for governor." The media are not the story; the story is the story. And the story is that a former party chairman has entered the race for governor. After leading with that and using his name, I would mention in the second sentence that he's joining a herd of entrants.

"We have a follow-up to the story of a melee at the Pontiac Correctional Center. A mini-war broke out between rivals of two Chicago street gangs." What we have is not a follow-up but a foul-up. We don't tell a story by referring to what *we* have. And we needn't mention that it's a follow-up. Many of our stories are follow-ups. So what? What we should do, without fanfare or further ado, is tell our audience what's new.

Mêlée is not an everday word, except perhaps in Malaysia. In the second sentence: what's a *mini-war?* Is it worse than a maxi-brawl? Or a near-riot? (*Near-riot* is a near-meaningless term. Also: shun *near-record* and *near-miss.* (If you stop to think about it, when two objects nearly miss, they hit.) And who was fighting? The gangs or *rivals* of the gangs? Perhaps the writer meant "rival gangs." (Aside: when you're writing about protests, be careful of *mob.* Be safe with *crowd.*)

The fourth sentence in that script presents the long-awaited "follow-up": **"Now prosecutors in the case say they hand down indictments against those involved."** That tense makes no sense. Further, indictments are returned by grand juries, not by prosecutors. And indictments are handed *up.* All in all, that writer should be sent to a reformatory, or a rewritery, and the editor should be sent to a correctional center.

"A letdown for the media covering a meeting this weekend of local Republican ward committeemen." Let's not start with a putdown by saying that writers who are caught up with the media are *mediocrities*, but they do need to be taught or reminded that news is not how an event, a near-event or a non-event affects the mood of the media. Too bad the media were disappointed, but that's not news.

"Pressure from the U-S Marines is apparently keeping former U-S embassy guard Clayton Lonetree from giving ___ News an interview." When I was a newspaper reporter and couldn't get an interview, my city editor would growl, "You flopped—again." But news-hungry as he was, he never said, "Write a story on why you flopped." Either you get a story or you don't. If you get it, tell it; if you don't, start working on your next story.

"The much-publicized case of Gary Dotson is taking another turn in the courts." What listener, on hearing the first few words, would think, "I'm dying to hear more about a 'much-publicized case'"? That lead, too, is media-oriented, emphasizing that the case has been heavily reported. But its having been much in the news is not newsworthy in itself. If anything, Dotson's frequent exposure is a turnoff.

"___ News [a network correspondent's script] **has been told the F-A-A will issue a mandatory directive to all U-S airlines, asking them to inspect their. . . ."** Since when is it news if someone tells us something? Almost every story depends on someone's telling us something. If the source of that story was an official who is reliable, the subject of the sentence should be the FAA, not the news organization, unless the news organization burns down, blows up or falls apart. Once we find out for sure what the FAA is going to do, we can simply report the news—without thrusting ourselves into the story and without resorting to the passive voice. Also: a directive *is* mandatory. It doesn't *ask*. Better: "The F-A-A will order all airlines to inspect. . . ."

When a person views everything that occurs in terms of himself, psychiatrists describe it as exaggerated self-reference. And the way some broadcast newspeople exalt *us* and *the media* could be called self-*rev*erence. Our job is not to write about ourselves and not about what someone "told us" and not what we told someone, not how we got the story or why we didn't, and not our views of the news. Our job is to get the news, write the news, tell the news.

Let's never forget—rather, let's always remember: Avoid author intrusion. News is not us.

34

Windy Scripts

The text for today's sermon comes from a British clergyman, the Rev. Sydney Smith (1771–1845):

"The writer does the most who gives his reader the most knowledge and takes from him the least time."

The Reverend Mr. Smith's message applies with equal force to broadcast writers. And with gale force to those who report the weather. The worse the weather, the worse the weather scripts. And even worse, what's *un*scripted.

First, a local script: **"Thunderstorms late this afternoon took their toll on Niles. There was no tornado, thank goodness, but the heavy downpour did cause some problems, nonetheless. Police were deluged with reports of downed wires and trees. Some of the trees blocked streets, and others fell on homes and garages. No injuries were reported."**

The script probably was written by a non-weatherman because the anchor did not introduce it with the tell-tale signs of an approaching word-storm: *"Next, Thaddeus Throckmorton's weather,"* or *"Thaddeus, what kind of weather are you going to give us?"*

No man, not even a superman, whomps up the weather. Now let's put that script under our weather eye: in the first sentence, the writer put the time element before the verb. Don't do it. At the start of a newscast, listeners assume that what follows is the latest news, so they first want to know *what* has happened, not *when*. If the writer had phoned a friend in another town, he'd probably have said, "Thunderstorms hit Niles hard late this afternoon." Or "Thunderstorms have hit Niles hard." I doubt that he'd say they *took their toll*. Let's hope he wouldn't.

Second sentence of the script: negative. Why tell us what did *not* occur? The interjection *thank goodness,* a euphemism for "Thank God," is acceptable in conversation but inappropriate for a newscaster. A downpour is a heavy rain, so *heavy downpour* is redundant. *Nonetheless* is a starchy way to say "even so," and it's no way to end a sentence.

Third sentence: Rather than rely on the passive voice for what police were told, we should use the active voice and tell what did occur. Facts are scarce, but here's a better way to write the story: "Severe thunderstorms struck Niles this afternoon. Damage is heavy, but no one is reported hurt. The storms blew down many trees. Some trees fell on homes and garages, some fell into streets and blocked traffic. And some falling trees tore down power lines."

Here's a script that was broadcast on a Thursday at 7 a.m.:

"Mother Nature unleashed her fury on the Detroit area Wednesday afternoon, knocking out electrical service to some 37-thousand Detroit Edison customers. Edison spokesman Marty Buffalini says crews worked throughout the night to restore service to the affected homes, and the battle appears to have been just about won. . . ."

First, don't mess with *Mother Nature*. She's so old, so tired and so trite, she deserves a long rest.

Next, if you go on the air at 7 a.m., don't start with what occurred the previous day. Start with the latest: "Power has now been restored to almost all the Detroit area homes hit by the storm. Detroit Edison crews have worked all night to fix. . . ." (In the original script, *electrical service* should have been clipped to *electricity*.)

After the newscast presented the voice of Buffalini, the script went on: **"Buffalini says the storm which moved through the Detroit area was kind of unusual in that normally outages are caused by lightning. In this case, there was little of that, and most of the homes were knocked out of service by high winds."** *Kind of unusual* is kinda klutzy. Also: The *homes* weren't knocked out of service; *power* was knocked out.

I'd boil down the tag: "Power outages in a storm are usually caused by lightning. But this time, the main cause was high winds." Original tag: 43 words; rewrite: 19 words. Shorter, sharper, stronger.

Now let's look at a transcript of a network weatherman's *un*scripted forecast, with my observations in brackets: **"Everybody's gonna be talking about what's happening in the Northeast again.** [Many people, perhaps, but not everyone. Anyway, start with action, not reaction.]

"It's another big snowstorm, or maybe a middle-sized snowstorm, anywhere from three inches to half a foot of snow is likely, and from Delaware and Maryland and West Virginia all the way up to southern New England there are travelers' advisories, so take heed if you're headed in this direction: 29 degrees around New York City; 31 in Philadelphia; 27 degrees in Pittsburgh and in Albany; in the 20s up through northern New England. [Weatherman, you've talked up a storm, but your patter is slushy. *Is* and *are* don't express action.]

"The Midwest is really rivaling what's happening in the East, because it's really very cold from Michigan across Illinois all the way through the northern Plains. [How many *really*s does it take to turn off a listener? How can the Midwest *rival* what's happening in the East?] **Temperatures are struggling to reach 12 and 13 degrees; 12 degrees later today in Chicago; only eight degrees in Des Moines; about one degree up in Minneapolis and Saint Paul.** [Temperatures can't struggle any more than weather can *cooperate*. Geographically, *up* and *down* are misleading: for people in northern Minnesota, the Twin Cities are *down,* not *up.* And he kept going:]

"Bitterly cold, winter-like weather is definitely here, and cold weather, even as far south as Dallas again in the 20s. [Why *winter-like* when it *is* winter? *Definitely* is definitely useless.] **Thunderstorms roaming across Florida likely later on today.** [Me not liking sentences lacking a verb with a tense.] . . . **That's a look at all of the weather. . . ."** That's not a look at *all* of it (or even most of it), but that's enough of it. At least he didn't dig out a relic of journalese and say the snow was *dumped* on a town. And he didn't trot out that flaky cliché for snow: *the white stuff.* (Save it for a story on dandruff.)

Whether we're writing weather or talking weather, those examples remind us that we must lay out our sentences calmly, clearly and crisply. All without sounding windy.

35

Do Drop the Ball

Sports jargon is often sent in to pinch hit for simple, clear English and usually strikes out. The arena where it almost always should be out of bounds is in general news stories.

A few f'rinstances from network scripts:

"The Soviets kicked off with a pre-summit news conference Western-style." When so many events are kicked off, aren't you ticked off?

"Just when you might have thought the biggest federal tax overhaul in decades affecting you and yours and everybody's wallet was on the fast track between President Reagan and Congress, think again. [Instead of telling us to *think again,* he should have given the copy another think.] **Today it was blind-sided and sidetracked, maybe even permanently derailed, doomed and ditched."** *Blind-sided?* That's a term football fans know, but it's not widely understood by a general audience. Eventually, tax overhaul did pass, so apparently the anchor who delivered that script was *blind-sided.* That's a term the writer might not have understood. How can a proposed tax overhaul be tackled on its blind side? And *sidetracked, maybe even permanently derailed, doomed and ditched?* The writer is guilty of piling on. He slung a string of strong verbs, but their quantity and comparability left at least one listener dismayed, distressed and disconcerted.

"One crewman died, three others were injured when the football-field-sized Helistat fell apart in mid-

air during a flight last night." And many listeners were lost when that jumbo sentence fell apart on takeoff. Why was a football field dragged into it? Comparing something to the size of a football field is a cliché; besides, a football field has only two dimensions. The blimp-helicopter might have been as long as a football field and as wide, but a three-dimensional object can't be the size of a field. And how many listeners know the size of a football field? Further, *football-field-sized* is clumsy and unconversational.

The writer fumbled: he starts with numbers and then backs into the action. When the writer says a crewman *died*, he leaves open the possibility the crewman died of a heart attack. The writer should have said *was killed*. And the accident occurred in flight, so *mid-air* is superfluous. P.S. Avoid saying that in an accident someone was *left dead*. It's blah.

"Congress heads into its August recess today, batting .500 on two major issues." The story went on to say that both chambers had passed a budget but that another bill was stalled in the Senate. How does anyone calculate batting averages for the House and Senate? If the Senate rejects two bad bills, is it batting zero? Can't a newscast report on Congress without applying—or misapplying—sports terms?

"Quicker than the flash of a knife, President Reagan's National Security Advisor, Robert McFarlane, is already cut tonight from the White House roster, believed by many to be the latest loser to the strong inside power game." And the story is a loser to the inside language of the jargonauts, where all the world's a game and all the men and women merely players. Haven't you had it up to here with references to participants in an event as a *key player?* Another sports term was misappropriated by a networker who said one of those *players,* in testifying, had "hit a hole in one." (One Player who *could* do that is Gary.)

"The President now is in the home stretch of his homework for the Geneva summit." If the Russkies can *kick off,* the President can saddle up. Too bad the writer didn't go the distance and think of a strong and suitable verb. Instead, he lifted a racetrack term and finished lamely.

"The issues are simple: The opposition says Marcos can't solve the nation's mounting economic problems. He says he can, and adds that things will just get worse without him. It could become a horse race. While government polls put [him] way ahead, independent surveys. . . ." *A horse race?* Listen up, pardner: Hold your horses! Don't trot 'em out for elections or other human contests.

"Terry Waite is a special assistant to the Archbishop of Canterbury. He's also a skilled hostage negotiator with a good track record." Horses have *track records;* humans have *records.* A record is a record is a record. And unless you're writing about a sport, disregard *ground rules* and go with *rules.* And while we're in the sports arena, shun *game plan* unless you're writing about a game. Likewise, shun *ballpark* estimate, unless you're making an estimate about a ballpark. And shun other sports terms (*huddled, struck out, hit a home run*) in non-sports contexts.

"After having their separate say in public about who has the better ideas on arms control, Secretary of State Shultz and Soviet Foreign Minister Shevardnadze met at the Soviet U-N Mission today to word-wrestle about it in private. All the talking and hard sell on both sides is a rehearsal for the main event. . . ." *Word-wrestle?* Why do two diplomats do that when they could simply *argue?* And how could Shultz and Shevy *rehearse?* And at a preliminary bout? An unscripted exchange was scheduled to take place between two other men, Reagan and Gorbachev, at the main event.

But the trophy for faulty writing goes to a sportscaster at a radio station. He's not a local yokel; he works in market Number One. He was talking about a major league pitcher who'd been suspended for putting sand-paper on his glove. Here's what the sportscaster said:

"If he's cheating, he'd better find a better way to do it." Find a better way to cheat? If the writer had thought more—or thought at all—about what he was say-ing, he'd realize that many listeners wouldn't see his script as sardonic comment. They'd see it as winking at cheating.

But sports lingo can serve in giving advice to writ-ers who frequently use—and misuse—sports terms: When in doubt, don't punt—or bunt. Find a better way to score—a better way to say it.

36

A New Look at "New Look"

The TV term "new look" needs a new look. News directors believe they can achieve a "new look" by hiring a new anchor, or building a new set, or using new graphics and a new format. But often the element that most needs a "new look" is overlooked: <u>newswriting</u>.

So let's look at a broadcast script, one that needed an unsparing second look. You'd probably do best by first reading the script, in boldface on the left, then my comments:

"A 32-year-old resident of Rome, Italy, was injured this morning on Interstate 90 in Harborcreek Township when the Jeep he was in flipped over on the slippery pavement. Robert Amirian was thrown from the Jeep in the accident shortly after 8:45 this morning.

What's in an age? Everyone has one. It's not critical, except for wine and cheese. And why say, at the top, the victim comes from abroad? There's no need to say *this morning* on an evening newscast; it's too long ago—and too long. "Today" will do the job. *The Jeep he was in* should be "riding in" or "driving." If there's time later, I'd like to know why it was slippery. Ice? Snow? Gas spill? *In the accident* is superfluous, the time is insignificant and the second *this morning* is repetitious.

222

Amirian was treated at the scene and then transported by Life Star helicopter to St. Vincent's Health Center, where he's listed in good condition this evening. Lawrence Park state trooper Jim Boniger said the driver of the Jeep, 29-year-old Jacqueline Amirian, was traveling too fast for conditions. She was treated and released at St. Vincent's.	Instead of repeating the man's name, which has four syllables and means nothing to listeners, it's easier to say "he." *Then* is of no use. *Transported* is a fancy way of saying "taken" or "carried." When writing about a chopper, "flown" will do. I'd use the active voice and say a chopper flew him. What are his injuries? *Is listed* implies "right now," so *this evening* is unneeded. The trooper might have been able to tell the reporter whether the driver is related to the passenger, and how. Also: how fast she was going. What speed was permissible? Was she ticketed? For what? What were the conditions? If someone is *treated,* that means the person was given treatment but not kept in the hospital, so *released* is unneeded.

The most important question the script raises: what relevance does the story have for our listeners? The story would be newsworthy if the driver and passenger were residents of our community, or if the accident were horrendous. Or if the Amirians were widely known. But apparently they came from elsewhere, not even from our county or country. Are they foreigners or Americans living abroad? What are they doing here?

The accident was minor. The story would be worth running if the names were recognizable or distinguished— or extinguished. Or if news is hard to find. Or if the site of the accident has been a trouble spot. It might merit using as a cautionary tale—but not delivered as a sermon: if you drive too fast, you might wind up dead. But that message, "Speed kills," is hardly new or interesting, and in that script, it's obscured. Also: safety-conscious listeners might wonder, "Was the man who was thrown out of the Jeep wearing a seat belt? And how about the woman?"

Here's a better way to write the story: "A Jeep flipped over on Interstate 90 in Harborcreek Township today, and a passenger was thrown out. A Life Star helicopter flew him to Saint Vincent's Hospital, where he's listed in good condition. His injuries: [bruises?] He's a tourist from Rome, Italy: Robert Amirian, 32 years old. A state trooper says the Jeep was going too fast for the slippery pavement. The Jeep was driven by Amirian's [wife, sister, cousin], Jacqueline, 29 years old. She was treated at Saint Vincent's Hospital for. . . ."

This rewrite helps point up my contention that the original script—and other TV and radio scripts—need a good, hard look to make a newscast worthwhile.

What's your reaction to this broadcast script?

"Philadelphia police are investigating a stabbing on the Broad Street subway line. Police say a man in his early twenties was stabbed when he attacked a woman on a subway car as the train pulled into the Allegheny Station northbound. Police say the woman stabbed the man in self-defense. The victim is in critical but stable condition at Temple University Hospital. He still hasn't been identified. Police aren't releasing the woman's name. No charges have yet been filed."

Let's examine the script: like too many broadcast scripts, it starts with reaction, not action. The news is the action: attack and counterattack. It's not news when police investigate. It would be news if they did not.

In the second sentence, the passive—*was stabbed*—keeps us from learning, until the third sentence, who did the stabbing, the woman or a third party. Whether the attack took place as the train was pulling into the station, or pulling out, or standing, is worth mentioning, but not so soon.

The third sentence is the third straight in which the subject is *police*. Give us a break, pleece! In itself, the sentence is O.K. But a succession of loose sentences—in contrast to periodic, or suspended, sentences, which build up to the key word or idea—makes for flabby story-telling.

The fourth sentence mentions *the victim*. Judging by the context, I presume it's a reference to the man. But can an attacker be a victim? And why identify the attacker's hospital? Do we want listeners to send a hit man?

Fifth sentence: does this mean that police haven't been able to identify the man or that police won't divulge his identity? When we write in the active voice, listeners know who's doing what to whom.

"The police *aren't* releasing" the woman's name? Never? Maybe they are, *even as we speak*. More to the point: was she hurt? How did she counter the attack? Was anyone else in the car? Did anyone help her? Was the attacker armed? Was it his knife or hers? How about her age? Height, weight? How big was her assailant? Had they been together? Why did he attack her? Was it rush hour? Within the hour? Is the guy an ex-con? A fugitive? A writer? Answers to all these questions may not be immediately available, but if I had any answers, I'd use *some* of them.

Finally: *charges* filed against whom? Him? Her? Them? When charges are filed, let's report them. Until then, why take time to say something hasn't occurred if it's bound to occur soon? Yet, an acceptable closer might be: "Police are trying to decide whether to charge him, her or them."

Now I'll take a stab at it: "A man attacked a woman on a Philadelphia subway train today, but police say she fought back and stabbed her attacker. He's in critical condition. The attack occurred on the Broad Street line as the train was pulling into the Alleghany Station. . . ."

The person who wrote the original script is typical of those who defer action in favor of reaction, the type of writer you might call reactionary. Some do serious damage by backing into a story, as in the next script:

"There were no injuries but there was extensive damage done to a home owned by Ernest Belford at 2220 Perkins street in Saginaw this weekend. Belford and his family weren't in the home at the time of the fire. Saginaw fire officials say the blaze began after some clothing that was placed too close to a hot water heater caught fire. There is no estimate available at this time as to the amount of damage done, but it took firefighters two hours to extinguish the blaze."

Let's zoom in for a closeup: the lead is negative, it tells us the outcome before telling us what happened, and it doesn't mention the most important element, the fire. *There were* and *there was* are deadly. And that first sentence uses them both. Which is why the script is DOA[2].

The second sentence is wordy: *weren't in the home at the time of the fire.* What other time would we be writing about? Simply put: *They weren't home.* A *blaze* is something that breaks out in a wastebasket or glows in a fireplace. *Blaze* is not a word that people say; they say *fire.* And *hot water heater* is redundant: *water heater* says it.

The last sentence of the script starts with the frail *there is.*

Extinguish? Firemen aren't extinguishers; they *put out* fires. (If you ever catch anyone writing *extinguish,* watch him carefully so he doesn't perpetrate *conflagration.*)

Here's another way to handle the story: "A fire in a home at 2220 Perkins, Saginaw, has caused heavy damage. The owner, Ernest Belford, and his family were not home. Fire officials say some clothing had been too close to a water heater and was set on fire. It took firefighters two hours to put the fire out. No estimate yet on damage."

I don't like to start a sentence with the indefinite *it,* but if I write, "Firefighters took two hours to . . . ," I may be suggesting that they dawdled. By saying it took them two hours, I'm saying they needed two hours.

Where did the writers of those two scripts go astray? They didn't think through the handful of facts they had. They didn't exercise sound news judgment. They didn't go to the heart of the story. And what they finally decided to go with, they wrote wordily, weakly and wrongly. That's *my* reaction.

37

The Power of Short Words

Grim, *grisly, gruesome:* That gaggle of G-words seldom adds anything to stories except girth. Yet we hear them often, as in these excerpts from recent newscasts:

"A grisly accident . . . in the capital. . . ."

". . . for injuries suffered in a gruesome accident this afternoon."

"They now face the grim task of removing bodies from the burnt wreckage."

Accidents worth reporting on air are bad enough without a writer's pumping them up. Most big accidents are a bloody mess. But there's no need for gory adjectives or graphic detail, especially at mealtime.

Even if adjectives are not unappetizing, they are usually unnecessary. What writers do need are strong verbs and solid nouns. The adjective, Voltaire said, is the enemy of the noun. And Mark Twain wrote, "As to the adjective, when in doubt, strike it out." In a letter to a 12-year-old boy, he said:

"I notice that you use plain, simple language, short words, and brief sentences. That is the way to write English—it is the modern way and the best way. Stick to it; and don't let fluff and flowers and verbosity creep in.

"When you catch an adjective, kill it. No, I don't mean utterly, but kill most of them—then the rest will be valuable. They weaken when they are close together. They give strength when they are wide apart."

228

The modern-day language expert Richard Lederer makes the case for short words in his book, *The Miracle of Language:* "Small words cast their clear light on big things—night and day, war and peace, and life and death. Big words at times seem strange to the eye and the ear and the mind and the heart. Small words are the ones we seem to have known from the time we were born, like the hearth fire that warms the home. . . . Here is a sound rule: Use small, old words where you can. If a long word says just what you want to say, do not fear to use it. But know that our tongue is rich in crisp, brisk, swift, short words. Make them the spine and heart of what you speak and write. Short words are like fast friends. They will not let you down."

The power of short words and short sentences animates the Bible:

"Jesus wept."

"And God said, 'Let there be light,' and there was light."

"His [Elijah's] word burned like a lamp."

"A word fitly spoken is like apples of gold in a setting of silver."

"The ear tests words as the palate tests food."

"He that hath knowledge spareth his words."

"Let thy speech be short, comprehending much in few words."

"Every idle word that men shall speak, they shall give account thereof in the day of judgment. For by thy words thou shalt be justified, and by thy words thou shalt be condemned."

"Think on these things."

Going back to *grim, grisly, gruesome*—and *gripping,* too—is *grueling.* And that last word is also suspect, at least in the eyes of Ambrose Bierce, a contemporary of Twain's. In his classic *Write It Right,* Bierce says of *grueling:* "Used chiefly by newspaper reporters; as, 'He was subjected to a grueling cross-examination.' 'It was grueling weather.' Probably a corruption of *grilling.*"

Bierce's book, subtitled *A Little Blacklist of Literary Faults*, was published in 1909. Bierce, a San Francisco journalist, disappeared in 1913. And his book almost disappeared, too. Now it has been rediscovered and reprinted by Edward B. Gannon and his son, Richard. They've re-subtitled it: *The Lost Book*. Bierce wrote in another era, and, as you know: "In one era, out the other." Yet, many of his strictures still stand. Here are some of the words he warned against, with boldface marking those he deemed correct, and his comments:

"*Appropriated* for **Took**. 'He appropriated his neighbor's horse to his own use.' To appropriate is to set apart, as a sum of money, for a special purpose.

"*Badly* for **Bad**. 'I feel badly.' 'He looks badly.' The former sentence implies defective nerves of sensation, the latter, imperfect vision. Use the adjective.

"*Compare with* for **Compare to**. . . . Comparison *with* may be for observing a difference; comparison *to* affirms a similarity.

"*Declared* for **Said**. To a newspaper reporter, no one seems ever to say anything; all 'declare.'

"*Deliver.* 'He delivered an oration,' or 'delivered a lecture.' Say, He made an oration, or gave a lecture.

"*Fail.* 'He failed to note the hour.' That implies that he tried to note it, but did not succeed. Failure carries always the sense of endeavor; when there has been no endeavor, there is no failure. A falling stone cannot fail to strike you, for it does not try; but a marksman firing at you may fail to hit you; and I hope he always will.

"*Got married* for **Married**. If this is correct, we should say, also, 'got dead' for died. . . .

"*Gubernatorial.* Eschew it; it is not English. Leave it to those who call a political office a 'chair.' 'Gubernatorial chair' is good enough for them. So is hanging.

"*Hail* for **Come**. 'He hails from Chicago.' This is sea speech, and comes from the custom of hailing passing ships. It will not do for serious discourse.

"*Inaugurate* for **Begin, Establish,** etc. Inauguration implies some degree of formality and ceremony.

"*Inside of.* Omit the preposition.

"*Lease.* To say of a man that he leases certain premises leaves it doubtful whether he is lessor or lessee. . . .

"*Loan* for **Lend.** 'I loaned him ten dollars.' We lend, but the act of lending, or, less literally, the thing lent, is a loan.

"*Scholar* for **Student** or **Pupil.** A scholar is a person who is learned, not a person who is learning.

"*State* for **Say.** 'He stated that he came from Chicago.' . . . We state a proposition, or a principle, but say that we are well. And we say our prayers—some of us.

"*Substantiate* for **Prove.** Why?

"*Try and* for **Try to.** 'I will try and see him.' This plainly says that my effort to see him will succeed—which I cannot know and do not wish to affirm. 'Please try and come.' This colloquoial slovenliness of speech is almost universal in this country, but freedom of speech is one of our most precious possessions."

A master wordwatcher, Lynn Slovonsky, has complained to me about a network evening newscaster's mention of an *armed gunman.* Along with that redundancy, Lynn has sent a splendid spoonerism from Herb Caen, the San Francisco chronicler: The F.B.I. agent who shot and killed John Dillinger, Public Enemy Number One, in 1934, moved to S. F. many years ago. Caen reported that at a dinner party, the hostess became flustered and introduced the famous agent, Melvin Purvis, as Mervin Pelvis.

38

Words to Watch: The Worst 40

If the big electronic ears of the National Security Agency listened to every U.S. radio and television newscast for 24 hours and N.S.A.'s supercomputers pinpointed the words used most often, we could easily spot the words that need watching most—a sort of WordWatcher's Worst 40:

Actually—Seldom useful. *Really.*

Advise—Often misused for *tell* or *inform. Advise = give advice.*

Announce—Seems to be in the first sentence of most press releases. Save *announce* for something of consequence, not the opening of a new fast-food restaurant.

Bizarre—A crutch word, used to prop up a story that doesn't need that kind of promotion. Also: *astounding, fantastic, spectacular, startling* and *weird.*

Blast—People don't *blast* with words; they *blast* with bombs or weapons.

Comment—"She commented that she's going to try again." Better: "She *said* she'd try again."

Conditions—"We have sunny conditions" = "It's sunny." Similarly, *situation* is usually an empty word, as in "flooding situation." Likewise, "crisis situation." *Crisis,* too, is misused and overused.

Continues—A verb that says—weakly—whatever has been going on is still going on. Use action verbs.

Controversial—What isn't? Aren't you irritated when you hear a newscaster tell of the release today of a *controversial* report? The newscast is the first public disclosure of the report, so it could not have stirred up a public debate. Perhaps the problem under study is controversial, but just about everything is. Have you ever heard of a new report or study on any subject greeted unanimously?

Dilemma—Not the same as *problem* or *predicament;* it's "two alternatives, equally undesirable."

Duo—Unless you're a music critic, save it for Batperson and Robin. As for *pair,* that's O.K. for twins, but not for gunmen. And don't write, "The gunmen fled." They never hang around.

Earlier—If something occurred today, it must have been *earlier* today. I'm going to end this sentence *later* today.

Expected—Don't say something is expected unless you identify the expector. As for *as expected,* something that has been expected hardly comes as big news. If you start an item with *as expected,* no listener would pipe up, "I *knew* you were going to say that." News is largely the *un*expected.

Here—Where is *here?* In your newsroom? No need for *here* in "Here at home." In fact, no need for "Here at home."

Hopefully—Careful writers shun it. I keep hoping it'll fade, *vainfully.*

Important—If the action or statement weren't important, we wouldn't be reporting it, would we?

Incident—Hollow when combined with certain words, as in "the shooting incident." Some newscasters use *incidentally* to preface a tag (or button). But if something is significant (and we don't broadcast the insignificant), it shouldn't be diminished with *incidentally* or *by the way.* Whenever I hear an item like this, I wonder: "Incidentally, the President is going to spend the weekend at Camp David." Does the anchor mean the visit is inconsequential to the President, or to the newscast, or to the listener?

Informed—As in "Newsradio 99 has been informed that. . . ." Informed by whom? Anyone who provides material *informs* us. And why should Newsradio 99 mention itself before reporting the news?

Involved—A detour word, Mitchell Stephens calls it, so imprecise it merely hints at a relationship. "He's involved in crime." Does that mean he's a criminal or that he's tracking criminals? Search me.

Issue—"Issue a warning" = warn. Subpoenas and warrants are *issued;* indictments are *returned, issued,* or *handed up. Controversial issue* is redundant.

Jail—A place for holding suspects, defendants, misdemeanants and felons awaiting transportation to prison. Misdemeanants serve up to one year in jail for misdemeanors, minor offenses like littering, loitering, and larceny. Felons serve time in prison for felonies, major crimes like robbery, burglary, rape and murder.

Kick off—Hold it for football. You needn't *kick off* a drive; you can *start* it, *begin* it, *open* it.

Learned—"Newsradio 99 has learned. . . ." Isn't everything we put in a newscast something we've learned, something we've either read or heard? Let's just report the story and leave ourselves out of it. A teacher's injunction, "Avoid author intrusion," still rings in my ears. (Or is it tinnitus?)

Local—As in "local residents." What other kinds of residents are there?

Lone—In "a lone gunman," *lone* is superfluous. When I hear "lone gunman," I think of one who pretends he wants a loan. And don't ever call him a gun*person.* Which leads to *spokesperson,* an ungainly, unnatural, unnecessary word. Would you ever roll up a snowball, shape it into a human figure and call it a *snowperson?*

Margin: "Stock market gainers lead losers by a margin of five-to-four." That's a *ratio,* not a *margin.* A margin is the *difference* between two numbers. Newscasters who report stock market news should learn the difference. And so should newscasters who don't report the market.

Meanwhile—Should be stamped out.

React—Stress action, not reaction, unless the reaction is the news. Or you need a second-day lead. Usually, you can report the reaction in a newsier way by skipping the verb *react* and the noun *reaction.*

Refute—Means to disprove or overcome conclusively; often misused for *rebut,* which means to present opposing evidence or arguments.

Report—The noun has two conflicting meanings: a rumor and a statement (or account). How can a listener tell whether "a *report* from Washington" is gossip or gospel?

Single—This was given a workout during Voyager's flight on a "single tank of fuel." What's wrong with saying "one tank"?

Sources—All our information comes from sources—including ourselves. Some stations (and networks) like to say, "Sources tell XYZ News that the President . . ." Which sources? Sources friendly to him? Unfriendly? Hostile? Imaginary? Be as specific as possible so the listener can consider the source.

Successfully—As in "She successfully swam the English Channel." Ever hear of anyone who swam it *un*successfully? (The "English Channel" does not refer to the BBC.)

There—Usually a space-eater, especially at the start of a sentence: "There was a gas tank explosion today near Gary." Better: "A gas tank near Gary has exploded." That's shorter and puts the emphasis on the key word, *exploded.*

Tragedy—Defined as "a dramatic or literary work depicting a protagonist engaged in a morally significant struggle ending in ruin or profound disappointment." Yet almost every day I hear about a baby's death in "a *tragic* fire." Heartbreaking, yes, but a *tragedy?*

Upcoming—An ugly, unnecessary word. Doesn't say any more than *coming,* just as *upsurge* doesn't say any more than *surge.* A newpaper editor once warned that the next reporter who used *upcoming* would be *outgoing.*

Very—"Use this word sparingly," say Strunk and White. "Where emphasis is necessary, use words strong in themselves."

Witnessed—In almost all cases, the best word is *saw.*

Worst—"They're calling it Fiji's worst air disaster." It might also have been Fiji's first. Save absolutes and superlatives for events of significance.

Youth—Do you ever say *youth* outside your newsroom? If not, don't use it inside your newsroom. Other non-conversational words: *slay, vie, foe, don, ax, accord.* Also avoid *gubernatorial,* which is probably not used even by gubernators.

My hearing isn't so good as N. S. A.'s, nor is my computing, but I've heard those Worst 40 words worked to death on radio newscasts—not to mention TV. (No, let's not.) Let me know if you have another word or two deserving dishonorable mention.

39

News Retardants

Remember my listing of "WordWatching's" Worst 40, words that newscasters most often misuse or overuse, words that need watching most? One I forgot: *remember*.

Remember deserves inclusion because it's a news retardant. Whenever a script starts with "Remember . . . ?" it usually postpones the point of the story. Often, *remember* serves only to remind us that that newsroom previously covered a story—or uncovered it. It's self-serving, and for anyone outside the newsroom, it's also meaningless.

An example from a network newscast: **"Remember . . . Correspondent __ __'s investigative report last __, which first revealed the existence of a nationwide murder-for-hire ring? Today, in Fayetteville, Arkansas, six people were indicted on charges of. . . ."**

No, I didn't remember. And if I had, would that have made the news any clearer? Most listeners have trouble recalling what they heard three minutes ago. Why expect them to remember a story carried three months ago? I don't remember what I had for breakfast this morning, or whether I had breakfast. But my faulty memory has nothing to do with the news. News is what's new. And news is not the newsman.

In case you don't remember, and even if you do, a previous chapter dealt with question leads. It said they are usually questionable. The main objections to question leads: they sound like commercials or quiz shows, they can trivialize the news, they can be hard to deliver, they don't inform and they delay delivery of the news. Still another objection comes from Tim Wulfemeyer: "If you ask a question, you might not like the answer you get." In some cases, he says, questions can simply be converted to a statement. For example: "Have you ever thought about going to college?" But Prof. Wulfemeyer says that question might bring answers he wouldn't like, so he would recast it and get rid of the question: "If you've ever thought about going to college, you'd. . . ."

Our goal is to answer questions, not ask them. Listeners tune in newscasts to hear news, not 20 Questions. The only questions you should ask are of yourself, your deskmates and people who have information. I don't want to insist that you never write a question lead. But if you allow yourself only one or two a year, you'll be on good paper with me—without question.

As for that script's reference to an *investigative report:* does that mean the story was distinctive because the correspondent investigated? Don't all reporters investigate? (They should.) And, yes, the script's use of *first revealed* is redundant. I was taught not to use *reveal* unless I was writing about the Book of Revelation. Which I took to mean only rarely and only about a disclosure that was of great significance. Instead of *reveal,* we should use *disclose.* Keep in mind: *disclose,* along with *reveal,* points to a fact, not a mere assertion.

Another lead that's a news retardant:

"Earlier this week, we told you about a 'highly charged' court battle involving a Damascus dairy farmer and his jittery cows. A Montgomery County jury has awarded Edward Burdette 420-thousand dollars in his lawsuit against Potomac Edison. Burdette says stray electricity from the company's power lines makes his 100 Holsteins too nervous to milk. . . ."

The fat content of that script is high. No need to tell listeners what you said *earlier this week.* Better: "A Damascus dairy farmer has won his case against Potomac Edison. A Montgomery County jury found that stray electricity from power lines made his cows too nervous to milk. And the jury said the company must pay him 420-thousand dollars."

I'm also tired of questions like this:

"Did someone stick their fingers into the Philadelphia anti-graffiti network till and stuff several thousand dollars into their own pockets? That's what's being investigated. . . ."

That lead turns a hard-news story into pap. (Zap pap!) And *someone* is singular. Certain other indefinite pronouns—*anyone, everyone, each, either, neither and no one*—also take singular verbs. When they are antecedents of pronouns, the pronouns, too, are singular: *he, she, it.* Also, those pronouns also require the singular possessive: *his, her, its.* In the spirit of the times, some writers avoid *his* or *her* by substituting *their.* That may be good for personkind, but in the eyes and ears of grammarians, faulty agreement is bad grammar. The writer of the script could have avoided this pitfall by writing a simple declarative sentence: "Police are trying to find out whether someone at the Philadelphia anti-graffiti network stole some of its money."

Another network example: **"There are various Swiss security personal and honor guards, each with their own fine hat."** *Each* is singular, and *their* is plural. One way to sidestep problems with agreement is to turn a singular subject into the plural: change *each* to *all,* and change *hat* to *hats* . That way it reads: "There are various Swiss security and honor guards, all with their own fine hats. Instead of writing, "Any employee who has held *his* job" or the bureaucratic "Any employee who has held *his or her* job," it's easier to write (and hear): "Any *employees* who have held *their* jobs." *Security* in that script seems superfluous. What's the difference between a guard and a security guard? And please be on guard against *there are.*

An editorial broadcast in Philadelphia suffered from a similar lapse:

"Let's not force a racial debate that neither can-didate says they want, and let's give the voters some credit for being intelligent citizens." That, too, can easily be corrected—and improved. I don't know what a *racial* debate is, but here's a rewrite: "Let's not force a debate both candidates say they don't want. And let's give voters credit for being intelligent." (No need to use *citizens*. Only citizens can vote.)

Writers can avoid mistakes in subject-pronoun agreement and subject-verb agreement by reviewing a good grammar. And they can keep this sermonette for a Remembrance of Things Lapsed.

40

Sources? What Sources?

A constant source of trouble in newsrooms is *sources*. We all know what the word means. But when newscasters use *sources,* we don't know what *they* mean. When they attribute a fact to *sources,* listeners haven't the foggiest idea who the source is: someone with a stake in the story? Someone who's mistaken? Someone who's trying to give the story a spin? Or a disinterested party who is knowledgeable and has no access to grind?

When you tell listeners that "sources say," you are saying almost nothing. Not even whether the source is a person or a piece of paper. "Sources say" can't help listeners gauge the reliability of our information because all news comes from *sources.*

When does a fact need to be sourced? Whenever we're writing about something we have not seen or that may be open to dispute. Broadcasters treat wire service copy as though it were written by a staff member, so we don't ordinarily attribute wire copy to the wires. But when we do use attribution, we should be as specific as possible and present it in broadcast style.

For source material, let's turn to a recent network script: **"The shooting occurred about a mile from General Noriega's headquarters in downtown Panama City, U. S. sources say.** [Hanging attribution at the end of a sentence is print style, *not* broadcast style. In fact, that sentence needs no attribution; both sides agree there *was* a shooting. Attribution *is* needed, though, for what they say led to it.]

"The Panamanian officer was hit twice, the sources say, in the arm and the leg. [Placement of attribution in the middle of a sentence is suitable.] **American soldiers are on high alert. But Panamanian charges that the U.S. might invade are not true, U.S. officers say.** [Again, attribution in print style.]

"Government officials [*which* government?] **this morning accused the U.S. military of threatening to attack, unless Panama explains the killing of the U.S. Marine officer. The soldier** [a Marine is not a soldier] **was in this car with three other U.S. servicemen when he was shot, the Southern Command reports.** [Another attribution in the wrong place. Besides, *whose* Southern Command?] **Panama says the servicemen in civilian clothes fired several shots at Noriega's military headquarters after running a roadblock.** [At last, attribution in broadcast style, with attribution preceding assertion. Better: "Panama says the servicemen ran a roadblock and fired several shots at Noriega's military headquarters."] **Three Panamanians, including a soldier and a one-year-old girl were wounded, Panama says.** [Wrong style again.]

"U.S. officials say the Americans, unarmed, were fleeing Panamanian soldiers, who had roughed them up when shots were fired. [Many editors would also attribute the *who* clause: "U-S officials say Panamanian soldiers roughed up the Americans, who, they say, were unarmed and were trying to get away when the Panamanians fired." That eliminates the passive—and vague— *shots were fired.*]

"U.S. soldiers and Panamanian troops have clashed at least 800 times since Noriega called a state of emergency in 1987. [What's the source for "800"? Also: do the math for the listener and say "two years ago."] **A typical incident: Panamanian soldiers arrested and searched six U.S. MPs, suggesting they were spies. . . ."** When? An arrest is an encounter, perhaps even a confrontation. But that arrest is more a *brush* than a *clash*.

Another *source* problem in a script broadcast by a major-market station: **"Fatigue is causing some airline pilots to wander out of assigned airspace, land on the wrong runways and even fall asleep at the controls. Government documents describe some 600 incidents in the past five years in which air crews blamed fatigue for fatal and potentially fatal mistakes.** [Voice-over] **Pilots, weary from flying many hours and across multiple time zones, say they are often exhausted and not fully in control of their actions. They blame deregulation and subsequent competition among the airlines for their overload of work. An unreleased report by the Canadian Aviation Safety Board cites fatigue as a factor in the 1985 crash in Newfoundland that killed 248 U.S. servicemen.**

[At last, we learn the source of the opening assertion: a *Canadian* report. And one not even released. Why not? Because the head of the board found the data inaccurate? The conclusions unjustified? The second sentence of the script refers to *government documents,* implying the government is ours—not Canada's.] **But the F.A.A. and Air Transport Association both say there is no evidence that fatigue is a problem."** Now we learn that the U.S. government rejects what the script presents as a key finding of the unreleased report. But the lead of the script has already presented the "findings" as fact—and forcefully.]

Another station: **"Philadelphia's police department is too slow to change ... and the city too weak to force it.** [Sounds like an editorial, but it's not.] **The Inquirer says a report expected out today blames the lack of a promotion program that's based on performance ..."** The strong assertions at the top should be preceded by the source, the *Inquirer.* And the lead should say the written report is *expected* today. Like the Canadian report in the previous script, this report may not be released today. Or ever. Or it may be revised significantly.

Whether the *Inquirer* reporter who wrote the article had read the report about the police or based his account on what someone had told him, he might have erred. It's not unknown for a reporter to misquote or misunderstand what he reads or hears. So a newscaster must take pains at the outset to identify the source. (Further, the script never says who's going to issue the report.)

The most reliable source for deciding on attribution—whether, where and how—is common sense.

Q. Doctor, what can you do for a nasty earache?

A. Tell me about it.

Q. I keep hearing such odd language in newscasts I can't believe my ears. And it hurts!

A. What's so irritating?

Q. Let me read from my notes, rather than play it by ear.

A. Shoot.

Q. This is the kind of broadcast script I'm talking about: **"According to sources, Presser was an F-B-I informant for nearly ten years, and, according to published reports, was authorized by the agency to break the law, presumably as part of an F-B-I probe into alleged ties between the Teamsters Union and organized crime."**

A. So what's wrong with that?

Q. What isn't? The correspondent starts by quoting *sources*. Are they government sources? Underworld sources? F.B.I. agents and U.S. attorneys rarely want to be quoted in a story like that. But just plain *sources* is too vague. *Sources* could be Presser's rivals—or the newsman's press rivals. Everything has a source, so writers should be resourceful and give us a better idea of where the story comes from.

A. Is that all that bothers you?

Q. Oh, no. That story goes on to quote *published reports*. A *report* can be either a rumor or a true account. So a published report might be a tidbit in a gossip column or it might be a thoroughly documented article. The word *published* doesn't sanctify the word *report*. Whenever I hear the term *published report,* it only raises a question: Is the *report* a factual article by a first-rate fact-finder, or is it by a reporter who couldn't cover a fire in a barrel with an asbestos blanket—and couldn't find a bleeding elephant in a snowstorm in a blind alley?

A. Sounds to me as though your hearing is fine.

Q. Well, I've enhanced my auditory acuity by mechanical means: recorders. That way, I catch newscasts word for word.

A. Is that your way of saying you're reliable?

Q. Yes, indeed. But I don't go around calling myself a reliable source. That reminds me of another sore spot. The lead of a second network story: **"A frequently reliable source has told ___ News in El Salvador that the government and rebels now have reached an agreement that would. . . ."** What irks me, Doc, is *frequently reliable.*

A. What would you have said?

Q. I know what I would not have said: I would not have said *frequently reliable.* I'd either try to nail down the story or else find another way to tell it. If the source is *frequently reliable,* it must be frequently unreliable. And if I were sitting on a jury, I certainly wouldn't vote to convict someone on the testimony of a witness who is *frequently reliable.*

A. Does anything else set your ears on edge?

Q. Yes, here's another source spot: **"Sources say we could use military force against Libya very quickly if that became necessary."** Who are the *sources?* A barber and a cab driver? Also, in conditional sentences, try to put the conditional (*if*) clause before the consequence clause, unless the whole point of the sentence lies in what follows *if.* Further: the key word in the script is *quickly.* So it shouldn't be buried in the middle of the sentence. I'd put it last. Although *quickly* often refers to rapid response, I might improve on it by using a snappy, one-syllable synonym: "[Sources more specific and substantial than *sources*] say that if it becomes necessary to use force against Libya, Washington could move *fast.*" By the way, what does the writer mean by *we?* Our station? Our nation? If you mean our station, we don't have any forces, except electromagnetic. Would you write, "We're going to start arresting youngsters on the streets after 10 p.m."? Forget about *We*—unless you're talking about Lindbergh's autobiography.

A. What can *I* do?

Q. Listen carefully. This type of lead is used more and more: "___ **News has been told the standoff took place when Italian troops blocked an American attempt to fly the terrorists directly to. . . .**"

A. What are you bellyaching—or earaching—about?

Q. A reporter should not start by saying that someone told him something. People are always telling us something. All kinds of things. Some are true, some aren't even close. If someone of substance tells us something newsworthy on the record, we might start by saying, "Senator Besser says. . . ." But I would never start a story by saying "X-Y-Z News has been told by Senator Besser that. . . ." That's no way to tell a story.

A. Why not?

Q. I'm glad you asked that. There are several reasons: No reporter—or network or station—is bigger than a story. The news is not that someone told us something. The news is the something itself. In writing broadcast news, attribution precedes assertion. But if we verify what we've been told, we should present it straightaway, not delayed or diluted. And we should try to write in the active voice, not the passive.

A. Anything else you want to get off your mind?

Q. Another kind of lead: "X-Y-Z News has learned. . . ."

A. Don't you favor learning?

Q. Yes. Especially by broadcast journalists. But there's no point in a newscaster's saying her network or station has *learned* something. Whatever news the station broadcasts is something they've *learned.* Probably they want to imply their story is exclusive. If you call a story *exclusive,* though, you prompt listeners to wonder whether you gather the rest of your stories while grazing with the herd. Or sipping in a pool—a press pool.

A. As I see it, or hear it, you're listening to too much news.

Q. Too much that's *not* news. Thanks, though, for hearing me out.

A. No matter how you label it, or libel it, I'm going to give you some simple advice: Don't listen so carefully. Just half-listen. Then you won't find listening so painful. And maybe you won't be such a pill.

41

Exclusive!

This column is exclusive! Every word, every script, every comment. Please forgive my crowing about it, but it's my first exclusive in 10 years of columny. And I've latched onto the word *exclusive* because it's in the air.

After the murder of Michael Jordan's father, James, investigators in North Carolina arrested two men. And one network evening newscast reported:

"James Jordan's brother spoke exclusively with ___ News." According to a transcript of the television program, he said:

"It's still sad, but I'm-I'm-I'm-I'm very much relieved."

That's it. All of it. Four seconds. Nothing worth calling *exclusive.* Nothing worth using. Nothing new. You can expect friends and family of the deceased to say his death is sad. That may be worth using locally. But not nationally. If family members ever say they're elated and that the deceased had it coming to him, then you've got yourself some news.

An anchor at a major-market station said on an early evening newscast: **"We conducted an exclusive Channel ___ news poll, asking hundreds of people** [whether they want ice skaters Nancy Kerrigan or Tonya Harding to win an Olympic event]. **The suprising results tonight."** But that night, an anchor on the 11 o'clock news—after plugging the *exclusive*—said: **"The results aren't all that surprising."** Instead of fretting about the two skaters, the producers should get their acts together. But who cares who's favored? (And what about the people hoping they'd *both* lose?)

An anchor on another station in that city introduced a piece with a roundabout way of saying *exclusive:* **"And we'll turn up the heat with more of the nation's most talked-about video. You won't see it anywhere else tonight."** What will this boasting produce worthy of such inflated language? Will it be a tape of the President slurping soup? Of the Chief Justice sipping soup through a straw? No, it's a new Madonna video. The anchor went on to say, **"Here's a look at one of the milder portions of the erotic fantasy video."** The release of the video may be news (if you have a huge news hole to fill), but it's not worth that kind of build-up. Except to Madonna. Worst of all, for serious cineastes like you (and me), the station showed only the *milder* parts. Not the wilder.

Many stations preface some stories with "Channel 86 News has learned." But isn't every story carried on newscasts something we've learned? The journalist Richard Clurman says *learned* signals that the information is exclusive, serving "no other purpose than bragging or calling attention to yourself." Yet the word *exclusive* pops up on many newscasts, often for stories that are not worth shouting about—or even whispering about.

"'Exclusive' is fast taking on an elusive meaning among New York TV stations," the New York *Daily News* said. (It could have been said today, but it was said February 26, 1990.) The paper reported two local stations had broadcast simultaneous interviews with Donald Trump that both stations called *exclusive.* And at the same hour, another local TV station was also running an interview with the real estate developer. The previous week, the article said, Trump's girlfriend (now wife), Marla Maples, was shown by four stations on five programs, and most of the appearances were called *exclusive.* All of which made *exclusive* meaningless. According to the *Daily News,* one of the news directors conceded the underlying motive of using *exclusive* is promotional: "It tells viewers you're aggressive and they'll get something here that they won't get anywhere else." Like what, a fit?

When you hear *exclusive* on a newscast, you wonder, Is that story worth all the hullabaloo? Is *any* story worth it? How come they have only one *exclusive* a day? Or only one a week? Are their other stories *non*-exclusive? Or are their other stories presented without fanfare because they're so ordinary? Are most of their stories picked up from other news organizations, stories that newscasters don't dare anoint with that super-charged word *exclusive?* Are some stories *exclusive*—which, strictly speaking, means "obtained by only one news organization"—because no one else wants them?

Some newscasters use other words to imply that their coverage is exclusive. A networker prefaced an item with a comparable self-congratulatory phrase: **"An important follow-up now to a** [name of news magazine] **story, and we're proud to say we were out in front with it.** [Voice-over] **Last July, __ __ told of a World War Two massacre that haunts Poland, the execution of over 4,000 Polish officers in the forest of Katyn. For 50 years, the Soviet Union had blamed the horror on the Nazis, even though it was whispered that Stalin had ordered it. A year ago, our cameras were there as the Polish people began to publicly honor** [correct: *honor the memories of*] **and grieve for their dead . . And today, the Soviet Union officially acknowledged its responsibility. . . ."** *Out in front* with the story? In fact, the Soviet role had long been known. That broadcast was made in 1990. But as far back as 1952, a U.S. Congressional investigation found that the crime was committed by the Soviet NKVD. So how could the news magazine be *out in front*—except in self-praise? And *proud?* Of what?

Two of the biggest and best sources of news, the *New York Times* and the *Wall Street Journal,* break many important exclusives, but they don't label stories *exclusive.* Why not? The director of the Freedom Forum Media

Studies Center, Everette Dennis, says the use of *exclusive* "may be a function of security and insecurity." Thus, the most insecure newsrooms use *exclusive* the most. So those two newspapers must feel secure. Apparently, they realize that the best way to attract attention to good work is to keep doing good work.

Please remember, you read it here last: Don't boast. Don't strut. Don't stoop. Conquer through hard work: Excel.

42

What's Next?

What's ahead for newswriters?

Plenty of news, but nothing new: no new writing rules, no new writing techniques, no new write-o-matic robots (turning out robocopy). We'll still be writing the same old way, the way we've been writing through the ages: one letter at a time—word after word, line after line, page after page. And when all our scripts have been aired, we'll still need to go back over them to see how we can do better next time.

Let's start painlessly by examining scripts of other writers: **"It's a beautiful day to be ice fishing . . . and you're safe if you're doing just that! The North Dakota Commissioner of Game and Fish—Dale Hennegar—says these past few warm days shouldn't pose a threat to fishermen on most frozen lakes and streams in the state. However** [*but* is better, shorter and sharper]**, he said, stay off any frozen portions** [better: *parts*] **of the Missouri River."** Is *safe* the commissioner's conclusion or the writer's? And even if the commissioner made that remark, would *you* feel safe? He's quoted as saying the warm weather *shouldn't* pose a threat—on *most* frozen lakes. *Shouldn't* doesn't sound too solid to me. And *most* means 51 percent or more. So it's probable that many places are not safe. If the writer attributed the observations properly, at least *he* would be safe.

"A Miami dog. . . . reunites with his owners. . . . after taking a seven-month. . . . 15-hundred mile walk.

Rocky. . . . a four year old Pomeranian. . . .is back home in Miami tonight. . . . with his rightful owner. He disappeared in February. . . . and was recently found in Cleveland. Because Rocky was wearing dog tags. . . . . the person who found him . . . was able to track down the owner in southern Florida. 15-hundred miles. . . . does Rocky have paws or Reeboks????"

Reunites? He *was reunited.* A seven-month *walk?* 1,500 miles? The owner knows how long the dog was gone, but he doesn't know *how* the dog got to Cleveland. The dog could have walked a couple of blocks from home and been picked up by a trucker bound for Cleveland. What kind of dog would walk away from Miami in February? And head for Cleveland instead of, say, Palm Beach or Palm Springs? The script was broadcast in September. *Rightful* owner? What other kind of owner is there? And why the shift from the plural *owners* at the beginning?

What were the circumstances of Rocky's being found? Begging at someone's door? Committing a public nuisance? Who found him? We don't need the finder's name but at least a few words telling us something about him. And how was the dog sent back home? By Greyhound?

Does Rocky have paws or Reeboks? It's not a case of either/or: a dog needs paws to wear shoes. And why the brand name? As for *15-hundred miles,* the distance by airplane is 1,080 miles. By road, it's 1,300 miles.

The script is slugged "LOST DOG." I'd make it "LOST WRITER."

The next script is slugged "KICKER":

"The people of Iran lost one of their most beloved actors this week. You could call him a giant in the industry. He is a seven-foot-tall actor named Mahmoud Lotfi. He was famous for his role in an Iranian sitcom called Uncle Napoleon. He played a butcher who was so jealous . . . he killed his wife's lover with a leg of lamb. Talk about violence on television!!" Talk about what passes for news! Why would an actor in the Mideast be of interest in the Midwest, where this story was broad-cast? Although the script says the people of Iran *lost* him, the script doesn't say Lotfi died or disappeared. The script's third sentence says he *is* an actor. If he's dead, he is not an actor. He *was* an actor.

The broadcast of that obit brings to mind a remark by the British writer G.K. Chesterton: "Journalism largely consists in saying 'Lord Jones Dead' to people who never knew Lord Jones was alive."

"A Springfield woman went to her car last night in a motel parking lot and was robbed there. Police say a youth about fourteen or fifteen years old approached her . . . shoved her against the wall and took her purse. Police don't know who the youth is . . . however . . . Crime Stoppers is offering a reward for information that leads to an arrest. The victim of the robbery wasn't hurt." Don't walk the woman to the car. *Cut to the chase!* The story is the robbery itself, not her going to the scene, not the robber's *approach.* Rather than *youth,* make it *boy* or *girl. Youth* is not a conversational word. Do *you* use it? Would you ever tell someone, "I saw two youths on the corner last night"? The reward—and the amount—should be mentioned last. How much is it? And how much money did the woman lose?

"An underground parking garage is the latest victim in the Colombian drug wars." Only living crea-tures can be victims.

"Tomato paste may be the culprit in a Springfield blast equal to nineteen tons of T.N.T. . . . It happened on board a tractor-trailer carrying barrels once used to hold tomato paste. Investigators say gases from the paste may have combined with metal shavings on the rig. . . ." Even if you're a victim of tomato paste, a veg-etable can't be a *culprit.* A culprit is a person who's an offender.

"A controversial management bonus program at the Port of Oakland that allows bonuses even if per-formance stagnates by up to 25 percent is expected to

[be] **recommended for major reforms tomorrow night."** Nothing can *stagnate up* or *down*. *Stagnate* means "stand still" and often applies to air, or water—or a mind.

"When we return . . . time for your flu shots . . . believe it or not . . . And would you believe their [*sic*] **may be chemicals in that hundred percent pure juice you're drinking?"** Why wouldn't we believe it? But please leave *Believe it or not* to Ripley. After all, we could use *Believe it or not* or a variation in half the stories we write. As for that juice, it's brimming with chemicals naturally. Everything in the universe consists of chemicals. We're all chemical factories. Believe it!

"If you didn't know it, it's Car Care Month . . We'll have some hints to help you conform . . when we come back . . . ." Most of us didn't know, and now that we do know, we don't care. *Conform?* Wrong verb. Perhaps *join in* or *take part.*

"It's a day of second guessing in Washington today . . Capitol Hill Democrats are blasting the President . . for missing a chance to. . . . ." *Every* day is one for second guessing in the capital—and in every newsroom. And in my workroom.

In the coming years, we'll have a lot to write about, so we'll have to write a lot. And we'll need to rewrite a lot. And a lot better. To improve our craft, we must learn a lot more about sharpening our tools. More about how to use tool chests like this *Guide*. More about words, more about how to use them effectively. And we must keep writing. And rewriting. And working at it. Hard.

Hard work does work. Take my word. Write on!

About the Author

Mervin Block has written news for Walter Cronkite, Charles Kuralt, Charles Osgood, Dan Rather, Tom Brokaw, Frank Reynolds, Harry Reasoner, Roger Mudd, Ed Bradley, Douglas Edwards, Edwin Newman, Marlene Sanders and Mike Wallace.

Block worked as a staff writer on the "CBS Evening News" and the "ABC Evening News," freelanced at NBC News and did a stint as a writing consultant at CBS News.

He also wrote and broadcast editorials for WNBC-TV, New York City; served as executive news producer, WBBM-TV, Chicago; and worked as a newspaper reporter and editor in Chicago.

Block writes a column on broadcast newswriting, "WordWatching," in *Communicator,* the magazine of the Radio-Television News Directors Association. And he conducts broadcast newswriting workshops for radio and television stations.

He holds the M.S.J. from the Medill School of Journalism, Northwestern University, and a certificate from Columbia University's Graduate School of Journalism, where he teaches part-time.

He has won first prize three times for TV spot-news scripts in the annual competition of the Writers Guild of America.

Block has also written two previous books: *Writing Broadcast News—Shorter, Sharper, Stronger* and *Rewriting Network News: WordWatching Tips from 345 TV and Radio Scripts.*

Index

A

"A" wire, 28, 111
Abbreviations, 133
Accident stories, 6, 9, 33,
    59–61, 71, 196, 219, 228
  rewrites of, 30, 56, 71–2, 83,
    88–9, 91, 94, 128, 148–9,
    159, 224
Accord, 236
According to, 40, 119, 183
Accuracy, 3, 11, 32–4, 45–51,
    57, 253
  in polls, 190
Acknowledge, 57, 80
Acree, Keith, 122
Acronyms, 39–40, 121, 133
Action, 8, 29, 63, 71, 87, 96,
    158, 216, 219, 224–5, 235
Action verbs, 3, 8, 10, 20
Active voice, 8, 44, 156, 215,
    225, 246
Actually, 232
Adjectives, 30, 154, 159, 175,
    228
  verbs buried in, 68
Adverbs, 36, 42, 66, 175

Advise, 232
After, 12–3, 20, 71, 105, 175, 179
Again, 13
Agreement,
  noun-pronoun, 36, 106, 120,
    131, 240
  noun-verb, 13, 67, 111, 152,
    160–1, 239–40
Alarming, 5, 132
Algren, Nelson, 195
All, 41, 73–4, 183, 217
Allege/alleged, 101, 176
Also, 9, 25
Amazing, 5
American Journalism Review, 48
Amid reports that, 78
And, 9, 201
Announce, 232
Another, 201
Anthony, Susan B., 110
Apparently, 96, 177, 182, 208
Appropriated, 230
Aquino, Benigno, 43–4
Arafat, Yasser, 112
Are, 3, 30, 68, 72, 158, 162, 164,
    185, 216
Arguably, 174–6

Around, 65, 184, 208
Articles,
    definite, 41, 56, 87, 183
    indefinite, 226
As, 162–5
As a result of, 12
As expected, 5, 233
As predicted, 5
Ashline, Susan, 122
Assertion, 4, 40–1, 45, 87, 121,
        140, 174, 183, 185, 194,
        238, 242–3
Associated Press (AP), 107–9,
        111, 114, 117–8, 246
*Associated Press Guide to News
        Writing, The,* 104
*Associated Press Stylebook and
        Libel Manual, The,* 191–2
At this hour, 25–6, 164
Attribution, 4–5, 13–5, 40, 43,
        45, 67, 71, 87, 94, 109,
        121, 140–1, 147, 155,
        176–7, 183, 185, 194,
        241–2, 244, 246
Audience, 2, 4, 8–10, 12, 39, 67,
        74, 76, 82, 86, 128, 175,
        185, 206, 221
    scaring, 130–3
Author intrusion, 210–3, 234,
        246–7
Authorities, 15, 95–6, 177
    Auxiliary verbs, 3, 20,
        36, 63, 68, 158–9, 162,
        185
Ax, 236

B

Babel, Isaac, 9
Bad, 5, 139, 230
Bad news, 139
Badly, 36, 230
Bakker, Jim, 128–9
Barbie, Klaus, 87
Barnes & Noble Inc., 48
Barron's, 48

Barzun, Jacques, 40, 136
*BBC News & Current Affairs
        Stylebook and Editorial
        Guide,* 78–9
Be, 3, 36, 63
Because, 9
Becomes, 3
Beethoven, Ludwig von, 152
Before, 71
Behind closed doors, 79
Bible, 229
Bierce, Ambrose, 31, 229–31
Big Bill of Chicago, 33
Billings, Josh, 139
Bizarre, 14–6, 232
Blast, 6, 91, 232
Blaze, 78, 226
Bliss, Edward, Jr., 39, 206
Boccardi, Louis D., 103
Bohn, Veryl, 122
Boutros-Ghali, Boutros, 187
Brace for a wave of violence, 78
Brackets, 29
Brecht, Bertolt, 139
Brevity, 3, 6–7, 10–1, 21,
        137–43, 147
Brix, Dale, 205
Broadcast News, 210
Broadcast journalism, 24
Broadcast style vs. print style,
        4–6, 8, 17, 40, 43, 51,
        100, 124, 241–2
Burchfield, Robert, 12
Bureaucratese, 13
Burg, Nelson, 119
Burgeoning, 78
Bush, George, 66, 140–1, 166
But, 9–10, 201, 252
Butler, Samuel, 51

C

Caen, Herb, 231
cannot / can't, 10
Cappon, René, 104

Cariker, Mark, 119
Carlin, George, 82
Carlyle, Thomas, vi
Casualties, 6, 128, 179
Centers for Disease Control,
    66–7
Chaos, 78
Charged, 15, 145
Charges, 101, 225
Chesterton, G.K., 254
Chicago, 47
Chicago Sun-Times, 44–5, 47
Chicago Tribune, 45–7
Churchill, Winston, 71, 126
Circulation, 34
Clarity, 3, 7–10, 21, 41, 65, 130,
    160, 196, 217
Clash, 78
Clichés, 6, 16, 26, 75, 78–9, 86,
    94, 121, 126, 175, 187,
    217, 219
Clinton, Bill, 36, 185, 187
Close quote, 27, 128
Clurman, Richard, 249
Comment, 232
Communicator, 1
Compare, 230
Conditional sentences, 245
Conditions, 232
Conference, news, 124
Confirmation, 25, 28, 33, 51,
    89, 92, 109, 125, 139–40,
    152, 157, 160, 203, 241,
    246
Conjunctions, 9, 162
Connectives, 9
Connolly, Cyril, 2
Consequence clause, 124, 245
Continued/continues, 5, 45, 168,
    232
Contractions, 10
Controversial/controversy, 45,
    99–100, 232–4
Cooper, James Fenimore, 67
Copy, source, 2–3, 6–7, 55, 116

wire, 6, 28–31, 109–10, 136,
    160, 189, 241
exercise source material,
    107–8, 111–4, 117–8
Corrections, newspaper, 45–50
Could, 3
Crisis, 232
Crisp, Quentin, 16
Crucial, 78
Culprit, 254
Cutlines, 48

D

Daley, Richard J., 32
Daley, Richard M., 45
Damage/damages, 33–4, 179
D'Amato, Alfonse, 47
Dangling modifiers, 15, 126, 183
Daring, 78
Dateline, 108–9
Daylight revealed, 78
Dead/die/died, 9, 21, 71, 80, 87,
    116, 136, 150, 180, 196,
    219
Dead phrases, 3, 68, 71, 185,
    226
Death, 6, 138, 150, 164, 178, 196
Declare, 10, 230
Deerslayer, The, 67
Defendants, 234
Definite articles, 41, 56, 87, 183
Definitely, 217
Deliver, 230
Dennis, Everette, 251
Descriptions, 5, 28, 52, 62, 71,
    74, 95, 142–3
Details, 178–9
Dilemma, 233
Dillinger, John, 231
Disaster stories, 6, 9, 14
    rewrites of, 69, 74, 97
Disturbing, 5
Do, 63
Don, 236

Dow Jones Industrials, 64, 76
Down, 8, 217, 255
Dramatic, 5
Duo, 233

E

Ear, writing for the, 2, 7–8,
    10–1, 24, 30, 39–40, 55,
    75, 84, 86, 121, 123, 154,
    163, 209
Earhart, Amelia, 111–6
Earlier, 133, 233, 238
Economic/fiscal woes, 78
Editing, self-, 81–98
Either, 60, 239
Electronic town halls, 191
Elements of Style, The, 11, 163,
    178
Eliot, T.S., 6, 91
Ellipses, 92–3
Elsewhere, 19
Empty words, 166–9
End quote, 40, 128
Equinox, 47
Erasmus, 33
Errors, 157
Esser, Doug, 115–6, 119, 122
Establish, 38, 231
Euphemisms, 6, 80, 136, 215
Exciting, 5
Exclusive, 247–51
Exercises, writing, 107–8,
    111–4, 117–8, 120–2
Expected, 243

F

Fact-checking, 3, 14, 33, 48, 51,
    92, 109, 152
Fact-finding, 135, 160
Factor, 122
Facts, 3, 25, 28, 51, 157, 160,
    174, 215, 227, 238, 241
Fail, 230

Fairness, 11
Farther/further, 202
Fatalities, 6, 128, 179
Father Time, 150
Felonies, 91, 101, 234
Ferry, 30, 128
Fighting, 78
First names, 110, 149
Fiscal/economic woes, 78
Fisk, Carlton, 38
Five W's, 17
Focus groups, 191
Foe, 78, 236
Follow-up, 8, 211
Following, 12–3, 20, 179, 209
For, 21, 23, 95, 105
Ford, Gerald, 192
Forecasts, 42, 79, 138–9, 176
Fort Worth Star-Telegram, 49
Fox Television Stations, 48
Fractions, 185, 202
Frailey, David C., 31
Free/for free, 95
Frequently reliable, 245
Frightening, 5
From vs. *of,* 68, 85, 112
From vs. *out of,* 22
Fronts, 38
Fry, Don, 3
Full-scale, 78
Funny, 5

G

Gallup, George, 192
Gannon, Edward B., 230
Gannon, Richard, 230
Garbarge, 31
Gates, Robert, 42
General Electric, 120–2
George V, 33
Get It Right!, 53
Gibbs, Wolcott, 75
Gilbert, William S., 115, 125
Giovanni, Nikki, 1

Gleason, Bill, 176
Going, 36–7, 159
Golden Book on Writing, The, 11
Good, 5, 139
Good news, 37, 139
Goodwill Industries, 53
Gorbachev, Mikhail, 92, 152, 220
Gorbachev, Raisa, 207
Got married, 75, 230
Grim Reaper, 150
Grueling, 229
Gubernatorial, 230, 236
Guinier, Lani, 36
Gunned down, 79
Gunshot, 79

H

Had/has, 3, 22
Hail, 230
Hall, Fawn, 61–2
Hall, Jerry, 75
Hall, Lee, 142
Halve, 141–2
Handouts, 14
Hard-news story, 198, 239
Harper Dictionary of Contemporary Usage, The, 106
Harris, Lou, 192
Have, 13, 20, 63
He, 194, 239
Headlines, 6, 46, 73, 78, 154
Headlinese, 150
Her/hers, 10, 35–6, 120, 239
Herald & Weekly Times Ltd., 48
Here, 8, 233
Hess, Rudolf, 28–9
High-speed, 20, 80
His, 10, 120, 239
Hit by fears that, 78
Hitler, Adolf, 28–9
Hoaxes, 50
Holes in scripts, 51–4, 70–7

Holm, Morgan, 122
Homonyms, 142
Homophones, 30, 128, 142, 167, 182
Hopefully, 233
Hospitalese, 86
Hosted, 79
How, 17
However, 64, 252
Huddled, 79
Humphrey, Hubert, 192
Hussein, Saddam, 151
Hustler, 142–3

I

I, 194
If, 162, 172
If clause, 124, 245
Immediacy, 68
Imperatives, 170–3, 185
Important, 233
In, 21, 30, 96
In [anyplace], 37–8, 42, 69, 99
In [business/science/medicine/ etc.], 66, 74, 204
In a bid to hammer out agreement, 78
Inaugurate, 231
Incident, 97, 233
Incomplete sentences, 99–102
Inconsistencies, 56
Indefinite articles, 226
Indefinite pronouns, 226, 239
Indictments, 8, 154, 211, 234
Inert verbs, 29
Informed, 234
Inge, William R., 31
*In*glish, 62–4
Initials, middle, 86, 95, 110, 133
Injured, 33
Injuries, 19, 60
Inside of, 231
Instant polls, 191
Interesting, 5, 198

Involved, 234
Irregular verbs, 184
Is, 3, 36, 68, 71–2, 75, 140, 158,
    185, 216
Issue, 234
It, 41, 61, 226, 239
It is, 3, 185
Its, 10, 121, 239

J

Jack Frost, 150
Jagger, Mick, 75
Jail, 91, 101, 234
Jargon, 6, 151, 187, 219
   sports, 77, 218–21
Jaroslovsky, Rich, 189
Jones, Donald D., 157
Jones, James Earl, 95
Jordan, Michael, 97, 248
Journalese, 6, 16, 24, 30, 78–9,
    203, 217
Journalism, 2, 254
Judgment, 103

K

Kauffman, Donald T., 46
Kelly, Edward J., 33
Kempton, Murray, 46
Kennedy, Jacqueline, 207
Kick off, 220, 234
Kid, 93
Killed, 15, 21, 196, 219
Kilpatrick, James J., 196
Kitchin, Bill, 29
Knight, Ted, 87
Knowles, Cameron, 122
Kogan, Herman, 33
Kuralt, Charles, 106

L

Labels, 5, 28, 52, 62, 71, 74, 95,
    142–3

Lady Luck, 150
Lambuth, David, 11
Lash out, 78
Last night, 38, 59, 72, 95, 156
Later, 71
Latin, 168
Launch, 24, 34
Lay / lie, 183
Leads, 3, 9, 37, 45
   in [anyplace], 37–8, 42, 69, 99
   in [business/science/medicine/
    etc.], 66, 74, 204
   list, 123
   negative, 181
   one-word, 154–7
   pronouns as first word in, 5,
    85–6
   question, 4, 237–9
   quotation, 4, 87, 155, 185
   shock, 9
   umbrella, 37
   words to avoid in, 5, 37–8,
    42, 45, 66, 69, 74, 85–6,
    99, 124, 153, 204
Learned, 234, 246–7, 249
Lease, 231
Lederer, Richard, 229
Legalese, 6
Lenin, Vladimir, 151–2
Like, 90, 162–5
Likely, 42
Linking verbs, 3, 20, 36, 63, 68,
    158–9, 162, 185
Listeners, 3, 10, 12, 39, 67, 74,
    82, 86, 128, 175, 185,
    206, 221
   scaring, 130–3
   vs. readers, 2, 4, 8, 27, 124
Litotes, 179
*Little Blacklist of Literary
   Faults, A,* 230–1
Live, 12
Loan, 231
Local, 60, 85, 112, 166–7, 204,
    234

Localize, 9, 141
Lone, 234
Lonetree, Clayton, 212
Longtime foe, 78
Look/looks, 3, 36
Loose sentences, 225
Los Angeles Times, 48
Lost Star, 116
Low-speed, 20, 80

M

MacDougall, Curtis, 135
Madonna, 249
Major, 38, 78
Making news/headlines/history, 5
"Man-in-the-street" interview, 192–3
Many, 74
Maples, Marla, 249
Marcello, Carlos, 25
Marcos, Ferdinand, 220
Margin, 234
Married, 75, 230
Martinez, Bob, 74
Marzullo, Vito, 45
Massive, 78
Mathematics, 57, 127, 134, 202, 234, 242
Mathews, Jay, 50
May, 3
Mayer, Louis B., 14
McFarlane, Robert, 219
Meador, Ron, 201
Meantime/meanwhile, 96, 201–2, 205, 235
Media, 106, 213
Meese, Edwin, 203
Mencher, Mel, 135
Metaphors, 8, 187
Michelangelo, 93
Middle initials/names, 15, 86, 95, 110
Might, 3

Millstein, Gilbert, 168
Minimal, 33–4
Miracle/miraculously, 79
Miracle of Language, The, 229
Misdemeanors, 101, 234
Modifiers,
   dangling, 15, 126, 183
   misplaced, 208
   squinting/swiveling, 13, 39
Montand, Yves, 46
Morgano, Todd, 122
Most, 42, 74, 252
Mother Nature, 150, 215
Mulroney, Brian, 58
Murdoch, Rupert, 48
Murray, Donald, 120
Murrow, Edward R., 7, 110

N

Names, 5, 142–3
   first, 110, 149
   middle, 15, 86, 95, 110
   place, 84, 99, 101, 109, 133
National Review, 191
Negative leads, 181
Neither, 239
Neuman, Alfred E., 110
Never, 82, 179
Nevertheless, 127, 215
New, 10, 12, 38, 55, 64, 124
"New look," 222
New Republic, The, 50
New York *Daily News,* 249
New York Times, 46–9, 250
New Yorker, The, 49
Newman, Paul, 159
News, 92, 121, 139
News, definitions of, 140, 246
News conference, 124
News Corporation Ltd., 48
News messengers vs. newsmakers, 210–3
News retardants, 237
Newscasterese, 24

Newsiness, 8, 21, 57, 68, 72, 74,
    93, 96, 140, 148, 158,
    180–1
Newspapers,
    as a source for scripts, 43–51
    corrections, 45–50
    guidelines for adapting
        scripts, 51
Newsweek, 50
Newsworthiness, 76, 213, 223
Newswriting,
    "39 Steps," 2–11
    exercises, 107–8, 111–4,
        117–8, 120–2
        acceptable scripts, 108–10,
            115–20, 122
    for the ear, 2, 7–8, 10–1, 24,
        30, 39–40, 55, 75, 84, 86,
        121, 123, 154, 163, 209
    guidelines, 2–11, 51, 130
    "tennis ball," 103–4
900-numbers, 191
911, 7, 144, 146
Nixon, Pat, 207
No, 9, 49
No one, 207, 239
Nominal, 33
Non sequitur, 94
Norfolk Virginian-Pilot, 49
North, Oliver, 61–2
Not, 9, 208
Nouns, 3, 26, 30, 33, 36, 56, 59,
    154, 175, 228
    agreement with pronouns, 36,
        106, 120, 131, 240
    agreement with verbs, 13, 67,
        111, 152, 160–1, 239–40
    verbs buried in, 3, 59–62, 79,
        94
Now, 10, 40, 71–2, 75, 80, 167
Numbers, 6, 29, 34, 39, 47, 49,
    57, 60, 73–4, 84, 87, 90,
    100, 121, 127–8, 134,
    175, 179, 184–5, 202,
    219, 242

O

Obituaries, 25, 45–6, 71, 87,
    150–1
    rewrites of, 25, 87
Obviously, 60
Of, 3, 52, 68, 85, 105, 112
Offbeat, 25–6
Oil-rich, 78
Old Man Winter, 150
O'Leary, Edward, 58
On, 65, 184
One-word leads, 154–7
Only, 138, 183, 208
Only time will tell, 79
Opdycke, John B., 53
Optimum, 34
Optional material, 29
Orwell, George, 187–8
Our, 8–9, 110
Out of, 22
Owen, Bill, 142

P

Paraphrasing, 27, 40–1, 128,
    194
Participial phrase, 4
Participles, 62–4, 68, 99, 159
Passive voice, 8, 44, 156, 215,
    224, 242, 246
Peale, Norman Vincent, 46
Peg, local, 9
People/person, 9, 58, 60, 63, 78,
    97, 145, 208
Per, 168
Percentages, 202
Perfect tense, 53, 68
Periodic sentences, 225
Personal pronouns, 5
Personification, 150, 216
Philadelphia *Inquirer,* 44, 243
Phrases,
    dead, 3, 68, 71, 185, 226
    prepositional, 90

Place-name, 99, 101, 109, 133
Plagiarism, 31
Plans, 182
Plato, 120
Players, 219
Pleaded/pled, 13, 84
Plots, 182
Plus, 26
Polls, 189–93, 248
  accuracy in, 190
  instant, 191
  straw, 189, 191
Positive form, 9, 38, 41, 66,
    85–6, 170, 178–81, 212,
    215, 226
Possessives, 10
Possibly, 174
Pratt, Jim, 122
Predictions, 42, 79, 138–9, 176
Prepositional phrases, 90
Prepositions, 26–7, 65, 72, 90,
    162, 231
Present perfect tense, 41, 53,
    72
Press conference, 124
Press releases, 14, 189
Print style vs. broadcast style,
    4–6, 8, 17, 40, 43, 51,
    100, 124, 241–2
Prison, 91, 101, 234
Privately, 124
Probably, 174
Probe, 79
Pronouns, 8, 10, 35–6, 59, 61,
    94, 120–1, 210
  agreement with nouns, 36,
    106, 120, 131, 240
  as first word in leads, 5, 85–6
  indefinite, 226, 239
  personal, 5
Property, 9, 109, 179
Protest, 41, 83
Prove/proven, 112, 121, 175,
    231
Public opinion, 191, 193

Published report, 244–5
Punctuation, 44, 61, 92

Q

Qualifiers, 208
Question leads, 4, 237–9
Quite, 42
Quotation leads, 4, 87, 155, 185
Quotations, 27, 40–1, 114, 128,
    194
Quote, 26–7, 40, 91, 128

R

Radio-Television News
    Directors Association, 1
Random House Dictionary for
    Writers and Readers,
    The, 150–1
Rates, 90
Ratio, 234
Reaction, 8, 87, 96, 216, 224–5,
    235
Readers vs. listeners, 2, 4, 8,
    27, 124
Reagan, Nancy, 207
Reagan, Ronald, 203, 219–20
Really, 151, 216, 232
Record, 15, 38, 64, 220
Redundancy, 12, 38, 64, 66, 80,
    86, 94, 99, 145, 150, 168,
    182–4, 215, 226, 231,
    234, 238
Refresher, 2–11, 51, 130
Refute, 235
Remember, 237
Repetition, 92
Report, 235, 244–5
Reportedly, 28–9, 145, 177
Reuters Handbook for
    Journalists, 50, 78, 202
Rewriting, 55–8
  examples of, 29, 127, 129,
    135, 140, 143, 155–6, 160

accident stories, 30, 56,
71–2, 83, 88–9, 91, 94,
128, 148–9, 159, 224
court stories, 53, 61, 90,
100–1
crime stories, 20, 54, 77–8,
85, 97, 124, 171–2, 176,
180, 206, 225
disaster stories, 69, 74, 97
economic stories, 40, 202,
208
fire stories, 88, 164–5
medical/health stories, 38,
67–8, 131, 141
obituaries, 25, 87
political stories, 41, 43–4,
141, 186, 240
wire copy, 28–31
Rocked by, 78
Rumors, 74–5
Rushed to, 79

S

Said, 40, 79, 114, 230, 232
Said to be, 28–9, 183
Sain, Johnny, 130
St. Valentine's Day Massacre, 35
San Antonio Express-News, 48
Say/says, 10, 55, 119, 230–1
Scaring listeners, 130–3
Schiller, Friedrich, 24
Schleier, Blanche, 189–90
Scholar, 231
Scope, 172
Scripts,
guidelines for adapting
newspaper stories, 51
holes in, 51–4, 70–7
newspapers as sources of,
43–51
weather, 214–7
Sczesny, Matt, 115–6
Seem, 3, 36
Self-editing, 81–98

Sentences,
conditional, 245
incomplete, 99–102
loose/periodic/suspended, 225
S-V-O structure, 7, 154
verbless, 99–102, 159, 217
Settlement, 103
Sevareid, Eric, 82
Shaw, George Bernard, 16
She, 36, 239
Shevardnadze, Eduard, 220
Shock leads, 9
Shock waves, 16
Shocking, 5
Short words, 7, 34, 228–31
Should/shouldn't, 3, 252
Shultz, Charles, 34, 220
Sibilants, 6
Sills, Beverly, 186
Similar to, 162
Simile, 187
Single, 235
Situation, 81–2, 167, 232
Slay, 236
Slovonsky, Lynn, 34, 231
Smith, Sydney, 214
Snyder, Mitchell, 151
So, 9
Soft-news story, 200
Solomon, Eileen Fredman, 146
Some, 13, 37, 74, 79, 225
Source copy, 2–3, 6–7, 55, 116
handouts/press releases, 14,
189
newspapers, 43–51
wire stories, 6, 28–31,
109–10, 136, 160, 189, 241
exercise source material,
107–8, 111–4, 117–8
Sources, 124–5, 139, 235, 241–7
Spark off, 79
Spell out, 79
Spelling, 49–50, 133
*Spokesman/spokesperson/spokes-
woman,* 13–4, 109, 234

Sports jargon, 77, 218–21
Squinting/swiveling modifiers, 13, 39
Statement came as, 78
States, 6, 231
Statistics, 175
Stay with us, 26
Steffens, Lincoln, 27
Stein, Laurie, 116
Stephens, Mitchell, 234
Stone, Vernon, 39
Stowe, Harriet Beecher, 95
Straw polls, 189, 191
Stretchers, 3
Strunk, William, 11, 38, 151, 163, 178
Subject-verb-object sentence structure, 7, 154
Subjectivity, 5, 21, 36, 44, 57, 66, 78, 131, 175, 195
Subpoenas, 234
Substantiate, 231
Successfully, 235
Sunday Times of London, 113
Superlatives, 6, 42, 61, 73–4, 82, 93, 124, 207, 217, 236, 252, 255
Supposedly, 208
Supreme Court, 61
Suspects, 234
Suspended sentences, 225
S-V-O sentence structure, 7, 154
Symbols, 132
Synonyms, 6, 10, 12, 57, 75, 101, 174, 245

T

Tallahassee Democrat, 48
Taste, 36
Taylor, Humphrey, 190–1
Tchaikovsky, Peter, 152
"Tell" stories, 171
"Tennis-ball writing," 103–4

That, 3, 68, 186
The, 3, 41, 56, 87, 163, 183
Their, 10, 120–1, 239
There, 3, 91, 186, 235
There are/is/was/were, 3, 68, 172, 185–6, 226, 239
Therefore, 186
"39 Steps" of broadcast newswriting, 2–11
This afternoon, 12, 96
This morning, 19, 222
Thompson, William Hale, 32–3
Tiananmen Square, 36
Time, 45
Time references, 124, 129, 164, 202, 215
 at this hour, 25–6, 164
 earlier, 133, 233, 238
 last night, 38, 59, 72, 95, 156
 later, 71
 now, 10, 40, 71–2, 75, 80, 167
 this afternoon, 12
 this morning, 15, 19, 96, 222
 today, 10, 12, 15, 21, 25, 39, 41, 61, 65, 80, 84, 88, 96, 101, 147, 168, 222
 tonight, 12, 25, 68–9, 156
 yesterday, 5, 14, 21, 41, 53, 144, 209
To be, 3, 36, 63, 68, 71–2, 185
Today, 10, 12, 15, 21, 25, 39, 41, 61, 65, 80, 84, 88, 96, 101, 147, 168, 222
Tonight, 12, 25, 68–9, 156
Total, 79
Toward/towards, 72
Tragedy, 196, 207, 235
Transitions, 201–3
 words to avoid, 97, 204–5
Transitive verbs, 76
Trigger, 79
Troubling, 5
Truman, Harry, 45
Trump, Donald, 249
Try and / try to, 231

Tucker, Jim Guy, 48
Turning, 68
Twain, Mark, 55, 67, 106, 209,
    228, 229
Tyson, Mike, 57

U

Umbrella leads, 37
Undoubtedly, 62
United States vs. U-S, 39
Unquote, 27, 40, 128
Unusual, 5–6, 158, 216
Unexpected, 182
Up, 8, 211, 217, 234, 255
Upcoming, 236
UPI Stylebook, 79, 175
Us, 210, 213
USA Today, 46
USS Dwight D. Eisenhower,
    107–10

V

Variety, 77
Verbal bridges, 102
Verbless sentences, 99–102,
    159, 217
Verbs, 5, 10, 19, 45, 154, 228
    action, 3, 8, 10, 20
    agreement with nouns, 13,
        67, 111, 152, 160–1,
        239–40
    auxiliary/linking, 3, 20, 36,
        63, 68, 158–9, 162, 185
    buried in adjectives, 68
    buried in nouns, 3, 59–62, 79,
        94
    inert, 29
    irregular, 184
    tenses, 41, 68, 53, 72, 76
Verification, 25, 28, 33, 51, 89,
        92, 109, 125, 139–40,
        152, 157, 160, 203, 241,
        246

Very, 42, 65, 151, 236
Victims, 17, 89, 225, 254
Victoria, Queen, 197
Vie, 236
Voice, active vs. passive, 8, 44,
        156, 215, 246
Voltaire, François, 228
Vowed, 79

W

Waite, Terry, 220
Wall Street Journal, 47, 250
Wambaugh, Joseph, 52
War, 16
Warrants, 234
Was, 3, 30, 36, 63, 68
Washington Journalism Review,
        48
Washington Post, 43–4
We, 8, 64, 194–8, 210–1, 245–6
Weather scripts, 214–7
Webber, Andrew Lloyd, 95
Weinberger, Casper, 34
Weiss, Ray, 117
Wendt, Lloyd, 33
Were, 3, 68, 77
What, 17, 214
When, 17, 214
Where, 17
Which, 3, 131
White, E.B., 11, 38, 137, 151,
        163, 167, 178
Who, 4, 17
Why, 17–23, 54
Wilder, Thornton, 110
Will be, 3
Williams, Ted, 175–6
Wimer, Arthur, 205
Wire copy, 6, 28–31, 109–10,
        136, 160, 189, 241
    exercise source material,
        107–8, 111–4, 117–8
    rewriting, 28–31
Wirese, 30

Witnessed, 236
Woes, 78
Words, 19, 21, 25, 28, 38, 42, 117, 172
  empty, 166–9
  misused, 26, 33–5, 39, 68, 71–2, 75, 85, 90, 94, 103–6, 116–7, 182, 208, 211
    jail/prison, 91, 101, 234
    Latin, 168
    lay/lie, 183
    meantime/meanwhile, 96, 201–2, 205, 235
  short, 7, 34, 228–31
  to avoid, 8, 16, 25–6, 62, 97, 127, 137, 141, 150–1, 187, 207, 211
    Ambrose Bierce's list, 230–1
    BBC News & Current Affairs Stylebook and Editorial Guide examples, 78–9
    bizarre, 14–6, 232
    following, 12–3, 20, 179, 209
    here, 8, 233
    in leads, 5, 37–8, 42, 45, 66, 69, 74, 85–6, 99, 124, 153, 204
    interesting, 5, 198
    local, 60, 85, 112, 166–7, 204, 234
    meantime / meanwhile, 96, 201, 205, 235
    obviously, 60
    our, 8–9, 110
    quote/close quote/end quote/unquote, 26–7, 40, 91, 128
    really 151, 216, 232
    Reuters Handbook for Journalists examples, 78

situation, 81–2, 167, 232
tragedy, 196, 207, 235
transitions, 97, 204–5
unusual, 5–6, 158, 216
UPI Stylebook examples, 79
we, 8, 64, 194–8, 210–1, 245–6
"WordWatcher's Worst 40," 232–7
youth, 18, 236, 254
"WordWatching," 1
Workbook for Radio and TV News Editing and Writing, 205
Worst, 121, 168, 236
Wounded, 33, 65
Wright, Frank Lloyd, 48
Write It Right, 31, 229
Writing,
  "39 Steps," 2–11
  exercises, 107–8, 111–4, 117–8, 120–2
    acceptable scripts, 108–10, 115–20, 122
  for the ear, 2, 7–8, 10–1, 24, 30, 39–40, 55, 75, 84, 86, 121, 123, 154, 163, 209
  guidelines, 2–11, 51, 130
  "tennis ball," 103–4
Writing Broadcast News— Shorter, Sharper, Stronger, 1
Wrongfully/wrongly, 106
Wulfemeyer, Tim, 199, 238

Y

Yawner, 37
Yeltsin, Boris, 25
Yesterday, 5, 14, 21, 41, 53, 144, 209
You, 189, 197–200
Youth, 18, 236, 254